A Stone in My Shoe

A Stone in My Shoe

Confessions of an Evangelcial Outlier

J. MICHAEL WALTERS

RESOURCE *Publications* • Eugene, Oregon

A STONE IN MY SHOE
Confessions of an Evangelcial Outlier

Copyright © 2021 J. Michael Walters. All rights reserved. Except for brief quotations in critical publications or reviews, no part of this book may be reproduced in any manner without prior written permission from the publisher. Write: Permissions, Wipf and Stock Publishers, 199 W. 8th Ave., Suite 3, Eugene, OR 97401.

Resource Publications
An Imprint of Wipf and Stock Publishers
199 W. 8th Ave., Suite 3
Eugene, OR 97401

www.wipfandstock.com

PAPERBACK ISBN: 978-1-6667-0198-2
HARDCOVER ISBN: 978-1-6667-0199-9
EBOOK ISBN: 978-1-6667-0200-2

05/18/21

To
Outliers everywhere,
who would rather live on the margins, than surrender
their faith-driven dreams.

Contents

Preface | ix

Introduction: It's Complicated! | 1

Chapter 1
The Making of an Outlier | 11

Chapter 2
Who Needs the Church Anyway? | 27

Chapter 3
The B-I-B-L-E: Evangelicals and the Good Book | 43

Chapter 4
Deciders or Disciples: Evangelism in a Post-Christian World | 60

Chapter 5
Sex, Lies, and Flannelgraphs: Rethinking the Facts of Life(Including Some We Learned at Church) | 79

Chapter 6
The Body Politic | 99

Chapter 7
American Idol(s) | 117

Chapter 8
Dinosaurs on the Ark | 135

Chapter 9
Too Wounded to Heal | 152

Epilogue: What Now? | 170

Endnotes | 177
Bibliography | 187

Preface

I THOUGHT ABOUT THIS book for eight years and then wrote it in three months. Years of musing about these things combined with a shelter-in-place order from my governor during the pandemic of 2020 accounts for its rapid completion. Because I've been thinking for so long about saying the things I talk about in these pages, I've arrived at some deep convictions about these matters, but the length of time also indicates a certain reticence on my part to "go public." As a pronounced introvert, I have, ironically, spent my entire adult life in the very public professions of pastoral ministry and college faculty member. Apparently, I have become adept at acclimating to circumstances that seem at odds with my inner self. Nonetheless, I have carried on a constant dialogue with that inner self in an attempt to quell the dissonance that inevitably arises in any thoughtful person's tenure in the aforementioned professions. Once the professional obligations cease and the need for adapting oneself to one's current job no longer exists, those inner dissonances do not go away. They end up in a book! This book.

My hope is that my own journey in the evangelical church has something in common with the journeys of others who I would also consider "evangelical outliers" like myself, particularly pastors. Outliers have all the usual evangelical bona fides, but due to a combination of our experiences and convictions about certain matters, find ourselves out of sorts one way or another with our mother church. It has been a great relief to me, through years of parish ministry and classroom teaching in the field of religion, to find like-minded souls who convince me, one, that I'm not crazy, and two, that I'm not alone. Many of these partner outliers have been faculty colleagues and/or members of my congregations. For them, I am forever grateful. It's hard for me to imagine my life being anywhere near as blessed as I now find it apart from these people and their unconditional friendships to me.

I owe special thanks to my wife and children. My daughter and son have gracefully and patiently endured my outlier idiosyncrasies through their developmental years without, thank God, excessively negative consequences. And as for my wife, well, she is the absolute center of my stability, the one who has unfailingly listened to my rants about what's wrong with whatever it is that had my attention at that moment in life. Her default response became, "you need to write about that." Even if that was primarily a defense mechanism on her part, it was, I hope, good counsel. Being the spouse of an outlier is, I think, a special vocational calling, and I'm thankful that Nancy graciously answered the call. Happily, she has the people skills, so lacking in me, to provide me the cover I have so often needed to continue my outlier ways in the church and the academy. Without her, this book does not exist.

I also want to especially thank two gentlemen who, each in his own way, made monumental contributions to this book. Nathan Danner rescued me from "software purgatory" on several occasions and enabled me to get my proposal to the publisher with both the manuscript and my sanity intact. Brad Wilber's work in editing this book was a wonderful gift to me at a crucial moment. His cheerful embrace of this kind of work, his considerable language skills, and his abundant patience amaze and encourage me. I am so grateful for his efforts.

While on sabbatical in 2005, my wife and I were on the South Island of New Zealand, near Queenstown. One day we visited the Kawarau bridge, the original commercial site for bungee jumping. We watched people pay a lot of money to plunge headfirst 440 feet. There is no scenario in which I would ever be one of those people. For one thing, I'm scared of heights, and just looking down into that gorge gave me the heebie-jeebies! But even if I were to don that harness and stand on the precipice of that bridge, I doubt that things would proceed smoothly. I am not, nor have I ever been, much of a risk taker. So I can easily imagine myself all harnessed up, ready to jump, but having serious second thoughts and delaying the entire process for everyone else standing in line awaiting their turn to take the leap.

Releasing this book for publication is, for me, the literary equivalent of bungee jumping. I've had some serious reservations about doing this, but once I take the plunge and free-fall my way into the unknown, my hope, my prayer, is that overcoming my risk aversion will prove to have been the right choice. Soli Deo gloria.

Trinity Sunday, 2020
Houghton, New York

Introduction
It's Complicated!

I DON'T KNOW. THESE three small words are both my refuge and my constant challenge. I can't begin to calculate how many times I have uttered these words. Sometimes I fantasize that in the afterlife there exists some capability of answering absolutely meaningless questions like "how many miles did I drive in my lifetime?" or, "how many tacos did I really consume?" But these would all take a back seat to "how many times did I say the words, 'I don't know?'" I'm guessing at least in the thousands. Or the number of times I said in my theology classes "I think I think . . ." I told students that if they wanted absolute certainty, they should head over to the math building! To be clear, my use of such words was not a claim to some virtuous sort of epistemic humility, although these days, such a trait can indeed be a virtue, particularly in Christians. My affinity for this phrase lies primarily in the fact that I really DON'T know. There are things I believe, things I affirm, but some of these would fall into the category of "I could be wrong about that." There are things I ardently believed in my younger days to which I no longer subscribe. On some issues, I currently have viewpoints that have evolved slowly through the years. I've been thinking about the matters in this book for a long time now and I have to confess that what has primarily prevented me from getting to it until now is the knowledge that I could well be wrong about what I am trying to say. I could be wrong about my take on Christian faith. I could be wrong about my analysis of the church. I don't know.

But this I do know: there is within me a kind of primal urge to, finally, get this out into the open, if for no other reason than to be honest with myself. Of course, I also hope to be honest with people who have known me across the years, and with anyone who happens to pick up this book. But most of all, I just want to deliver myself of what has been churning within for far too long. My reticence up to now has been born of a combination of accommodation, personal cowardice, and just wondering if anything I say would make any difference at all. This and the ever-present fact that *I don't know*. I can't adequately explain why suddenly I feel emboldened to put these thoughts on paper. Perhaps it is the knowledge that if not now, when? I'm seventy years old and who knows how much longer I'll be here, let alone be able to think clearly about such matters. At any rate, what follows is my awkward and humble contribution to a conversation that I've been wanting to have with the church for the better part of my adult life.

The title, *A Stone in My Shoe*, seems an appropriate way to summarize my relationship with the church for most of my life. My faith journey with the evangelical church in America has been uncomfortable for me at times. It is my observation that American evangelicals, too often compromised by the winds of the prevailing culture, have effectively lost much of their "saltiness." I believe that cultural accommodation has resulted in a church that fails to fully embrace its earthly mission and to adequately differentiate itself from the regnant culture. The well-publicized role of American evangelicals in the election of Donald Trump only magnifies these concerns exponentially.

The entire course of my faith journey has been done within the auspices of the evangelical wing of the church. I am an evangelical, always have been. I am quite confident that I fall within the parameters set out by British historian David Bebbington, in his well-known description of Evangelicalism. Bebbington identifies what he terms "the four primary characteristics of evangelicalism":

- Conversionism: the belief that lives need to be transformed through a "born-again" experience and a life-long process of following Jesus

- Activism: the expression and demonstration of the gospel in missionary and social reform efforts

- Biblicism: a high regard for and obedience to the Bible as the ultimate authority

- Crucicentrism: a stress on the sacrifice of Jesus Christ on the cross as making possible the redemption of humanity[1]

I embrace these characteristics. Without any hesitation whatsoever I affirm what Thomas Oden has called "Classic Christianity"[2] as summarized in the Nicene-Constantinopolitan Creed. I have been spiritually birthed and nurtured by the evangelical church and I will forever be indebted for that. But having served over four decades in the trenches of evangelicalism, both as a pastor and religious educator, I sometimes found myself unable or unwilling to go where this particular expression of Christ's church seemed intent on going. I want to believe that on such occasions my hesitancy has been the result of a reasoned and theologically based response. But I'm sure that my actions weren't always clear to others. The image that has often come to my mind in this regard is that I have been "chasing" the bride of Christ for all these years, trying to find my rightful place. I just can't seem to catch up and find my seat at the table. And, honestly, sometimes, I have viewed the American evangelical church as a kind of "runaway bride," revealing its own uncertainties about its God-ordained purpose in the world. Hopefully, this book will reassure readers that I have had, and continue to have, the desire to be vitally joined to the church as the earthly expression of Christ's body. The question is: can I do this in the current context of American evangelicalism?

This book's subtitle, *The Confessions of an Evangelical Outlier*, intends to describe my vantage point and the origins of the material that is discussed within. Although I have been an ordained minister of the church for nearly fifty years, much of the time I have worn this designation with all the comfort of the proverbial hair shirt. I suspect that my introverted self bears some responsibility for this. Lord knows, I never wanted nor envisioned myself in the sorts of roles I have filled that, together, add up to the substance of my adult life. But, beyond personal quirks, there has been, indeed there is even now, a sense that I never fully made peace with the vocation of ministry. This was largely due to some gnawing doubts I had about my fit within the church I served and its ministry, along with an almost constant undertow of dissonance over what I believed or what I was asked to affirm as an officer of the church.

As I've written these pages, I have harbored "dangerous hopes." They are dangerous stemming from my belief that I write my observations herein at some personal and professional cost. But even if that is an overblown concern, the fact remains that the viewpoints towards which I would hopefully move the church are, in themselves, fraught with some risk. Change always brings with it uncertainty. But these are my "hopes" in the best sense of the word. I believe that the church is called to "serve the present age" and therefore I hope to see the marshaling of Christ's bride in a manner that reflects this kind of contextual engagement.

My subtitle is something of a cheap knock-off of a book I read my final year in seminary, a book that altered the way I looked at virtually everything. Over forty years ago, sitting in a seminary classroom, I heard a favorite professor of mine reference a book that had deeply affected him and the way he looked at matters within the church. Because I admired him so, I noted the title of the book, *Include Me Out!: Confessions of an Ecclesiastical Coward*, written by an English Methodist missionary to Zambia named Colin Morris

(Abingdon Press, 1968). As fate would have it, a few days later, browsing in a small bookstore in Lexington, Kentucky, I found this book on a sale table! I paid fifty cents for it and proceeded to have my ecclesiastical world turned upside down. And that may be an understatement. The storyline of the book involves Morris opening his front door one morning to discover the body of a little African man who had died there from hunger during the night. Later that day, the mail brings Morris the latest church paper from England, filled with church politics and typical ecclesial bluster about things like the proposed Methodist/Anglican union, how to properly dispose of leftover communion bread, and other issues that are figuratively juxtaposed beside the emaciated body of a hunger-riven Zambian man. The almost obscene disconnect of these events is more than Morris can endure, and he "includes himself out" from further involvement in that kind of ministry, in that kind of church. Thus begins the prophetic rant of a self-confessed "ecclesiastical coward."

This ninety-nine page book has been read and re-read throughout my nearly fifty years in ministry. It has rained all over my neat little ecclesiastical parades, challenged me to try to focus on what truly matters, and castigated my pride whenever I felt like I had "arrived" in any sense of the term. Of course, Morris engages in some literary hyperventilation, but his basic point that the church exists to meet the needs of real human beings was an arrow that lodged deeply in my heart from the moment I read the book. Over the years, I have had members of my pastoral staff read the book, and although it is long out of print, I secured copies to give to my two children once they were old enough to read it with understanding, telling them that it might be the best way to understand this mysterious person who happens to be their father.

As I look back at what Colin Morris did in his book, I have come to see it as a case of what I call "table flipping." Mirroring Jesus' episode in the Temple, Morris figuratively walked into the halls of the church and started flipping over tables that had become obstacles or hindrances to what he viewed as the church's real purpose. His story illustrates how easily, good intentions notwithstanding, the church often becomes its own worst enemy. Our ideas for making things better, for becoming more efficient (shall I say "purpose-driven"?), so often become more non-essential furniture in the ecclesial foyer barricading the way of the very people who are at the center of our mission and reason for existence in the first place. It happens. So, from time to time, men and women possessed with particular visions and burdens have walked into churchly courts and begun to flip over tables, "driving out" that which complicates things for people who need to get in. But it's a dicey proposition, because just like the temple authorities of Jesus' day, ecclesiastical leaders have never been known to take kindly to those who overturn the status quo and mess with the entry way of the church.

I have no doubt that Colin Morris paid a personal price for his venture into table flipping. Going back to the original temple table flipper, Jesus himself, it's not likely that anyone can question the powers-that-be or the methodologies of the moment without paying some kind of cost. In fact, some years after I first encountered Morris' book, I was talking with a missionary who had connections in Zambia and asked him if he had ever heard of Colin Morris? His face reddened as he veritably spit out the name of Morris and proceeded to condemn him in no uncertain terms as a troublemaker and all-around headache for the church. As far as I can tell, that's par for the course with table flippers. There is an oft-used phrase that rightly describes the risk of flipping ecclesiastical tables in any age: They Hang Prophets! Or, as one wryly noted, they ignore them, which in the long run is far worse. So all of what follows is, in the best sense of the word "a dangerous hope."

Over the past four decades, I have served the church as a pastor or theological educator. I served as Senior Minister in a highly visible and influential church, where one of the founders of the National Association of Evangelicals was a member. I chaired the Department of Religion and Philosophy at a nationally known evangelical liberal arts college. I have lived in close association with American evangelicalism for all of my adult life. I have profited measurably from my associations with the church and met wonderful, devoted people. All my previously stated reservations aside, I do not regret the way my life has unfolded as a servant of the church. However, like Morris, I have observed and experienced things that have affected me deeply, at gut level. Now, at the end of my "active" ministry, I find that there are a host of signs, trends, approaches, etc., in the church which strike me as extremely worrisome. In fact, I believe that these matters could well place the church in grave peril.

Let no one misunderstand. I'm no saint. I'm not even a crusader in the best sense of that, now, questionable term. My record as a champion of the poor and downtrodden is spotty at best. But Morris' book drilled into me a deep suspicion of "business as usual" even when it was done in the name of God. In short, this is what has turned me into an outlier. The dictionary defines an outlier as a person or thing situated away or detached from the main body or system; or, a person or thing differing from all other members of a particular group or set.[3] I would view my forty-plus years of ordained ministry as "situated away or detached from the main body." I know that I differ in a variety of ways from other members of this particular group known as evangelicals. I have often perceived myself as one who is "looking in from the outside," and further, I know that I am not alone. I believe that the evangelical church in America has a growing number of outliers. And a lot of them hold ministerial licenses.

My desire to speak out in critique, to openly express my "dangerous hopes" for the church, is driven by a desire to speak for many others in ministry who, I know, resonate with much of what I am about to say. As a pastor and ministerial educator for more than forty years, I have often found myself in conversation with pastors who share with me their misgivings about the direction the church is taking with regard to particular issues. I know these men and women to be faithful shepherds of God's church, and yet the political realities of the ecclesial world requires that they mute their voices lest they raise questions about their fidelity to the church, or even risk subtle and not-so-subtle forms of retribution. They are not paranoid; these things happen. Much of my own frustration and concern for the church lies right at this point: namely, that we can't even talk honestly about certain issues lest we are branded as somehow suspect. There's nothing heretical about having an honest conversation! This is how theology has always been done. The concerns of these men and women, who so faithfully embody what officers of the church ought to be, prompt me to attempt to speak for them. Not that they will find themselves in agreement with me at every turn. I sincerely doubt that will be the case, in fact. But I want to model an atmosphere of honest dialogue about matters of great importance, which is something I believe the church needs as it finds its way into a new century.

Continuing to account for my willingness to write—more explanation of "why now?"—brings me back to an image, I even see it as a vision, that I have not been able to dismiss. A few years ago, I was on sabbatical in Australia, working with Aussie pastors and with men and women who needed ordination and licensing coursework in the areas of my teaching experience. Because Australia is both like and unlike American culture, I have found it a most useful context for thinking about the role of the church in today's world. Despite the best efforts of European and American missionaries, Australia remains a mostly secular country, particularly in comparison to the U.S., and thus I'm conscious that it may be providing me a glimpse into where the church in America is likely headed. To put it mildly, the church's joust with post-modern culture is not producing a surplus of "feel good" moments!

Near the end of my sabbatical travels, I was particularly concerned hearing about certain methods some Aussie churches were employing in their evangelism ministries. In my opinion, these methods were essentially American imports which, truthfully, hadn't even worked all that well in Bible-Belt USA. I couldn't see why they would garner any positive results in a country like Australia. While I refrained from being the "American know-it-all," and "setting them straight" (an all-too-frequent occurrence in the interactions between the Aussie and American churches), I found this extremely frustrating. The next day I commuted into the center-city of Melbourne to meet an Aussie friend for lunch. I found myself rehearsing the previous day's frustrations as I rode the train into the city. As I left the train station and walked to my destination, I encountered a young woman, maybe twenty or so, walking towards me. She was typical of Aussie young people in many ways—tattoos, body piercings and the like—but what was most noticeable about her was that she wore a sweatshirt that proclaimed in large black letters, "WE'RE FUCKED!" That's all it said. This is not a word that I use personally, nor do I wish to offend any reader, but it seems to me that the ramifications of the message on this young woman's clothing ought to be given all due attention, particularly for those of us who believe in something we claim to be "good news."

The message emblazoned on the front of a nondescript tan sweatshirt was an eloquent, if graphic, summary of the challenges confronting the Christian church. I couldn't pick this young woman out of a lineup if I saw her again. But the testament she bore was, to me, a blunt and angry sermon to the church and to me as a minister of that church. Since I never engaged this young woman, it's hard to say with any precision exactly what she meant by the words on her shirt. But, it seems apparent that her words were designed to communicate a combination of young-adult judgements on the current state of their lives and their world. It's easy to imagine that these words speak anger, dismay, frustration, and, perhaps more than anything else, a kind of resigned hopelessness that nothing can be done about this state of affairs. And whether one encounters such young people in a major cosmopolitan city like Melbourne or engages young adults from virtually any other area of the world, a little honest conversation will lead sooner rather than later to the kind of realities that foster profanity-laced sweatshirts.

How has this happened? Why have the profane sentiments of this woman's shirt come to symbolize the outlook of a generation, particularly in relation to the way they view the church? Anyone serious about Christian faith and the church's mission in the world must weigh such questions carefully. To the extent that these blunt words accurately portray the outlook of young adults in our world, the church must find an appropriate response. I believe that we dismiss this young woman's sentiments as mere adolescent rebelliousness at great peril. While the language is hard for some to hear, it is, in fact, an accurate and concise summary of what this generation is saying to everyone in general, and to the church in particular. That many within the church recoil at such language simply underscores the growing gap between those on the streets and those who would speak for God and His church. *This* is how they feel! And no amount of squeamishness on our part relative to how they communicate their anxieties is going to change that. The real question is: how will the church respond to the "we're fucked" generation? Do we care enough to leave our comfort zones to even try?

As a Christian, I clearly believe that we have something hopeful to say to this young woman and her peers. I don't believe that this generation is inescapably "fucked" in any final sense of that term. I know that God loves this young woman and her peers unconditionally and longs to be in relationship with her and them. I have been hugely blessed to enjoy this kind of fellowship with the Creator and have no doubt that it is indeed good news for everyone. But, I completely understand why members of this generation have come to feel the way they do about their prospects in the world and, particularly about the inability of the church to do much of anything to change matters. This book is an attempt to speak to the church about taking steps to engage, in redemptive and relationally meaningful ways, the "sweatshirt generation." And these steps begin with taking a long, hard look at ourselves. For, whatever else this sweatshirt prophecy means, it clearly implies that the church has fallen well short of what it has been called to be and do in our world. We must be willing to see the church the way those on the outside see it. We who have grown up in the church have seldom been able to see what others on the outside see. Or, like the proverbial man in James' epistle, we look at ourselves in the mirror of reality only to immediately forget what we saw as we turn our attention back to "church work." Such an exercise of honest assessment is not for the faint of heart, nor for those into quick fixes. As one aptly put it, "yes, the truth will set you free, but only after causing you a great deal of pain." Some painful self-reflection on the part of the church is called for in order that we might redemptively engage a world that seems to be, well, "fucked."

Although I have made, and will make, acknowledgments to many who have put me in their debt due to the role they have had in shaping my life and thinking, this book is significantly driven by the memory of that chance encounter on the streets of a large Australian city. Much of my motivation to write these words is vested in that young woman, whoever she is, and, to all the other people, young, old, black, white, straight, gay, and so on who would share her "darker" outlook and its prospects for the largely forgotten majority.

As I alluded to earlier, my greatest fear about the things I am writing here is that some will take my words as just one more self-pitying rant from an embittered member of the clergy, a sucker punch at a church that doesn't hit back, at least not usually in any tangible sense. To any who might read

Introduction

this kind of motive into what follows, all I can say is this: I write from a deep love of ministry and the vocation of ministry. In many ways, I have had a wonderful experience in serving the church as one of its clergy. I can't imagine what my life would have been like apart from this kind of service. I have a profound regard for the church, but this regard is coupled with an ongoing sense of frustration at the way the church often presents itself or is represented in the world. What I hope readers might do is to consider these words a kind of "lovers' quarrel," a conversation that originates not out of rancor or rejection but out of a desire to engage the beloved bride of Christ in a frank and open manner. Doubtless, some will find this difficult to grasp given the issues and viewpoints that they will find within. But, to all who read these words, I pledge that this is my best attempt at "speaking the truth in love."

I am acutely aware that because of some of the positions I lean towards, or even because of the questions I raise, some will assume that I have "given up my faith" or, at best, have entered some kind of faith crisis. Neither is the case. Never in my fifty-plus years as a Christian have I not consciously determined to follow the teachings of Jesus as best as I knew how. If some choose to question my fidelity to Christ and His Church, there is nothing I can do to prevent that. But I take heart that such a judgment lies in God's hands alone. It is to Him that I must ultimately account. As the title suggests, I have been walking with the church for many years, but the walking has been with some discomfort. I do not for a moment discount the possibility that some of the "stones" in my shoe creating that discomfort are my own weaknesses. I humbly confess those weaknesses and desire to submit them to the ample resources of God's grace, but I also believe that the concerns I raise herein are shared by a large number of my fellow-travelers. Some of them have found their relationship to Christ's bride has been strained and virtually broken. How can that not bring great harm to the church and to those who love it?

By nature, I am an introverted, non-confrontational, even cowardly, person. I have never sought to pick a fight with anyone, least of all the church. I have been an expert at keeping quiet and then thinking afterwards, "you know, what I should have said was . . ." I am not naturally given to flipping tables. Whether the new daring is owing to the increasingly real notion that my days of active ministry are drawing to a close, or to the cumulative effect of a lifetime of watching the church shoot itself in the foot with regards to its intended mission, I will leave to the reader's judgment. But at this moment in my life, I have a compelling need to march into the halls of the church and have at it! I repeat that my greatest fear is that this will be misinterpreted as some long, simmering tirade of one more church cynic. All I can say to that is that I am not cynical regarding the church. My greatest hope is that this will be received as a kind of love letter to an institution that I have tried to serve faithfully throughout my adult life. It's "tough love," to be sure, but as God is my witness, it springs from a deep and abiding love for the church. What I know for sure is that I/we owe it to that sweatshirt-wearing young woman to have this conversation. With the memory of her so clear in my mind, I cannot remain silent. It would be an absolute betrayal of my calling, my church, and most importantly, my Lord.

For nearly forty years now, I have served the church either in parish ministry or in theological education. I have been a pastor of small, medium and large congregations and helped to prepare dozens, if not hundreds, of men and women for Christian ministry. I have graduated from a Bible college, a Christian liberal arts college, two seminaries, and a university-level graduate school. I have served on licensing and ordination boards, worked with denominational task forces, and assisted with any number of assignments related to the church and its mission in the world. I have married, buried, baptized and administered the sacrament to people from virtually all walks of life. I have sat at the bedsides of dying saints, and had anguished conversations with the angry, apostate grandchildren of those same saints, on their way out of the church. In short, I have seen and experienced a great deal inside and outside of the church over my lifetime. I do not come to my current judgments regarding the church naively or without experience and context. But, like Colin Morris' little man with the shrunken belly, there is a young woman walking down the streets of a major city, wearing a tan sweatshirt with a crude, provocative message on the front, who has taken up permanent residence in my head. What I say to the church, I say on behalf of this young woman and the countless millions of others whom she represents. The tables I flip over in my own ecclesial temple are items and issues that I believe stand as a barrier between that young woman and the Christ who so ardently wants to become her savior and friend. Everything written herein is penned with sincere humility, sobriety and even a healthy dose of fear.

> They angered the Lord at the waters of Meribah,
> and it went ill with Moses on their account;
> for they made his spirit bitter,
> and he spoke words that were rash. (Psalm 106:32–33)

God forgive me if I am being rash. It really is complicated. And besides all that, I don't know.

Chapter 1

The Making of an Outlier

> Fear of being written off by friends, family and colleagues is frightening, but something is more frightening: living a life of faith that is fake and inauthentic. Silence, like every form of dishonesty, is life-destroying.
>
> —Jacqueline Bussie[4]

No one starts out with the goal of becoming an outlier. I mean, who honestly *wants* to be an outsider? Being outside looking in through the window is not anyone's dream scenario. And when those windows are stained glass, the prospects of such an outside vantage point become all the more unappealing. But outliers persist nevertheless, and some accounting for that persistence must be made, for the simple reason that there are a lot of us sitting in the pews of evangelical churches these days, unsure of what to do. "Do I stay, or do I go? And where would I go?" This is my dilemma as I write these pages. "Am I still an evangelical?" "Do I even want to be?" "Can I remain in a church where it seems that I have so many minority opinions?" I have found such questions persistent and torturous as I try to discern just how I ought to relate to the church tradition in which I have been born, raised, and nurtured. In many cases, particular circumstances or an obvious force would appear to explain how persons become marginalized from their original place of refuge or safe harbor; a hurtful church experience, an overly authoritarian pastor, or an intractable theological issue can all be the source of one's outsider status. In my case, it's more complicated. That's what this chapter aims to explain. Previously, I suggested that some of my personality traits might help explain my feelings towards the church. The role of temperament in one's choice of a church is much more significant than we might imagine, and I'll admit to feeling intuitively much more at home in some of the mainline churches. But because that's far from the whole story, I'll fill in some further context and background that should map out my journey to the margins and clarify how I have come to view myself as something of an evangelical black sheep.

BEGINNINGS

I am awake. With a nod to Charles Dickens, these words aptly describe the beginnings of my journey in the church. I can't prove this, but for all of my conscious life, my earliest memory has been one of me waking up on my mother's lap in church. That's not hard to imagine; my family spent a *lot* of time in church! I am the eighth of ten children (seven girls, three boys) and collectively we logged more time in church buildings than many pastors. So the odds are pretty good that my first memory would be located in a church environment. "Waking up" also serves well as a recurring metaphor of my relationship with the church of my youth and adolescence. I have awakened often in church, in a variety of ways.

My early faith was nurtured in the congregation of a small "holiness" sect centered, mainly, in the state of Ohio. Shortly before I was born, my family had moved from central to southern Ohio (technically, Appalachia), where I spent my first ten years. Our church would rightly have been viewed as "revivalistic," and worship was a lively, intense, and often highly emotional event. In my youth I observed people shouting spiritual words and phrases, running through the aisles waving handkerchiefs, and actually walking on the backs of church pews in a demonstration of religious fervor. I even saw people "slain in the spirit," which struck me at that stage of life as strange and even a bit frightening, but it was how our faith was "done." We prayed "unitedly," or all together all at once; we were "almost Pentecostal," stopping short of glossolalia. That was forbidden in no uncertain terms! My own children grew up in a much more reserved, formal kind of church atmosphere and never saw or experienced anything remotely similar to what I've described above. When my son was in seminary, he sent me a paper he'd written, needing a proofreader, and I noticed he mentioned that his father had grown up in the Pentecostal tradition. Based on what he'd heard from me around the dinner table, that was a reasonable conclusion!

I spent my early childhood carving Bibles from huge bars of Ivory Soap, turning Quaker Oat boxes into ersatz drums for the annual Vacation Bible School rhythm band, and going to camp meetings in the summer. I was raised on Southern gospel music, creek-side baptism services, and innumerable potlucks and church picnics. For reasons I can't recall, in those days, attending Sunday school was considered even more important than attending morning worship. I can remember skipping the church service from time to time to get an early start on a day trip, but we would never consider missing Sunday school. I have, even now, a medal I received for not missing Sunday school for six consecutive years! I wore that medal every Sunday with childish pride, and only our eventual move away from that small community prevented me from adding another bar or two to my trophy. Church was clearly the centerpiece of the Walters family. All this seemed very normal. I didn't know anything else, and at that point in my young life I considered churches where things were done differently inferior to my own. So, I cut my religious teeth in the heart of the southern Ohio Bible belt in a church that was revivalistic, sect-like in its wariness of other churches, and highly emotive in its worship and practice of the faith. My initial awakening in church introduced me to a particular expression of Christian faith that seemed right to me in that moment, but I would come to question elements of that early faith heritage as I grew older.

In the spring of 1960, the Walters family was rocked with news that would forever alter my life. My father was diagnosed with a serious lung disease, most likely attributable to his work as a foreman in a steel mill during World War II. There was no cure for his condition, only remedial steps that could slow the development of the disease and prolong his life. The doctors recommended a major step: a move from southern Ohio to a dry climate.

We learned of our father's illness in April. Four months later, my parents—having sold their business and their home—loaded up their six unmarried children, said goodbyes to their four married children and a dozen or so grandchildren, and moved southwest to Tucson, Arizona. The eight of us made the trip in a 1959 Ford station wagon (un-air-conditioned!) pulling a U-Haul trailer that held whatever household belongings had not been sold at auction.

Moving from southern Ohio to the Sonoran desert was the mother of all paradigm shifts for our family! In Ohio, my parents had owned their own business, but now they sought employment wherever they could find it. My older teenage sisters struggled with leaving their friends and adjusting to new schools. My young brother and I, blissfully oblivious to these concerns, reveled in our new surroundings. We had traded in the oak, mulberry, and hickory trees for saguaro and prickly pear cacti, mesquite and palo verde trees, and neighborhood streets paved with sand. The lizards, horned toads, and tarantulas we found right around our house made us think we'd moved to Mars! But beyond the change in flora and fauna, the human world suddenly grew much larger for me. In Ohio, I had rarely seen people of color. I doubt that I'd ever seen a Latino, Native American, or Asian person. I had only glimpsed an African American from a distance when we went to a nearby city. But in Arizona all that changed. I encountered not only different races, but different religions; there were Roman Catholics, Jews, Mormons and every kind of Protestant you could name. Our immediate neighborhood was heavily Roman Catholic and I suppose, given the number of children in our family, neighbors easily assumed we were as well, at least until they saw how often we went to church! We went Sunday mornings, Sunday evenings, Wednesday evenings and any number of other occasions when there were special services such as fall and spring "revivals" every year. The availability of a church in the same holiness denomination we had associated with in Ohio was an important factor in choosing Tucson for relocation.

I spent the next eight years of my life in that church, constantly aware that the virtually endless variety of faith and life that the city and culture presented was both invigorating and threatening. As my own personality and temperament developed, I also increasingly sensed a subtle disconnect between my inclination toward shyness and aloof rationalism and the overly demonstrative brand of Christian faith I saw modeled in our church. Not that I doubted its validity in the lives of those who embraced it, not at all. My own parents remain, to this day, two of the most consistently Christian people I have ever known. Whatever I say in this book, I feel nothing but deep gratitude for their faith and the heritage that I received from them in authentic Christian living. But as far back as Tucson, expressions of faith in the emotive vein didn't readily appeal to me.

During my sophomore year in high school, I began to deal with what I would eventually come to see as a "call" to ministry. Initially, I found this appalling. As an introverted, painfully timid person, not given to the kind of emotional expressions that I associated with Christian faith, there was nothing I wanted less than a life in the church! I dealt with this as best I could—in other words, I kept it to myself hoping it would go away. It didn't! It was always there, somewhere. I graduated from high school and entered the University of Arizona, still edging away from this strange sense of calling. After one year of denial marked by a number of personal failures, which seemed at the time to be unmistakable omens, I relented and applied to a denominational Bible college affiliated with our church.

It was the late 1960s. In that era, moving from the virtual anarchy of a major university campus to the completely regimented life of a tiny

Bible college was a complete culture shock to me. But I did my best to adjust. I believed I was doing the right thing, my dis-ease notwithstanding. I found wonderful friends there who loved God deeply and served Him wholeheartedly. Inwardly, though, I continually struggled with my inability or unwillingness to join in the highly emotive expressions of personal faith. Mercifully, I found ways to cope. One of my strengths—and weaknesses—is the ability to blend in, to "go along to get along." It's a necessary survival tool for outliers! I employed it as needed. Fortunately, I met a new faculty member during my junior year who became a mentor and later a life-long friend. He encouraged me to consider going to seminary following graduation, even though that was not at all typical for graduates of this college in those days. The prevailing feeling was that "Bible School" was sufficient "book-learning." I actually had a meeting with an administrator who tried to talk me out of my decision to attend seminary. Happily, he was unsuccessful.

Seminary opened the Christian world up for me in important ways. I met men and women from different backgrounds and faith contexts who clearly loved God as much as I did. I discovered worlds of scholarship that I didn't know existed. Best of all, I met my future wife, who was matriculating across the street at a small Christian liberal arts college. My seminary years represented the beginning of my desire and willingness to "color outside the lines" with respect to some of the things I had been taught and had accepted in uncritical ways.

After seminary, I spent two years as an assistant pastor and youth minister at the Houghton Wesleyan Church in western New York State. Since the town was home to Houghton College, I had the opportunity to interact with disciplined scholars, many at the top of their fields, who took their Christian faith very seriously. This, along with my earlier awakening to academic life in seminary, birthed a desire in me for further education. After two years in Houghton, we moved to San Antonio, Texas, where I would work as an assistant pastor/youth pastor at a modestly sized Wesleyan church. I made the move intending to pursue a Master's degree at a local university, but on the day I went to enroll in classes, I learned that the program had been cancelled! I turned to San Antonio's St. Mary's University and found a Master's program in theology there, one of the most serendipitous events of my life. At St. Mary's, the Marianist and Oblate Fathers treated me like a long-lost cousin! My unflattering caricatures of Roman Catholicism were shattered as I met men and women who were deeply spiritual and committed to God. I discovered there my love of the sacramental life of the church. Best of all, it was at St. Mary's where I discovered and fully embraced my Wesleyan heritage. With the full encouragement of the Marianist Fathers, I explored Wesley more deeply than ever before and wrote my thesis examining his "social consciousness." I cannot adequately state how important my time at St. Mary's was in terms of shaping my viewpoints and forming me spiritually.

After finishing that degree, I spent four years on the faculty at the bible college from which I'd graduated six years earlier. It was an important part of my development, as I was required to teach in a variety of areas, and that forced me to venture into new avenues of thought and practice. Probably most importantly, these four years convinced me that my "fit" within this particular culture was never likely to be comfortable. I enjoyed my time there, made good friends and had some very fine students, but I learned when to keep my head down, when it was safe to speak out, and when it wasn't. I had no illusions about the ease of making this type of environment a long-term part of my life, so I began to make other plans. In 1982, I applied for and was accepted into doctoral studies at Drew University for the following fall, but I decided to delay my studies for a year and continue on faculty at the Bible college due to some personal and family concerns. In late July, I received a phone call from my old "employer," the Houghton church in New York. Their pastor had suddenly resigned to accept a position on the West Coast. The church had heard that I was in transition and asked if I would consider serving as the interim pastor of the Houghton congregation for a year while they conducted a search for a full-time pastor. Since I had already determined to postpone doctoral work for a year, and my wife and I had both enjoyed our earlier two-year stint in Houghton, we agreed to this.

One year! I spent the next thirteen years of my life as the Senior Pastor of Houghton Church. It was, and will always be, the single most transforming experience of my life. For one thing, it turned me from an ambivalent and suspicious "60's Jesus person," into a "churchman" in the best sense of that term. Second, I fell in love with pastoral ministry in a way that I never anticipated. I continue to prize those years of my life. In 1995, I left pastoral life and joined the Department of Religion and Philosophy at Houghton College as Professor of Christian Ministry. Leaving parish ministry was a hard choice, but I was keen to work at preparing women and men for ministry. I soon learned that the world of church-sponsored higher education puts faculty, particularly religion faculty, in the crosshairs of critics, many of whom seem deeply suspicious of virtually every aspect of higher education. My twenty years on faculty included numerous occasions which raised difficult questions about my fit within the broader evangelical community.

Since retiring and leaving the faculty, I have continued to wonder about the church and my relationship to it. Specifically, I've wondered, "What are the reasons that I have felt detached?" In the following chapters of this book, I will address specific issues that have become "stones in my shoes." But before getting to those matters, I want to articulate some foundational concerns that have prompted me to question whether my relationship with evangelicalism can or even ought to continue.

ECCLESIASTICAL COMPLICATIONS

As I pondered this writing, a line from Colin Morris's book *Include Me Out!* repeatedly came to mind. He said that "as a pastime, reviling the church from the inside has much in common with kicking one's mother inside the womb. It is aggression without consequences, a mock heroism that allows the strut of bravado secure from retaliation."[5] While I don't imagine that what I write herein is clearly "secure from retaliation," I am acutely conscious of the possibility that my words could be interpreted as a kind of sucker punch aimed at a target that is easily attacked. I am committed to doing whatever I can to allay that judgment. I've always detested bullies, so the furthest thing from my mind is to be one more ecclesiastical bully and pick on the church that birthed and nurtured me, knowing that it will not hit back. I merely endeavor to share with readers why it is that, for me, the suit doesn't seem to fit! At least it doesn't a lot of the time. I am trying to address the question of whether there is room in today's evangelical church for outliers like me. I honestly don't know the answer to that question. Much of the time I suspect that I have a good inkling of where things are headed, but in the end, of course, I don't know. It's at least somewhat likely that this book will bring that question to resolution.

So, to borrow an old cliché, I have a stone in my shoe. Actually, I have several. A quick glance at the Contents page reveals many of them. But here, I wish to paint in much broader strokes. I want to address certain aspects of today's evangelical church that I find both uncomfortable and worrisome. I'm troubled enough by these issues that I question my ongoing ecclesial future, and I'm worried that these issues deeply affect the church as it pursues its mission in the world. Painting in broad strokes involves generalizations, always perilous. Of course, there are churches that are clear exceptions to the concerns I raise. The fact is, I can name some of them. And, I am truly grateful for the courage and vision they show in choosing an ecclesial "road less traveled." But overall, the fact remains that there is an evangelical "brand," though these days it is subject to a variety of interpretations. Here, I'm offering mine.

Years ago, I audited a class in "The Sociology of Religion." It was an eye-opening experience for me that continues to help me assess both the church and my own personal faith. But the most enduring thing I took from that course was this: "Whatever is perceived *as* real, *is* real in its consequences."

Two points to make before picking up my brush: first, there are widespread perceptions about the evangelical church out there which, regardless of their veracity, exact heavy consequences from the general population. The church forgets that, or denies that, at great cost. Second, what I am cataloging below and throughout this book are *my* perceptions. They may be arguable, and they may turn out to be mistaken, but they are my perceptions, and I can poignantly vouch for the reality of their consequences.

DON'T ASK DON'T TELL

I readily admit to being a huge Bruce Springsteen fan. I love his music because I think it so accurately catches the vibe of blue-collar America. But I'm also struck by how he has this knack for getting below the surface of human life and relationships. In his song "Code of Silence," he sings about a couple whose relationship is in deep trouble. The root of the problem is the "code of silence" between them that prevents them from the kind of communication and truth-telling that healthy relationships require. If there is any hope for this relationship the silence can't go on. Clearly, the Boss didn't have the church in mind when he wrote this song, but the truth it conveys is all too applicable to relationships within the church. As it turns out, silence isn't golden after all!

One of the first indications that you may actually be an outlier is that you instinctively know when *not* to say anything. You know that the church is often no place to speak freely. There is a steep price to pay if you are too outspoken or self-revealing because it causes anxiety in the group. In systems theory, this is referred to as "homeostasis," the delicate tranquility and systemic equilibrium that is highly sought after and desperately guarded in any "anxious emotional system." The "code of silence" is all too real in the church. But this is problematic in a variety of ways and indicates a fundamental weakness in the church's self-understanding. In *Life Together*, Dietrich Bonhoeffer contends that "the final breakthrough to fellowship" cannot occur until there is fellowship *as sinners*.[6] What he means is that people must be real! This kind of fellowship necessitates a kind of honesty and authenticity in the body that is all-too-rare because it is messy, uncomfortable, and even a bit risky. So the message comes through loudly and clearly: "Don't rock the boat!" When someone is faced with this reality, the choice ordinarily comes down to living one's life silently, stifling authenticity, or leaving the community all together.

The truth is that people *want* to talk. They want to be authentically themselves. And this includes saying things that aren't always considered kosher. Many of the people who hold the church at arm's length aren't looking for easy answers. Rather, they are "looking for a place to ask questions, where they can rest comfortably with few answers, learn new questions, and to be accepted by others in a faith community."[7] A "code of silence" stymies this kind of atmosphere and community. Psychologist Leon Festinger coined the very useful concept of "cognitive dissonance," meaning information that contradicts previously held views *in which we have a stake*.[8] The questions people want to ask, the burdens they long to share, are those in which they have a personal stake! To discover that what you have long thought and believed may be questionable in some way is an anxiety-inducing experience. If church isn't the place where such questions can be asked, where is that place?

As a member of the clergy, I find the practice of keeping silent particularly onerous and counterproductive for pastors. Most pastors have questions; ideas that they'd like to discuss, and yes, even some doubts about matters of the faith that they'd like to share with someone. But they quickly figure out that being forthcoming and honest can become a fast track out of the church. And there is some evidence to suggest that they are right. Muzzling pastors may preserve the ecclesial peace, but it is short-sighted and in the long run pushes clergy towards cynicism. I know this all too well, personally and professionally.

This concern goes well past simply talking and being candid and honest. Without exception, every church has boundaries. Sometimes they are tangible things like membership, baptism, or basic doctrine, and sometimes the lines are more "sentient" such as traditional practices, historical connections, or congregational views on lifestyle issues. Whether clearly defined or sentient, boundaries are very real. And crossing those lines in a church is risky business. Coming to a place in life where one makes the choice to cross such boundaries requires a person to weigh the likely repercussions of their decision carefully.

I was in seminary during the Watergate hearings. I had cast my first-ever ballot in a presidential election a few months before. Raised in a Republican home, I honestly hadn't given politics much thought at that point in my life. I pulled the lever for Richard Nixon and moved on. When Watergate first became an issue, I was convinced it was nothing more than some partisan attempt to undermine a duly elected president. But as I became more informed, I began to think differently, and it was at that point that I knew I was crossing a line. That process eventually led me to a whole new perspective on politics, one that I have found interfaces best with my faith understanding, even if it has put me in a precarious position with some of my family and other old friends. But importantly, Watergate and other occasions of line-crossing have shown me the fallacy of simplistic binary choices between upholding my heritage and surrendering my faith! Seriously, there are church people who view political commitments in just such a manner (see Chapter 6)!

While most of these "boundary" decisions fall far short of denying the faith, they clearly complicate matters. They complicate things because in the churches I have been associated with over the years, when you cross a boundary, or color outside the lines, you get branded as an instigator. Trying to live authentically always carries with it seen and unforeseen costs. Outliers know this from experience, but why is this the case? Why must the church present a choice between conforming to the boundaries or being viewed as a rebel and a potentially dangerous person to the rest of the body? Especially when perceived boundaries have nothing to do with basic Christianity. Is the church not any different from any other club or social group in its essential character? Of course, there should be limits to openness, but in my view, the typical evangelical church has miles to go in this regard before they are anywhere near a dangerous precipice.

Despite the damage done, these ecclesial battles over tradition and boundaries continue virtually unabated. The ultimate squelch in evangelicalism is to pin someone as a "liberal." "L" has become the new scarlet letter! The Liberal/Conservative divide in the church has become just that—a convenient reason to divide. I don't get it. As I stated earlier, I subscribe to classic Christianity in every way, and yet there are many evangelicals who would dismiss me out of hand as a dangerous liberal. Nancey Murphy observed that "there are often deeper divisions between liberals and conservatives *within* a denomination than there are between one denomination and another (emphasis mine)."[9] I have certainly found this to be true. I have taught religion and theology across the spectrum, including seminary classes comprised of people from all the "main-line" denominations, even Universalist/Unitarians, and I can say without hesitation that the most pressure I've felt to carefully weigh my words was in the classes populated by self-professed evangelicals. I have seen faculty colleagues hauled before committees of pastors and church officials and forced to defend statements they have made in their classes (often misunderstood or taken completely out of context by the student who brought the matter to the attention of authorities). Do such inquisitions actually help? Isn't the church bigger than this? It is entirely appropriate to have people properly vetted as pastors and teachers, but it is another thing altogether to question the orthodoxy of deeply committed servants, who have sacrificed more than most understand to gain the credentials necessary to practice their craft. They deserve the benefit of the doubt. And by the way, there's a huge difference in a classroom setting between "ideas" and "beliefs." I think that should be clear to those who want to "steady the ark" and guard their traditions and viewpoints, but apparently it isn't. Exploring ideas is part and parcel of "doing theology." Speculating about *ideas* is the coin of the realm for theologians, while *beliefs* are in an entirely different category. Understanding the difference is crucial.

Ultimately, the unwritten "code of silence" and the marginalization of those who trespass boundaries reduces back to the problem of dealing with diversity within the church. Frankly, I've concluded that much of the talk about church unity is mostly pietistic malarkey! The reason that there are several hundred distinct Christian bodies in the United States, and Lord only knows how many "independent" churches, is that the church struggles continually with the issue of unity. Doubtless, many will claim that *their* particular church needed to arise or separate to safeguard doctrinal purity or to take some particular stand on an issue, but at the end of the day, the gospel truth is that we prefer being with people like ourselves! Scripture takes very seriously the tangible real issue of unity, but we subtly move the goalposts and focus on something more aptly described as uniformity. "We're one," we say. "Just look at how we agree on everything." "Everything" typically being some set of doctrines, or worship styles, or positions on "social or political" issues, and so on. But, such pleasant talk about "unity" is belied by all of the previous discussion of how people are silenced and socially coerced into towing particular lines on church boundaries. And, let's be straight about this: uniformity isn't unity, not even close! A church of a hundred or so people, who all agree on what music they like, how they vote, and how stylish the pastor's spouse should dress etc., are talking about something other than what Scripture means by the unity of the church. Look it up: diversity in the church is not only to be tolerated, it is to be celebrated!

So, that brings us back to the outliers, like me, who want to be part of the body but who also wish to live and speak authentically as members of that body. Not everyone is alike. It's not possible, and it's not healthy to pretend that it is. Again, as Bonhoeffer put it, "Our community with one another consists *solely* in what Christ has done . . . I have community with others and I shall continue to have it *only* through Jesus Christ," (emphasis mine).[10] I take this to mean that if the church builds its unity around *anything* other than Christ it will inevitably go off the rails at some point. Is sourcing unity in Christ alone risky? Yes. Is it messy? Yes. But that's what the church is supposed to be doing. John Pavlovitz put it this way:

> The church is capable of being a beautifully restorative community, one where disparate people are invited to bring the full weight of their inconsistency and hypocrisy and vacillation and

to be lovingly received as they are. It can and should be a place of loving renovation and healing and growth, but only when we allow everyone—both up front and in the pews—to be exactly who they are, to ask the truest questions of their hearts, to confront the deepest recesses of their personal darkness. It should be the very last place that pretending should be required or encouraged. And the wonderful truth is, a God worthy of worship can totally handle such naked honesty. It's sad when we who call ourselves the Church cannot.[11]

I've been looking for this community. I haven't found it yet, but I'm hopeful it's out there. You don't have to be an outlier to figure out that the code of silence can't go on.

HEARTS OVER MINDS

As a long-time faculty member in Christian higher education, I can say without hesitation that the professors' biggest frustration is the unending issue of trying to convince good, evangelical students that there is no contradiction between having a clear head and a clean heart. Some, thankfully not all of them by any means, show up for their college education virtually "learning-foreclosed," a term with which Christian higher education faculty are all too familiar. The irony of students paying thousands of dollars of tuition so they can sit in class and resist any suggestion that they ought to take a fresh look at their faith never ceases to flummox me. But, as they say, they got it honest! The evangelical churches from which they came have had a long history of harboring suspicions about education. And that has become a major disappointment and painful stone in my shoe across the years.

I make no pretense of being a scholar in the best sense of that term. I have been in higher education long enough, and rubbed elbows with enough genuine scholars, to know that I am not in that league. But I have a profound appreciation for the educational process because of the doors it has opened for me and the gut-level conviction that loving God with our minds is not something that applies only to people with graduate degrees. It applies to any and every serious Christian. I went to seminary and graduate school out of the belief that Christians should take advantage of every opportunity to learn and go deeper in the understanding of their faith. Becoming the pastor in a college community only served to deepen this conviction. But such commitments wrestle with the almost constant paradoxical reality of a faith tradition that, in many ways, remains deeply suspicious of education and its "liberalizing" tendencies. Church people, especially those of a more conservative bent, have long had a tendency to pit the mind against the heart. Diana Butler-Bass wrote, "In many religious circles, the life of the mind is deemed dangerous because of its potential to challenge authority or reject church teachings."[12] I've endured numerous church meetings where the dangers and limitations of "book-learning" and education are solemnly intoned as cautionary tales. Listening to these caveats, it has often occurred to me that the person making this plea rarely has had much in the way of education, and I couldn't help but wonder what was truly motivating the speech. In her book, *Apostles of Reason: The Crisis of Authority in American Evangelicalism*, Molly Worthen says that "Of all of America's religious traditions, evangelical Protestantism, at least in its twentieth-century conservative forms, has ranked dead last in intellectual stature."[13] Having spent most of my life on evangelical campuses I both understand and regret Worthen's assessment. Not that there are no wonderful exceptions to this. There are, of course. But the unfortunate generalization holds true in most instances. The reluctance, or even fearfulness, I've witnessed in church people and Christian students to open themselves to expanding their understanding of God and the faith is puzzling, to say the least. Worthen notes that many evangelicals "seem more inclined to listen to amateurs and demagogues with little interest in subtle theology or close attention to history."[14]

I did a seminar once at a summer conference in which I made a statement about how the Pentateuch we have today came together. Despite the scene in "The Ten Commandments" movie where Charlton Heston—I mean Moses—walks up and hands Joshua the first five books of the Bible, I don't believe that Moses was the sole author of these books. While talking about these matters, I noticed a woman busy on her cell phone. After the session, she accosted me with some Googled information which basically allowed her to discount everything I had said and to dismiss me as "one more ivory-tower liberal." I knew the web resource she was using, one well-known for its rigidly literalistic readings of Scripture. For her this was a matter of defending her faith against the educated elite. For me, it was painful to realize that many people do not want to "grow up" in their faith, and thus they perceive people like me, my faculty colleagues, and thoughtful pastors as the "enemy." Dave Tomlinson put it this way: "Many evangelicals relate to God and their Christian faith in the compliant Child mode. What is even more remarkable is the number of such people who have extremely well-developed Adult modes of behavior in other areas of their lives. A friend recently spoke with despair of the way in which doctors, lawyers, and business people in his church settled for an incredibly simplistic version of faith, despite their training and professional responsibilities. They walked into church, seemed to switch off their critical faculties, and proceeded to go along with virtually everything."[15] My dilemma, shared by many, is this: "do we want to be part of this kind of church, where thinking critically about matters of the faith is viewed as unnecessary, unhealthy, and even dangerous?" "Do we want to have to constantly feel apologetic about getting educated?" I invested thirteen years of my life in being educated so that I could be useful to the church. The realization that many evangelical believers fail to value that is grievous to me. In 1995, Mark Knoll, a historian at Wheaton College, wrote a book titled *The Scandal of the Evangelical Mind*. His book is summed up with these words: "The scandal of the evangelical mind seems to be that no mind arises from evangelicalism. Evangelicals who believe that God desires to be worshiped with thought as well as activity may well remain evangelicals, but they will find intellectual depth—a way of praising God through the mind—in ideas developed by confessional or mainline Protestants, Roman Catholics, or perhaps even the Eastern Orthodox."[16] In the absence of an "evangelical mind," I know many who have found their way into other churches or traditions that value the mind in obvious and healthy ways. As an admitted outlier, I think about that, a lot.

SIN IN THE SYSTEM

In 1973, Psychologist Karl Menninger wrote a widely read book titled, *Whatever Became of Sin?* (Hawthorn Books, 1973). In that book, he lamented the hesitancy, even refusal, of modern people to speak meaningfully of sin. My final generalization about my struggles with evangelicalism focuses on what I believe is the tendency within evangelicalism to "cherry pick" when it comes to how they understand and remedy sin, the most empirically verifiable of all Christian doctrines. It is a paradox of no small order that a movement which champions the idea of confession, forgiveness, and redemption repeatedly fails to consider the full implications of what it means to live in a fallen world. Of course, I'm talking here about the concept of "systemic" sin or evil. While evangelical churches readily call out personal sins, as they should, for some reason they seem loath to explore the deeper ramifications of evil in our world. Back in the late 11th or early 12th century, Anselm of Canterbury wrote these words: "You have not yet taken full account of sin." I think about that line from time to time when I see or hear of evangelicals looking the other way when some form of injustice becomes apparent, opining that the church should "stay out of politics," arguing that systemic racism does not exist, or generally resisting any perspective that would embrace the presence of evil in things like governments, economic systems, or corporate entities. When I hear evangelicals buy into some of the extreme rhetoric afoot in our culture that would encourage people of faith to "run away" from any notion of "social justice" I am reminded of Anselm's words. We truly haven't yet taken full account. Obviously, several of the later chapters of this book will deal with specific manifestations of what I would consider "systemic evil," but this particular stone in my shoe has been uncomfortable enough that I want to call it out as one of the issues that has rapidly accelerated my status as an outlier. Selective theology is not actually theology at all. To fail to see that God's redemptive purpose in Christ transcends the forgiveness and restoration of individuals and envisions the transformation of the entire world is to close one's eyes to *the* major theme of Christian faith.

I remember, years ago, hearing Orlando Costas, a fiery Latino theologian, who lit up the Houghton chapel with his powerful and passionate call to justice for all. He excoriated the tendency to keep the good news personal and individual rather than viewing it as God's proclamation of liberty for all. He said, "The content of a gospel without demands in respect of justice, peace, and equity suggests a conscience soothing Jesus, with an un-scandalous cross, an otherworldly kingdom, a private, inwardly limited spirit, a pocket God, a spiritualized Bible, and an escapist church. Its goal is a happy, comfortable and successful life, obtainable through the forgiveness of an abstract sinfulness by faith in an unhistorical Christ."[17] I find his words compelling and convicting, and I want to be part of a church that grasps the cosmic implications of evil, while celebrating God's provision for evil's removal from God's world. This is not some newfangled idea from theological eggheads, not at all. This is "gospel 101." Our unwillingness to accept this as part of the reality of the church's mission in the world will forever hamstring its ministry and give serious pause to those who grasp this greater vision. Colin Morris said, "The judgement upon us is not that we have failed to bring our theology into line with its best modern thought, though that may be true, but that we do not act to the limit of the theology we already have."[18] The church's broad failure to live up to its own theology is what prompted Dallas Willard's observation that, "The post-evangelicals among us—and they are among us, in large numbers—are for the most part those who, *because* of their evangelical insights or suspicions, cannot accept a *form* of evangelical religious culture that makes the heart of evangelical faith irrelevant and the heart of the prophetic biblical tradition anything but subversive."[19] This goes for "outliers" as well.

So, this is where I find myself these days: a cautious, largely silent participant in a church that doesn't encourage diversity and openness, since that can complicate matters. I take some solace that I am far from alone. There are many outliers within the evangelical church. And their common predicament is that they're stuck! Chained, in many cases, to a fundamentalist past, convinced that it cannot get them where they need to go, and still not sure that they can go where some of their questions might be taking them. Frustrated, anxious, and yet at the same time, hopeful that there might yet be a place for them. For us. For me.

Chapter 2

Who Needs the Church Anyway?

LEARNING THE PERILS OF ECCLESIOLOGY LITE

> Evangelicals were once known as 'the serious people.' It is sad to note that today many evangelicals are the most superficial of religious believers—lightweight in thinking, gossamer-thin in theology, and avid proponents of spirituality—lite in terms of preaching and responses to life.
>
> —Os Guiness[20]

ABOUT TWO YEARS AGO, my daughter and her family moved from the center of the city where they lived to the suburbs. She enrolled her son in a church-related daycare, and she decided to visit the church as a possible church home. When I asked her about the visit, her impressions were less than stellar. I can't recall any of the specifics except for this line: "Dad, I don't need the church to give me coffee." Raised as a "preacher's kid" for much of her life, she obviously has a more acute sense of what the church is and should be than some, but her comment spawned a number of thoughts and seemed to validate concerns I have had about the church, particularly about its evangelical version, over the past two decades.

For the past twenty years now, my theological antennae have been dialed in on that branch of theology called "ecclesiology," the study and doctrine of the church. In a post-Christian and postmodern culture, the church in its incarnational presence is the single most important manifestation of what Christianity is about. But, as my daughter's comment attests, general impressions of the church often leave much to be desired. At least my daughter's evaluation arose from some sense of knowing that the church ought to be about more than providing some caffeine. The much more troubling phenomenon that characterizes today's ecclesial reality is the growing number of people who question whether the church is actually needed at all!

Anyone unaware of the disturbing data regarding church involvement in America in recent times is either not paying attention or is in denial. George Barna estimates that the number of unchurched Americans is growing by about one million each year, and the percentage of Americans with no religious preference has skyrocketed since the 1990s.[21] Fewer than half of those who claim affiliation with any Christian church in America actually attend on a given week. The percentage of adults in the U.S. who identify themselves as Christians has dropped dramatically. Millions of adults who were regular churchgoers as teenagers will no longer be active in a church by the time they reach thirty. This leads to the statistical probability that, given these numbers, most Americans will be non-Christians by the year 2035.[22] The immediate net effect of such data is that approximately 3,700 churches close their doors permanently in a given year (seventy-one per week).[23] And this is not just a "mainline" problem. Increasingly, the "who needs the church?" crowd has a past history in the evangelical church. This has clearly attracted the attention of church leaders, even if they don't say much publicly about it. Reggie McNeal, a well-known church analyst, pointed to the dis-ease he sees among church leaders: "In every arena I am running into an increasing number of people who are expressing fundamental doubts about the viability of the church. These are not critics from outside who don't like what the church is doing. These are connected leaders who don't like what they are experiencing in church."[24] McNeal paints an even direr long-term scenario when he questions the sustainability of the church in its present form. "The current church culture in North America is on life support. It is living off the work, money, and energy of previous generations from a previous world order. The plug will be pulled either when the money runs out (80 percent of money given to congregations comes from people aged fifty-five and older) or when the remaining three-fourths of a generation who are institutional loyalists die off or both."[25]

Whether this analysis is hyperbole or the proverbial "canary in the coal mine," it calls for anyone concerned about these matters to take a long look at why people are not only staying home from church services on Sundays but questioning the very idea of church itself. The sustainability of the church matters greatly to me. The church should be unsettled, and undertake serious self-reflection, when it hears people, particularly younger people, adopt a "whatever" attitude towards Christ's church.

Much has been made in recent years of the so-called "rise of the nones." This phrase describes the growing number of people who make no particular religious claims whatsoever. The move towards a more secular culture has been afoot at least since the 1960s. But the rate has markedly accelerated in the past couple of decades. This has occasioned much hand-wringing in church circles and produced many studies aimed at answering the question of why this is happening. In 2007, David Kinnaman and Gabe Lyons wrote, *UnChristian: What a New Generation Really Thinks About Christianity . . . and Why it Matters* (Baker Books). To this day, it remains a sobering wake-up call to anyone who may be tempted to think that "young people have always rebelled against the church and their parents' faith; once they get married and start having kids, like always before, they'll be back." *UnChristian* bluntly explains why this assumption could be patently untrue. Summarizing their findings, Kinnaman and Lyons write: "Most people [we] meet assume that *Christian* means very conservative, entrenched in their thinking, anti-gay, anti-choice, angry, violent, illogical, empire builders; they want to convert everyone and they generally cannot live peacefully with anyone who doesn't believe what they believe."[26] They go on to add that, "Many of those outside of Christianity, especially younger adults, have little trust in the Christian faith, and esteem for the lifestyle of Christ followers is quickly fading among outsiders. They admit their emotional and intellectual barriers go up when they are around Christians, and they reject Jesus because they feel rejected by Christians."[27] There are points to be argued here which might debunk some aspects of this statement, I'm sure. But, remember, *that which is perceived as real is real in its consequences!* I have no doubt that Kinnaman and Lyon are accurately reporting what they have found. The way Christianity and the church are perceived by the younger generations portends disaster.

But, as worrisome as the "rise of the nones" and all of its attendant issues may be, there is, I believe, an even more pressing issue that highlights the perils of what I am calling "ecclesiology lite." Beyond my concern with the "nones," there is the issue of the "dones"—those people who are simply "done" with church. They have grown up in the church, found meaningful faith for their lives, yet they have come to a fork in the road when it comes to their further participation in the institutional church.

This exodus out of the church is characterized by one major rationale—to preserve their faith! These folks "contend that the church no longer contributes to their spiritual development. In fact, they say, quite the opposite is true."[28] To quote Julia Duin, "Sunday mornings at church have become too banal, boring, or painful. Large groups of Christians are opting out of church because it is impossible to stay."[29] These "churchless Christians" have been described as perhaps the fastest growing denomination in America; David Barret estimates that there are over 100 million "churchless Christians" worldwide and that this number could easily double over the next twenty years.[30] Some of these do find their way into other denominations. Duin quotes a seminary classmate who switched from an evangelical to an "older" denomination because, "There's no training in sanctification," she said. "If you compare the church to a spiritual hospital, all evangelicals have is the obstetrics ward."[31] I've heard versions of this complaint often, and I think it has some validity. On her blog *Rethink Church*, Maggie Nancarrow said, "The church is not dying. It's failing. There's a difference."[32] Clearly, many Christian people are seeing something in the church that is disturbing enough to cause them to walk out and have a go at their faith apart from an institutional faith community. Most of the rest of this chapter is dedicated to suggesting why this might be the case. Tim Morey and Eddie Gibbs suggest that the "typical de-churched person approaches the church with the caution of one who has been burned and expects to be burned again."[33] The seemingly endless list of anecdotal episodes involving abuse, intolerance, and staggering insensitivity on the part of the institutional church towards people who sought sanctuary there (in the broadest sense) explains the "rise of the dones."

In his book *The Continuing Conversion of the Church*, Darrell Guder suggests that the "institutionalization" of church itself has contributed to the disaffection of many church goers.

> Over the last century, the Christian religion has become a big American business. We have centralized for efficiency and good management, developed major headquarters, accepted numerical and financial growth as the most important indications of success, introduced statistical measurement to determine that success, and made religion into a product. Denominational headquarters have generated programs and curricula. Marketing has become an essential function of religious management. Public relations and the canons of effective advertising define our activities. Local congregations are run as businesses, where giving, membership numbers, growth and attendance are all evaluated as evidence of a healthy religious bottom line.[34]

In Guder's eyes, the church has become data-driven. Perhaps we can compare that to the world of sports, recently revolutionized by the phenomenon of analytics. The data-driven approach to running a sports team was made visible in the 2003 movie *Moneyball*, where general manager Billy Beane used analytics to bring a World Series title to the Oakland Athletics. And nothing breeds imitation like success! These days, virtually every professional sports team has an analytics department. But, for a lot of us, this data-driven approach has taken much of the fun out of being a sports fan. Who cares about statistical minutiae? Just play the game! I find myself wondering if the same is not true of churches built on the business and marketing approaches Guder alludes to. My millennial children have taught this old 1960s flower child something about institutions: younger generations aren't impressed with corporate business plans, statistical summaries, or buttoned-down marketing strategies. They don't like to eat at chain restaurants, either! In both restaurants and churches, they are looking for honesty, authenticity, and some personal creativity. They don't want a "clubhouse" where "religious people hang out with other people who think, dress, behave, vote, and believe like them."[35] The "ecclesial analytics" characterizing so many evangelical churches today effectively blurs distinctions between the corporate world of market-place capitalism and the church, and yet younger people desire those sharp distinctions. They're looking for the church to be a peaceful, open faith community. The late Rachel Held Evans, who herself became a "done," at least for a while, put it like this:

> When I left church at age 29, full of doubt and disillusionment, I wasn't looking for a better-produced Christianity. I was looking for a truer Christianity, a more authentic Christianity: I didn't like how gay, lesbian, bisexual and transgender people were being treated by my evangelical faith community. I had questions about science and faith, biblical interpretation and theology. I felt lonely in my doubts. And, contrary to popular belief, the fog machines and light shows at those slick evangelical conferences didn't make things better for me. They made the whole endeavor feel shallow, forced, and fake.[36]

The "dones" do not respond well or commit long-term to "ecclesiology lite." They view this approach to church as trying much too hard to mirror marketplace strategies and forgetting the "saltiness" that made the church distinctive and attractive to them in the first place. Instead of finding high-efficiency, "purpose-driven" congregations attractive and inviting, the "dones" see them as "religious chaplains of the dominant system, purveyors of religious goods and services to keep its supporters spiritually preoccupied and thus pacified."[37] And they are done with that. Little wonder that "the church now finds itself discarded as an irrelevant institution of a past era. We got in bed with the forces of modernity, and once they had their way with us, we were sent back to the street, abused, confused, and of no further use."[38]

So, here's my outlier dilemma: I completely get why so many people have thrown up their hands in resignation and declared, "I've had it with the church!" I not only understand where the "dones" come from, I have wondered on occasion what it might entail to join them. But that's where this becomes a dilemma. As a Christian who has taught in the theological disciplines for so many years, I simply have nowhere to put these feelings, no matter how exasperated I become with the church. On the one hand I resonate with much of what the "churchless Christians" are saying, but on the other hand there's a biblical/theological red line that I cannot cross. I began my own faith journey in the late 1960s when suspicion of institutions and all things "establishment" was at its zenith, and as I look back now, I see I brought a good bit of that suspicion with me into my own faith journey and educational preparation for Christian service. It wasn't quite as pronounced as the "I like Jesus, but not the church" viewpoint so prevalent in recent times, but it was close. Ultimately, though, I had to face up to the incongruity of claiming to love Jesus but not loving what Jesus loves, and make no mistake about it, Scripture is clear on this: Jesus loves the church! (Ephesians 5:25). The church is, indeed, Christ's beloved bride. So, while I can empathize with people who are so frustrated with the church that they feel that they must separate from it, I cannot commit myself to such a radical step because I see it as a betrayal of a fundamentally important aspect of my Christian faith. And so, my painful walk continues, with me trying to deal with the stones in my shoes. Taking solace, as so many seem to do, in some invisible, "universal" church will not do. As Guder put it, "Any understanding of the Christian church which does not emphasize the concrete and historical reality and the centrality of local and particular communities is docetic: it is not taking with great seriousness God's mission and the incarnation of that mission in Jesus Christ and his church."[39]

However, the problem persists. There is no getting around the reality of a church that struggles to win and keep the people who represent its essential mission in the world. I want to suggest that a huge part of the problem is the church's tendency to look outside for solutions instead of looking within at its own biblical and theological resources. Americans, in particular, have a deep faith in our ability to "fix" things. And this extends to the church. Religious bookstores and web sites hawk all the latest church "success stories." Pastors' email boxes fill up with yet more "easy-button" solutions to what ails the church. But, as Guder notes, these solutions tend to be methodological. He continues, "the answer to the crisis of the North American church will not be found at the level of method and problem solving. The real issues in the current crisis of the Christian church are spiritual and theological."[40] I couldn't agree more. Yes, I'm really saying that theology, and specifically, ecclesiology, needs to come front and center as we deal with the "Who needs the church, anyway?" multitudes. Years ago I heard a United Methodist bishop say, "Your system is perfectly designed to produce the results you're getting!" I'm suggesting that we would do well to look at the ecclesiological foundations of the church in Scripture and theology, and then compare our findings with our current church "systems." Perhaps then we can judge how we might regain a proper theological bearing, rather than settle for mimicking the culture's enslavement to the latest attractive fads and technological gizmos. Too many of the current quick fixes thrown at the church do not address the real issues. It's not about attracting a crowd. And it's not about learning how to "do church better." Reggie McNeal puts it bluntly, "the culture around us does not wake up each day thinking they would go to church if only there were a good one to attend!"[41]

Ecclesiology helps us understand the intended nature and purpose of the church. It answers the questions "what is the church?" and "what is its purpose in the world?" We begin to answer these fundamental questions by understanding that ecclesiology, the doctrine of the church, flows necessarily out of missiology, or "what is God doing in the world?" The answer to that question, in turn, must be found in Christology, the study of the person and work of Jesus Christ. And that order—Christology, missiology, ecclesiology—is non-negotiable! Looking at the life and ministry of Jesus, which the church, as his body, continues, it's easy to see why this is so. As I often reminded students, "there's a reason it's called CHRISTianity!" It is God's intention to continue the redemptive mission begun in Jesus Christ through the auspices of the Christian community that bears His name. James Davison Hunter summarizes the implications of this: "If Christ has overcome the powers, then the task of the church is to proclaim it and to live it out. This task certainly finds expression in the personal life of the believer, but its primary expression is collective. It is as an alternative community that manifests a new form of social relations. Ecclesiology, then, is the form by which engagement with the world takes place."[42]

A robust, not "lite," appropriation of ecclesiology is critically necessary to guide the church through a culture that is constantly attempting to remake everything in its own image. Apart from a deep commitment to a biblical and theologically sound charter, the contemporary church easily becomes just one more "store" competing with other "stores" to sell something to increasingly wary consumers. Huge numbers of people who have at least some rudimentary commitment to Christian faith are telling us, by their absence, that they are tired of being "sold" a product, no matter how desirable the product may be. I believe that they actually want to imbibe the rich traditions of a community that has lasted for two thousand years, at times improbably. They want to be a part of something bigger than themselves, something that tells a story far more compelling than whatever tale the current culture is selling. Earlier, we saw Rachel Held Evans express her disillusionment with the church and why she left. But she returned. "What finally brought me back," she says, "wasn't lattes or skinny jeans; it was the sacraments. Baptism, confession, Communion, preaching the word, anointing the sick—you know, those strange rituals and traditions Christians have been practicing for the past 2,000 years. The sacraments are what makes the church relevant, no matter the culture or era. They don't need to be repackaged or rebranded; they just need to be practiced, offered and explained in the context of a loving, authentic and inclusive community."[43]

The value of "practiced authenticity" came home to me powerfully on my first trip to Australia. In this largely secular country, where the church has been marginalized, I was struck, one day, by a billboard that said simply, "Thank God for the Salvos." (Aussies shorten everything!) This board announcing the work of The Salvation Army was obviously intended to engender good will and some contributions to that organization. But that billboard truly reflected the attitude of the casual Australian towards this visible expression of the Christian church. Say what you will about the "Salvos" but there is no mistaking what they are about and how consistently they practice what they preach.

YOUR KINGDOM COME

The real genius of The Salvation Army lies in the fact that, though they are a "church" in virtually every sense of the term, they are mostly recognized for the ways in which they demonstrate the Kingdom of God. Again, Christology underscores that Jesus came proclaiming the coming of God's kingdom into this world. The "Salvos" unmistakably live out their belief that such a kingdom has, indeed, come among us. Unfortunately, the kingdom's presence is often conflated with, or misunderstood as referring to the church itself. The theological reality is that the church is NOT the kingdom. Rather, the church is *evidence,* a sign that the kingdom of God has come to earth. The church becomes the best possible witness to the reality of God's kingdom, but if the church views itself *as* the kingdom, then the tendency is to view the church as an end in itself rather than an incarnational means to God's redemptive purpose in the world. We see this amply demonstrated by the numbers of churches that seem completely oriented towards their own ends, however noble such ends might be. The success of a church is not measured by its size, budgets, or even the extent of its ministries. A church's success is measured its ability to turn people into agents of God's kingdom in the world.

> The church is the offspring of the divine reign. It is its fruit, and therefore its evidence... The church must not be equated with the reign of God. The church as a messianic community is both spawned by the reign of God and directed toward it. This is a different relationship from what at times has captured the church's thinking. The church has often presumed that the reign of God is within the church. The two have been regarded as synonyms. In this view, the church totally encompasses the divine reign. There church extension or church growth is the equivalent of kingdom extension or kingdom growth, and the reign of God is coterminous with the people who embrace it through faith and gather together as the church. This view leads easily to the affirmation that there is no salvation outside the church. The church then sees itself as the fortress and guardian of salvation, perhaps even its author and benefactor, rather than its grateful recipient and guest.[44]

For some time now, I've thought about the concept of a church's "kingdom footprint." In the same way that we speak today of human beings and various industries having a carbon footprint that impacts the environment in specific ways, I believe that local congregations ought to be finding ways to ascertain and evaluate the effects of their kingdom footprint. They should ask, "What about us, our life together, our work and ministry, bears witness to God's kingdom in this time and place?" And, I don't think it has anything to do with size. I know of large churches and small churches that have huge kingdom footprints. Their witness to God's kingdom in their respective communities is significant and fruitful. The communities served by such churches would be negatively affected if those churches were not there. In the same way, I know of large and small churches with little to no kingdom footprint. They could close their church doors tomorrow, and the world around them would barely notice. This reminds me of a conversation I had a few years ago with a well-known church historian. We were talking about the witness of the church in the world and he said to me, "Remember that there are times in history where God was doing more outside the church than on the inside!" I believe that is the case; however, I do not believe that is God's intention. I believe wholeheartedly that God wants the church to be the best possible evidence of His kingdom come. Stanley Grenz put it this way: "In the final analysis, we dare neither equate nor radically separate the church and kingdom. Rather, the church is best seen as the *product* of the kingdom."[45]

A further peril of "ecclesiology lite" is akin to the church/kingdom issue, but it's the opposite of conflating church and kingdom. This issue involves the intentional separation of the sacred and secular dimensions of life and our being in the world. This was a huge issue in the church of my youth and adolescence, where most everything outside the church was viewed as "worldly." In those days, this largely had to do with forms of entertainment, certain personal choices like smoking and drinking, and generally, most anything of interest to teenagers! I exaggerate only slightly. The first time I got myself into some hot water in ministry was as a youth pastor. In that position, I reported to the Board of Christian Education, and at a monthly meeting I was asked if it was true that, at the recent youth group roller-skating party, I had failed to give a "devotional." I replied that this was true, and when they asked me why, I told them, "because I invited kids to go roller skating, not to listen to me preach." Needless to say, the Board of Christian Education didn't see it my way, clearly supposing that such activities needed some kind of "sacred moment" to be baptized as legitimate. I can't say I won that particular battle, but I'm still happy with my response. Today, the sacred/secular divide is more muddled and complicated. We tend to compartmentalize life into a "religious" dimension which mostly happens on Sundays in a church building, and then the "rest" of our lives. But the church isn't the church only on Sunday! And following God's kingdom absolutely involves life outside of the church facilities. Such a bifurcated approach flattens life out in a manner that is completely unrealistic, not to mention uninspiring. In his book *Seeing God in the Ordinary*, Michael Frost begins with a quote from Walter Brueggemann: "The gospel is . . . a truth widely held, but a truth greatly reduced. It is a truth that has been flattened, trivialized, and rendered inane." Frost then goes on to say, "We have thought of the gospel as a fragile and precious object. We have held it too tightly, and it has become shapeless and uninteresting."[46] I'm convinced that this is a major issue with people who are fed up with the church. They aren't in the least interested in living regimented, compartmentalized lives. And why should they be? The world doesn't fall neatly into categories in this way. If the life of Christ teaches us anything, it is that he wasn't at all concerned about observing the strict boundaries between sacred and secular which had been erected by the religious establishment of that day. Frost quotes the great Jewish philosopher Martin Buber as saying, "rather than separating the sacred from the profane, we should see our world as a division between the holy and the not-yet holy.[47] As Christians, we believe that this entire world belongs to God and that one day, Christ will be recognized and revered as its rightful King. Sound theology would dictate that the church ought to live that way here and now. The entire world is valued in God's eyes. He loves it and means to have it as His own. The world does not exist simply as raw materials for the church. This has too often seemed to be how the church views the world around it.

> It's okay to tear people out of their neighborhoods as long as we get them to church more. It's okay to devalue their "secular" jobs as long as we get them involved in church work more. It's okay to withdraw all our energies from the arts and culture "out there" as long as we have a good choir and nice sanctuary "in here." It's okay because, after all, we're about salvaging individuals from a sinking ship; neighborhoods, economies, cultures, and all but individual souls will sink, so who cares? . . . Is the world a mountain to be clear-cut and strip mined for the benefit of the church? Or is the church a catalyst of blessing for the good of the world?[48]

Who among us likes being used? Fair or not, that's precisely the way some would construe how the church relates to the world around it. The church stays separated in its holy cocoon until it sees something it needs or desires, then it appropriates it and returns to life behind its sacred curtain. "One of the outcomes of a truly monotheistic view of the world is the annihilation of the dualistic category of sacred and secular. If one God is the source of reality and the reference point for life, how can life be fragmented?"[49] People who struggle with "church," including outliers like myself, long for a holistic spirituality that covers every aspect of existence and which lives in a profound sense of gratitude for the wonders and beautiful evidence of God's amazing grace throughout our world. We long for a spirituality that applies to *all* of life, to anything that is of interest and concern to human beings. We long to celebrate the beauty and creativity of the arts; we want to join in the dance (yes, that's right, the dance!) that resides deep in the hearts of all of God's children. Like C.S. Lewis, we want to share a pint with our friends at the neighborhood pub while talking about the mysteries of the Trinity. We want to be awed with the talents and gifts of men and women who, whether they acknowledge it or not, sing, act, and perform to the glory of their Creator. And maybe we'll even go see "The Boss," or U2, or Garth Brooks, or Alicia Keys, or whoever, because . . . well, just because it's fun! The strict separation of sacred and secular is not something that squares at all with a biblically sound conception of the world. As Abraham Kuyper famously said, "There is not one square inch in the whole domain of our human existence over which Christ, who is Sovereign over all, does not cry, 'Mine!'"

CHURCH AND THE BOTTOM LINE

Although I came to love the pastoral vocation, I have to confess that I found one thing completely tiresome and irritating. I didn't care at all for the subtle pressures I felt to constantly be doing and saying things primarily designed to grow the church in statistical ways. Let me be clear. I have no problem with the idea of healthy, growing churches. Healthy churches will, in fact, grow. I have no problem with large churches. I pastored what was, at that moment in history, one of the largest churches in my denomination, and I was happy to see it grow in a number of ways. My irritation isn't about size. It's about a kind of ecclesiological miscalculation that, I believe, has left many pastors burned out and has contributed to the exodus of many from the church. Darrell Guder explains what I mean by "ecclesiological miscalculation."

> In *The Churching of America, 1776–1990: Winners and Losers in Our Religious Economy*, Roger Finke and Rodney Stark argue that the choice made early on in the United States not to have an established religion meant that an economic understanding of religious life and practice was inevitable. They contend that "where religious affiliation is a matter of choice, religious organizations must compete for members, and . . . the 'invisible hand' of the marketplace is as unforgiving of ineffective religious forms as it is of their commercial counterparts . . . Religious economies are like commercial economies in that they consist of a market made up of a set of current and potential customers and a set of firms seeking to serve that market." Indeed, they suggest that it is appropriate to use "economic concepts such as markets, firms, market penetration, and segmented markets to analyze the success and failure of religious bodies." In their view, then, the clergy are the church's sales representatives, religious doctrines its products, and evangelization practices its marketing techniques.[50]

What Finke and Stark describe could be referred to as "social-Darwinist ecclesiology," or put another way, a "survival of the fittest" approach to church that employs ideas and strategies more appropriate for marketplace capitalism than for church life. "Some churches succeed, while others fail. That's just how it goes in the dog-eat-dog world of church life." What? How in the world did it come to this? When did growing the church numerically come to justify a spirit of competition, of win/lose strategies, and, let's face it, blatant proselytizing? There are many studies suggesting that much ballyhooed church growth is, in fact, transfer growth, euphemistic church-speak for rustling sheep from other churches. The ecclesiological miscalculation in all this is the view that the church is mostly a social organization that can be marketed and managed utilizing the methods of the marketplace. Along with this, the so-called "Church Growth Movement" adhered to a core principle of homogeneity, which means that churches are more likely to grow when people do not have to cross social barriers. This movement justified such social segregation in the name of winning more people to Christ and to the church. But all kinds of dissonance happens when measuring growth against the common understandings of the church as necessarily transcending barriers of race, class, and culture. There is no getting around the fact that this movement has profoundly influenced and shaped much of the evangelical church in America for the past several decades, but the irony should not be lost on us that in spite of numerous success stories, church growth emphases have failed to halt the overall decline of the church in America and the rest of the Western World. Even in the "successful" churches that have employed these methodologies, there are indications that all is not well. The dreaded "back door" is wide open in these huge congregations, and people are leaving by it, having decided they need to move on. As I suggested earlier, the pressure this puts on clergy is often unbearable. "Growing a church on steroids," as one put it, is not a recipe for long-term pastoral flourishing. Young people seem increasingly put off by some of these growth strategies, opting for smaller faith communities or simply dropping out altogether. And I have to admit that I get very concerned about the long-term sustainability of multimillion-dollar church buildings, and increasingly, "campuses." The financial pressures on these churches must be unrelenting. Growth in such cases is not an option; it is necessary for survival. And this kind of desperation brings with it a potentially harmful kind of pragmatism, of doing whatever is necessary to "feed the bulldog." As a friend of mine said to me years ago, "if you really have to survive, you will. But, you may not like what you become."

The pressure for churches to survive whatever the cost can be readily seen in the frantic efforts of some churches to claim the mantle of "relevance." In my hometown, there has been a church named—I kid you not—"The Cool Church." This church was started in the early to middle 1990s and is still going, although they have recently changed their name. I suspect they grew tired of the snarky comments that claiming to be "The Cool Church" brought with it. But give them this: at least they owned it. At least they were up front about something a whole lot of other churches just down the street from The Cool Church are desperately trying to do—make themselves appear relevant. In the *Washington Post* opinion piece titled, "Want millennials back in the pews? Stop trying to make church 'cool,'" cited previously in this chapter, Rachel Held Evans noted that younger people are leaving the church, so, "In response, many churches have sought to lure millennials back by focusing on style points: cooler bands, hipper worship, edgier programming, impressive technology. Yet while these aren't inherently bad ideas and might in some cases be effective, they are not the key to drawing millennials back to God in a lasting and meaningful way. Young people don't simply want a better show. And trying to be cool might be making things worse."[51] I think she's right. My thirty-plus years with Christian college students have convinced me that they have a deeply-held aversion to being "played." They can sniff out sales pitches like foxhounds on a chase. Gabe Lyons said that, "though 'relevance' was once a useful adjective, the word has become the idyllic Holy Grail for churches craving the cool factor. When they talk about being 'relevant,' they are describing their agility to adapt the message of Jesus *or* their ability to become like others in order to relate to them well. Their desire seems harmless, but relevance is the exact opposite of counter-cultural, and the unintended consequences are significant."[52] I saw this firsthand when I visited a well-known mega-church. Plastered across the entire front of the sanctuary, in huge block letters, was the word "Relevant." My impression, shared by a good number of others who have written about this church, is that they seem to be chasing the grail of relevance a bit too hard. Os Guiness, himself something of an evangelical outlier, put it succinctly:

> After two hundred years of earnest dedication to reinventing the faith and the church and to being more relevant in the world, we are confronted by an embarrassing fact: Never have Christians pursued relevance more strenuously; never have Christians been more irrelevant. . . . By our uncritical pursuit of relevance we have actually coveted irrelevance; by our breathless chase after relevance without a matching commitment to faithfulness, we have become not only unfaithful but irrelevant; by our determined efforts to redefine ourselves in ways that are more compelling to the modern world than are faithful to Christ, we have lost not only our identity but our authority and our relevance. Our crying need is to be faithful as well as relevant.[53]

"Faithful, as well as relevant." How does the church do that? Remember, earlier I said that proper ecclesiology emerges from proper missiology, which, in turn, emerges from proper Christology. As clichéd as this may sound, it all comes back to Jesus. He, his life, and his teachings are the measuring stick of the church's faithfulness. And, by the way, I've never heard anyone fairly and truthfully consider the life and teachings of Christ and conclude that he has no relevance.

St. Paul's Cathedral is the seat of the Archbishop of Melbourne for the Anglican diocese in the Australian state of Victoria. It sits on the busiest intersection in the city. Diagonal to it is the city's main train station, out of which thousands of people pour daily, bound for the central business district. One day, I slipped into St. Paul's to gain some respite from the noise and crowds of the city. As I sat there silently enjoying the peaceful quiet and the beauty of that edifice, a small Asian woman, a tourist no doubt, tapped me on the shoulder and asked me, "Is this Jesus' church?" I assured her that it was, and that seemed to satisfy her as she made her way down the aisle gazing at the stained glass. I don't know what prompted her query, but it strikes me as the central question with regards to the evangelical church of today. Is this Jesus' church? The disciples in the Book of Acts were charged, by Jesus himself, to continue what He had begun, in the power of the Holy Spirit. Jesus' church, the "body of Christ," would, in the power of God's Spirit, carry on what Jesus started. No matter how simple or complicated you want to make the church, ultimately it must be judged by its fidelity to Christ, and Christ alone. Like Jesus himself, the church is to be "in the world, but not of the world." From any vantage point, that is a whole lot easier said than done. It cannot be done apart from a constant assessment of where the church is and where it is going in relation to what we see in Jesus. Trevor Wax says, "Ironically, in our earnest and sincere efforts to transform the culture around us, we have actually been transformed ourselves. Instead of being salt and light, we have become unsalted and lite."[54] Looking broadly at the evangelical church today, I see churches that I fear have been overly influenced by the culture around them in various ways. Whether becoming overly pragmatic in methodology, becoming too self-focused, or becoming too "Americanized," there are troubling signs that the church needs some ecclesiological recalibration as it makes its way into the future. Any such adjustments must necessarily begin with Jesus. It's not just outliers or "nones and dones" who recognize that something is amiss. The unease is pervasive. Stanley Grenz, back in the early 1990s, sounded the alarm. "The ferment within our ranks exhibits a deep-seated desire among contemporary believers for a new understanding of the relationship between the personal life of faith and the faith community. The disquiet within many evangelical churches is in effect a postmodern cry to the church to be the church."[55] Can the evangelical church submit itself to the discipline of Christological fidelity necessary to shed the "lite-ness" that has characterized it all too often in recent years? Such discipline comes at a cost, but the alternatives are all likely much more costly.

The biblical and theological truth is that we all need the church. Stanley Hauerwas' and William Willimon's words have always struck me as a wonderful summary of why ecclesiology matters. "From a Christian point of view, the world needs the church, not to help the world run more smoothly or to make the world a better and safer place for Christians to live. Rather, the world needs the church because, without the church, the world does not know who it is. The only way for the world to know that it is being redeemed is for the church to point to the Redeemer by being a redeemed people. The way for the world to know that it needs redeeming, that it is broken and fallen, is for the church to enable the world to strike hard against something which is an alternative to what the world offers."[56] Our world needs the church. My doggedly individualistic outlier self knows that full well. I hope and pray that I can find my way into it, and cultivate sufficient vision to recognize Jesus' church when I see it.

Chapter 3

The B-I-B-L-E
Evangelicals and the Good Book

> When we let the Bible go as a modern answer book, we get to rediscover it for what it really is: an ancient book of incredible spiritual value for us, a kind of universal and cosmic history, a book that tells us who we are and what story we find ourselves in so that we know what to do and how to live. That letting go is going to be hard for you evangelicals.
>
> —Gabe Lyons[57]

At the end of the hallway in my family's house in Arizona there was a double cupboard. The bottom half held linens and other household items, while the top half was used as a kind of catchall for whatever required a home. One of the shelves in this upper half contained books. We didn't have a lot of books, so the content of this "library" was pedestrian at best. There were a few classics (Mark Twain, Robert Louis Stevenson, etc.), and few of those old Reader's Digest Condensed Books, compilations which promised to boil popular novels down to more readable size. Not a memorable collection, by any means. But there was one book that I distinctly remember being on that shelf. It was a dark-red, hardcover Revised Standard Version Bible. I have no idea how it came to be in our home, but I clearly remember looking at that dark-red volume and thinking, "That's not really a Bible." I don't know why I thought that. I don't recall ever being told that by my parents or anyone else at the time. I'd never seen it anywhere but on that shelf. I suppose that, as an eleven- or twelve-year-old, I might have compared it to the black leather-bound Bibles my parents carried to church, or to the huge black family Bible that sat on a coffee table in our living room, but for whatever reason, the "hermeneutic of suspicion" was in full flower when I looked at the dark-red RSV in the cupboard. Eventually, I came to know more about such matters and changed my opinion about that questionable book, actually claiming it for myself during a Christmas trip home from seminary. It sits, yet still today, on my own library shelves. The story of my coming to include the RSV as acceptable is offered as a kind of a parable of my biblical awakenings.

It is deeply ironic to me that the way I now view the Bible would so readily confirm my outlier status with many in today's evangelical church. I graduated, originally, from a "Bible" college, but I didn't really know much of the Bible, or much about it. That began to change in seminary, where my exposure to some excellent biblical scholars ignited a new kind of interest and passion about Scripture that I'd never known before. But beyond everything else, my tenure at the Houghton church took me to places of intellectual and spiritual growth in my interactions with Scripture that continue to amaze me even now. As Senior Pastor at Houghton, I administered the church and multiple pastoral staff and gave leadership to the church's liturgy, which largely meant I preached a lot. The responsibility of regularly speaking before a congregation made up of college faculty, staff, and students presented me with the weekly opportunity to spend multiple hours in Scripture. I reveled in this. There were days when I could hardly believe I was getting paid to do it! Without hesitation, I affirm that the most transforming experience of my own spiritual formation were the thirteen years I spent in my pastoral study at Houghton preparing to share Scripture with that congregation. That hardly sounds like the qualifications of an outlier, but when it comes to the matter of the Bible within evangelicalism, I've learned that it takes very little to find oneself on the outside looking in. I hope to explicate my views on the Bible as a means of pointing out what I consider to be some problems that shadow the evangelical church and its approach to Scripture.

While I'm driving down the road, I'm often amused to read the various church signs that proliferate in these United States. The signs always seem to convey a warm family orientation that invites one and all to what must be the friendliest, most vital—and most orthodox—church in those parts. It makes me wonder how every church seems to view itself as the best of the best. Of all the different phrases one might see on church signs, my absolute favorite is this: "Bible Believing." One might ask, "What's special about that?" Would not *any* Christian church automatically be Bible-believing? But, of course, that's not what these church signs are intending to say at all. "Bible-believing" is code for, "Don't be fooled by all those other places, we *really* take the Bible seriously here." Some even go so far as to proudly proclaim their fidelity to the King James Version of the Bible, and others add words like "fundamentalist" or "Pentecostal" to the mix. At the end of the day, however, the dilemma is this: precisely which kind of Bible-believing *group* are you? The fact is that it's possible to claim a lot of different things, always citing Scripture as one's source.

People often ask me to suggest a book that gives "the biblical view" on a particular problem or set of issues. These people want answers, so they don't typically like my response to their request. I tell them that there are multiple "biblical" views on the issue for which they are seeking clarity. I mean, think about it: if the issue was clear, they wouldn't need my input on a book. Many issues can be extremely complicated, which ordinarily means there's more than one way of looking at them. I usually try to steer people towards sources that can enable them to frame the issues in ways that are conversant with Scripture, or books that I've found helpful, but I can see the disappointment in their eyes when I fail to point them to *the* biblical view. It's not that I don't believe the Bible takes strong positions on many of the issues of our day. Far from it. But I don't want to encourage more "black and white" thinking in an increasingly gray world, and I don't want to exacerbate the problems of how the Bible often gets used and abused. As I noted, Scripture means the world to me. I dearly love the Word of God and I know it to be an invaluable instrument in the hands of God's Spirit. It is a primary conduit of grace, and the church must give it proper place in its life, mission, and worship. It's become far too easy to simply mouth certain words or phrases from Scripture without actually submitting to its authority. Not long ago, I was asked to be a guest speaker at a "Bible" church. This independent congregation obviously took great care to advertise to one and all their commitment to Scripture. The funny thing, though, was that apart from the four or five verses of Scripture I read that morning for my sermon text, there was no other Scripture or mention of the Bible in the worship of that congregation. Bible Church? What does that even mean? To put it bluntly, every Christian church is a "Bible" church, or at least it should be. In the fall 2018 edition of the *Wesleyan Theological Journal*, Rob Wall and Daniel Castello wrote, "We believe the church formed the Bible under the direction of God's Spirit to form the church." If this is so, it requires that we look at Scripture as much more than a mere catalog of information about God and Jesus. We must acknowledge that the Word of God is, in itself, a critically important means by which God relates to us. Through His Spirit,

God uses the Bible to initiate, sustain, and bring to completion the restoration of humankind that we believe is at the heart of the gospel. The Bible is, in truth, the church's book. We can surely all agree on that. Unfortunately, it often appears that we don't agree on much more.

SWORD FIGHTS IN THE CHURCH

Draw Swords! Every kid who grew up in an evangelical church knows what these words mean: lift your Bible up above your head in preparation for a mad dash to be the first one to come up with the answer to a question about some verse in the Bible. I suppose there isn't anything terribly harmful in teaching youngsters about the "sword of the word," although the hermeneutical methodology of such exercises might leave something to be desired. But that can be remedied later down the line. My concern here is with the ongoing "sword fights" in the church, the never-ending battles between Christians over the Bible. I have spent most of my professional life in Houghton, New York, first as the pastor of the only church in a college town and later as a faculty member at the college, and still later as chair of their Department of Biblical Studies, Theology, and Philosophy. Houghton is a denominational college whose student population has never been more than 20% of that sponsoring church. As pastor, I quickly learned that a lot of students, and even more of their parents and pastors (especially pastors!), wanted to know my "view" of Scripture. I knew what they were after—certain catchwords or some popular evangelical bromide. This question was put to me often enough that I finally adopted this response: "Come and listen to me preach three or four times, then *you* tell me what my view of Scripture is." I wish I could tell you that answer satisfied my interrogators, but you already know better than that.

I finished seminary and entered full-time ministry in the heyday of the so-called "Battle of the Bible," which was not so much a battle as it was the church's latest episode in the never-ending theological serial designed to ferret out the "true believers" from the rest of the bunch. So perhaps it's no surprise that this "battle" continues today, in subtly different ways but with the same inconclusive results. One day during my faculty years, a church official suggested that all of the college religion faculty should pose together for a photo, taken underneath a banner reading "We believe in Inerrancy!" Gospel truth, this actually happened! My reaction at the time was that I would be willing to do it under one condition—that we misspell the word "inerrancy." It's probably a good thing the department didn't take up my suggestion, but it did accurately portray how I felt about the issue then and how I continue to feel about it now. There is a long-standing uneasiness in the evangelical church regarding how the Bible is presented and taught in the halls of Christian higher education. The suspicion with which Christian college faculty are viewed is born of great fear that something precious will be lost or forfeited in the name of scholarship. This fear comes somewhat naturally in evangelical circles. "The doctrine of inspiration came to play an especially important role in conservative American Protestantism in the nineteenth century, in response to the same threats to religious authority—higher criticism, modernism, and so on—that prompted Catholicism to promulgate the doctrine of papal infallibility."[58] When the Roman Catholic Church defined the doctrine of papal infallibility in 1870, conservative Protestants, equally concerned about evolution as well as the onset of "higher criticism" in biblical studies, began to look for ways to vouchsafe the Bible from such threats. Early in the 20th century, the movement known as "fundamentalism" arose, aimed at defending traditional beliefs from "modernism." One of the chief steps in this defense was championing biblical inerrancy. While it can be argued that such a response was at least plausible in terms of the historical context, arguing for an inerrant Bible was, in the eyes of many (including myself presently), misguided. The claim of an inerrant Bible is an empirical claim. In other words, if you make an empirical claim it must be empirically verifiable. If I claim that it is snowing outside, a quick look out the window should either validate or invalidate my claim. But when we claim that the Bible was inerrant (completely without error) in its original manuscripts, we are making an empirical claim that is unverifiable. We don't have the original manuscripts. So, at best, inerrancy is a faith assumption, but I would contend that it's an empty faith assumption, a kind of theological rabbit-trail that distracts from the more important questions of biblical inspiration and authority.

    This inerrancy battle persists under a variety of different guises. During my department chair days, I had a phone call from the mother of a prospective student. She told me that she had some questions for me, to which, she said plainly, she wanted "yes or no" answers, nothing more. She proceeded to ask me a series of questions designed to demonstrate to her that I believed in an inerrant Bible that was meant to be read literally and implicitly agreed to without nuance or discussion. She couldn't possibly have known that virtually no one in higher education, especially in religious studies, agrees to simple "yes or no" answers to much of anything! But her call demonstrated the longing on the part of so many for absolute certainty about matters of belief, coupled with the fear of even considering alternative ideas and approaches. That kind of certainty is problematic, however, in the sense that it bypasses the kind of faith we are called to exercise in our lives as Christians. The extent to which conservative Christians employ the tools of modernity to try and anchor their faith is puzzling and ironic. Employing the canons of scientific empiricism to argue for the trustworthiness of the Bible is a poor strategy for anyone truly concerned about the denigration of Scripture in the current culture.

In one of my classes in introductory theology, I used to show students the Italian master Caravaggio's 1602 painting titled "St. Matthew and the Angel." It shows Matthew earnestly at work at his desk, writing instrument at the ready, intently listening to an angel whispering into his ear. This painting was modeling a widely held belief in those days regarding Scriptural "inspiration." But such a view hardly elevates the Bible. The idea that God, or one of God's angels, literally dictated the words of Scripture misses the beauty and wonder of inspired writers, in widely divergent historical circumstances, finding ways to speak of the acts of God in their own words and cultural milieus. One of the most amazing things to me about the Bible is how such a disparate group of authors, representing radically divergent contexts, can nonetheless consistently allow a redemptive metanarrative to course through the pages of Scripture, from book to book, in ways that captivate scholars, theologians, and readers across all stations in life—past, present, and, undoubtedly, future.

While the "battle *of* the Bible" may have abated somewhat in the recent past (though it reignites periodically), the battles *over* the Bible continue uninterrupted. I find various attempts to weaponize Scripture in support of a particular group's ideas or convictions very troubling. I also consider the selective applications of certain parts of the Bible, while ignoring other parts that might prove problematic, as illustrative of the battle's continuation. Many Christians appear unable to control their tendency to *use* Scripture to pursue specific agendas rather than *submit* themselves to Scripture's repeated admonitions to incarnate God's shalom in the world. Ironically, much of this is done under the guise of somehow "protecting" the Bible, which is a curious assertion given the Bible's centuries-old demonstration of inexplicable resiliency. Does the Bible honestly need our safeguarding? What usually comes of such efforts? Barbara Brown-Taylor notes, "As a general rule, I would say that human beings never behave more badly toward one another than when they believe they are protecting God." She adds, "In the words of Arun Ghandi, grandson of Mohandas, 'People of the Book risk putting the book above people.'"[59] Rather than trying to defend the Bible's authority, we should be incarnating that authority via the witness of our lives, individually and corporately. Beyond the way these quarrels undermine the church's witness in the world, they betray a fundamental flaw in how the Bible itself is perceived by those who feel compelled to "protect" it. Kent Blevins puts it this way:

> The Bible is not a treasure that needs defending, as though its truth is so fragile it cannot stand on its own. The Bible is a resource best wielded in the hands of truth-seekers. It calls us on a journey of discovery. Perhaps a better image for understanding the function of the Bible as an authority source is to compare our faith journey to a voyage. The ship of discovery awaits, ready to sail, beckoning us to come aboard. The journey is not a solitary voyage; Christians are part of a community, and the Bible serves as a community authority. The Bible is like a map for our journey that opens up vistas and possibilities. Where do we wish to go today? What do we wish to explore? What new things await us? The image of a voyage helps us better see and understand both the diversity among Christians as well as the fact that Christians are not the only ones on this journey of truth-seeking. Those of other religious traditions have different maps, and part of our journey involves comparing maps, exploring points of similarity and difference.[60]

I'm fairly confident that Blevins' reference to "different maps" will likely evoke a reaction akin to, "Aha, there you go saying that the Bible is just one of many sacred books." Well, on the one hand, that's correct; the Bible *is* one example, among many others, of "sacred texts." But, Blevins aims to help us see that the Bible is a peculiarly Christian book, one that we believe can be trusted to guide us on the journey of our lives. The mere existence of other sacred texts should not threaten us in the least when it comes to asserting our confidence in the Bible. But Blevins' words further push us to explore exactly why we believe that the Bible is special. Exactly what is the Bible, anyway? What is the nature of Scripture? What makes it so special?

As expected, the answer to these questions depends on who is asked. For many people, the Bible is a kind of "owner's manual," a guide to how we should live. This "heavenly instructional manual" has been downloaded from heaven, as it were. If we follow the directions we will flourish, but if we ignore the manual, we will pay an unthinkable price in this life and the next. While I would admit that the Bible does indeed have much wisdom to share with us in directing our lives towards fulfillment and wholeness, this view of Scripture falls far short of what the Bible truly is. Peter Enns expands on this common misconception of Scripture by saying, "The Bible is not a Christian owner's manual but a story—a diverse story of God and how his people have connected with him over the centuries, in changing circumstances and situations. That kind of Bible works, because that is our story, too. The Bible 'partners' with us (so to speak), modeling for us our walk with God in discovering greater depth and maturity on our journey of faith, not by telling us what to do at each step, but by showing us a journey of hills and valleys, straight lanes and difficult curves, of new discoveries and insights, of movement and change—with God by our side every step of the way."[61] The commonly held view of Scripture as "life manual" is further complicated by the fact that so many people interpret the "manual" so differently. If the Bible is primarily given to guide us in life by a God who loves and cares for us, why can't we all just agree on what it is saying to us? Returning to Peter Enns' contention that the Bible is mostly a story (a library of stories, actually), we can easily begin to grasp how stories affect people differently, in fact, how they affect us personally in different ways depending on our circumstances and where we may be in life's journey. I can say without hesitation that the Psalms speak to me in very different ways at this point in my life than they did when I was in my twenties. This should only be expected of a book that we believe is "living and active" in specific ways. So when we speak of the Bible we are, necessarily, speaking about a very different kind of book; for those of us in the Judeo-Christian tradition, it is a book that transcends all other books. But additional problems arise as we begin to unpack how we relate to this very special book.

BIBLIOLATERS R US!

It was the first Sunday of a new school year. At that point, we still had a Sunday evening service, and while the college was in session, we held both Sunday services in the college chapel. As I looked over the Sunday evening crowd, I could see that it numbered somewhere between four and five hundred. That's a lot of people, but in a chapel that seats close to 1,300, four to five hundred people tend to spread out like current-day social distancing. One person whom I noticed almost immediately was sitting all by himself in the first row of the balcony. He stood out because he wore a black suit with a white shirt and black tie. Students didn't tend to dress up at all for evening services, so this guy was impossible to miss. I stood up to preach and read my sermon text, closed the Bible and laid it next to me on the lectern and proceeded to deliver the sermon. The sermon was an expository treatment of the text that I had read at the beginning. At the close of the service the well-dressed student in the balcony made a beeline for me, quickly ascending the steps onto the chapel platform. Before I could even acknowledge him, he said, "You closed the Bible!"

"Excuse me," I replied. "I did what?"

"You closed the Bible. You spoke your words, not the Bible."

This young man, a new student, was extremely upset by the fact that, from his balcony vantage point, he could see that I closed my Bible after reading the sermon text. As I talked with him, I gathered that he was from a church tradition that not only revered the Bible but essentially worshiped it. To them, Scripture had an almost magical aura about it. Anything that could be interpreted as disrespectful made one's faith profession immediately suspect. Unfortunately, this young man left college at the end of that first semester, clearly unable to deal with what he likely perceived as many unforgivable breaches of proper reverence for the Word of God. While reverencing God's Word is praiseworthy, elevating the Bible to a place where it is virtually worshiped is idolatrous.

Each year, we had a special week at Houghton College devoted to world missions. One year the guest speaker was a winsome woman who had served many years as a Bible translator. She was a very good speaker who wonderfully represented the important work of Bible translation around the world. But there was one thing about her that I found a bit unsettling. In every session she would, at some point, lift a Bible into the air and proclaim, "It's all about this book!" Given her life's work in Bible translation, I could appreciate her passion, but I have to admit that I wanted to say in response, "No, it's not all about that book. It's about the God who is revealed to us in that book." The truth is, Christians don't "believe" in the Bible, they believe in the living God who is revealed to us in the Bible. The Bible is not an end in itself, but rather the critical means of God making Godself known to us through the stories of Israel, Jesus, and the early church. Importantly, Christianity is indeed a "revealed" religion, which means that the substance of our faith has been given to us. And Scripture is a primary source of revelation, although, as we will see later, not *the* primary source. When people elevate the Bible to the point of idolization, even in benign ways, crossing that line has only deleterious outcomes. The late Stanley Grenz wrote, "We must not idolize the Bible itself, as some non-evangelicals accuse us of doing. Scripture is not an end in itself. Rather, we honor and ought to honor, the Bible as the Spirit-inspired and Spirit-illumined means to knowing God."[62] Whenever we try to read the Bible as an encyclopedic guide to life, or all-knowing answer book, we are making the Bible into something it isn't intended to be. This easily becomes a kind of idolatrous quest to find some absolute source of truth that we can hold and use for our own purposes. That's basically the textbook definition of idolatry—using the sacred to manipulate and control, perpetuating the myth of our own sovereignty.

Beyond this, we need to be very clear about what we *don't* mean by inspiration. We do not mean that the Bible is "magical" in any sense. It is not to be used to hold power over others in ways that we have often witnessed by far too many pastors posing as little popes. Moreover, the Bible was never intended to allow us to unlock all the secrets of the universe. We actually "see through a glass darkly" in our present lives. Human experience is filled with mystery. The Bible must never become a sort of talisman that we use to fend off or deny the undesirable elements of human life. And let's be clear: trying to turn Scripture into a science, economics, or even an ethics textbook constitutes a kind of textual abuse that substitutes our own expediencies for the real purpose behind the Bible. Mark Knoll is surely correct when he writes, "Evangelicals display a gnostic strand when we treat the Bible as if it were an esoteric code to be deciphered as a way of obtaining privileged information about the creation of the natural world, the disposition of historical events, or the unfolding of the future. This tendency, unfortunately, leads evangelicals to shortchange the Bible, as well as the serious study of nature, history, or the more general world of human affairs "[63]

But, just as importantly, the Bible is not a mystery book. Understanding Scripture is not the special privilege of a select few. Basic knowledge of things like grammar, historical context, and certain interpretive principles can unlock, at least to a degree, most of what is in the Bible. Scripture is meant to reveal, not conceal, God. And, as should be obvious at this point, the Bible is not dictated by God or his angels. The Bible represents a unique sort of synergy, namely God and human authors in a special and unusual kind of partnership. As Peter put it in his second epistle, "Above all, you must understand that no prophecy of Scripture came about by the prophet's own interpretation of things. For prophecy never had its origin in the human will, *but prophets, though human, spoke from God as they were carried along by the Holy Spirit* (2 Peter 1:20-21, emphasis mine). The Greek word translated here "as they were carried along" (pheromenoi), is a navigational term which depicts the wind filling the sails of a ship and propelling it to its destination. That is a beautiful picture of how Scripture is, literally, "in-Spirited," though employing human agency. Through the years, increasing my understanding of the human element in Scripture (the author's intentions in writing, their historical circumstances, their theological vantage points, etc.) has immeasurably deepened my respect and reverence for this exceptionally good book. But unlike many other books we may pick up, reading the Bible with maximum understanding means that it must always be read with certain realities in play.

THE ART OF READING OLD BOOKS

For several years, a faculty colleague and I created and directed an off-campus program known as "Houghton Down Under." This was a semester-long experience in Australia, taking courses in things like Australian literature, Australian history etc., taught by Aussie professors. Each year, we took Houghton students, along with students from a variety of other American Christian liberal arts colleges, for an intense, exciting semester of learning. Because the program was designed as an immersive cross-cultural experience, watching these American students deal with "Aussie" culture was both enlightening and highly entertaining. Since Aussies speak English, the students tended to think that, other than driving on the "wrong" side of the road (a peculiarly American way of putting it!), and having some really odd animals, Australia wasn't much different from back home. In a way, they were right, at least on a surface level. In Australia, they found McDonald's, Starbucks, Burger King (called Hungry Jack's there), and Kmart, among others. And they had *Crocodile Dundee* and other pop portrayals of Australia under their belts. So the first few days in-country typically produced a huge amount of confidence ("Nothing much different here," etc). But within a week or two, as they actually began to talk with Aussies, visit places that tourists didn't typically go, and attend uniquely Aussie events like "Footy" (Australian Rules Football), the realization that they were no longer in Kansas began to sink in. That's what crossing cultures is intended to do: force you take a closer look and see things you didn't know or see previously.

When most people pick up the Bible, at least one written in their own language, they tend to read it without ever crossing cultures. But failing to realize that the Bible represents a variety of cultural contexts, across several centuries, can easily give us a false sense that we can readily discern what is being said right from the comfort of our La-Z-Boy! Now, I'm not backing off my previous statement about the Bible being accessible to ordinary people, not at all. But we have to know that we are reading Scripture with a mindset different from those people who lived thousands of years ago. Some of the questions we might bring to the text would never have occurred to the biblical authors or those to whom they wrote. In the Bible, we are reading of an ancient people's experiences with God, using their colloquialisms, dealing with their questions, all expressed in a language different from the English texts that most of us read. In addition, there are at least three immediate problems that modern readers encounter in the biblical text. First, there is a pre-scientific worldview that appears to be in serious conflict with modern science (more on that in a later chapter). Second, there are moral and ethical viewpoints that seem problematic to us today, on things like slavery, polygamy, genocide, etc. Finally, there are some instances where Scripture seems to be in conflict with itself. Think, for example, about Abraham, the paragon of "righteousness," blatantly lying about being married to Sarah on a couple of occasions. What's that about? Reading Scripture responsibly necessitates cultivating some ability to see what it meant for ancient Israelites, for example, to speak about God in the way they did. We simply have to refrain from imposing our expectations onto biblical texts written long ago in cultures very different from our own. Gabe Lyons contends, "One thing that both modern liberals and conservatives have in common is that they read the Bible in very modern ways. Modern conservatives treat the Bible as if it were a modern book. They're used to reading modern history texts and modern encyclopedias and modern scientific articles and modern legal codes, and so they assume that the Bible will yield its resources if they approach it like one of those texts. But none of those categories even existed when the Bible was written."[64] We do injustice to Scripture when we impose our understandings of "history" onto these ancient texts. Those biblical storytellers are not trying to do history in the modern sense. Rather, they are preserving the traditions of Israel in a manner that serves a specific purpose, a specific motivation for writing. They were not trying to be objective in the modern sense of the word. They were trying to persuade and inspire their original readers to some larger purpose. Remember that "the people who wrote the Bible didn't know they were writing the Bible," as Kent Dobson writes. "There was no Bible, no obsession with the truth being confined to words on a page. Paul wasn't hoping his letters would make the cut for the New Testament canon. He might have laughed at words like *inerrant* and *infallible*. He spoke from his experience, for better and for worse."[65]

Yes, the Bible is the inspired Word of God, absolutely, but we always need to keep in mind that there are two voices speaking. One of the voices is a human being that is trying to communicate something significant to the people addressed in the written text. The human author also becomes the primary doorway into what God is saying to people like you and me, separated by centuries from the original text. So, for example, when we read Genesis, we are reading a very ancient text and should limit our assumptions about that text to ideas and questions that would have been appropriate for the original readers. Far too many Christians today try to read Genesis through a modern scientific lens when such questions would not even have occurred to the post-exilic people of Israel who appear to be the original audience for this text in its current form. Our failure to cross cultures and our insistence, instead, on reading these ancient texts with a mindset shaped by modernity is at the root of so much misunderstanding and conflict about the Bible.

A further indicator of the general failure to grasp the Bible as an ancient source lies in the prevalence among some modern evangelicals to insist that Scripture must be read and interpreted "literally." A while back, I spoke at a newly planted church about forty miles from my home. I preached that day from Matthew 5:33–37, where Jesus talks about the use of oaths, teaching the truth that in the kingdom of God, oaths are unnecessary, because the citizens of the kingdom are truth-tellers. A simple "yes" or "no" is sufficient. After the service, a man came up to me and said that he appreciated my sermon because he "believed in taking the Bible literally." I have to confess that the thought ran through my mind, "if I slapped this guy on the cheek, I wonder if he'd turn the other one to me for a second go around?" Of course, I didn't say that, much less do it, but statements like his are absolutely absurd. The idea of parents stoning rebellious teenagers, or forcing surviving sons to marry the widow of an older brother, or any number of other Old Testament practices, demonstrates how untenable taking the Bible literally can be. We really have what Christian Smith terms an "uneven and capriciously selective literalism."[66] We find things we like and take them literally. Those things we don't like we relativize or adopt alternative interpretations. Even Jesus used language in such a way as to obviously forgo literal interpretations, such as "hating one's parents" or "plucking out one's eyes." Reading Scripture literally fails to take the nature and character of the Bible seriously. Biblical literalism is ultimately a road to nowhere.

To briefly return to a previous point, Christianity is a "revealed" religion. The substance and basis of what we believe is given via revelation. Whatever we know about God, about God's nature, and God's ways, is given to us. We know because God wants us to know it and has revealed it to us. But at the same time, we have to understand that nowhere does the Bible pretend to provide us with anything resembling a full-blown theory of knowledge. The Bible doesn't tell us everything. Revelation as a doctrine is primarily concerned with "saving" knowledge, a knowledge that bears decisively on the meaning and wholeness of our lives in relationship to God and others. That's why I insist that "I don't know" can be a most appropriate theological judgment. Confessing that God has been revealed to us in the Bible is not the same thing as claiming that we know everything about God that can be known. While God does reveal Godself in Scripture, God remains God and never becomes a possession at our disposal. God never becomes our prisoner. He remains free, ever a mystery, ever hidden, in some sense, from us. What we do find in this compendium of revealed truth we call the Bible are stories, lots of stories. These are stories which accurately portray the dominant God-consciousness of that day, so alongside stories that we may find repugnant or morally questionable (like violent conquests and wholesale massacres) we also "cross cultures" and read in such a way that we see the emergence of radical ideas about equality, justice, compassion, and love.

One further example of how reading things into the biblical text prevents us from truly grasping the message of Scripture, is, in my opinion, the most outrageous of all. I speak here of the way that biblical eschatology has been almost completely hijacked by sensationalism, money-hungry hucksters, and some well-intentioned yet misguided conservative Christians. Eschatology, a term for the study of "last things," holds all kinds of potential to deepen our understanding and appreciation of the Bible, particularly for the contemporary church and its life in the world. But when eschatology is overrun by a popular form of escapist theology, exemplified in the *Left Behind* series of books and others, it leads to a rationality-defying kind of chaos in biblical interpretation. In his book, *Reading Revelation Responsibly*, Michael Gorman critiques the *Left Behind* books thus: "This is a thoroughly misguided approach to the Bible, theology, and the Christian life. It could be passable fiction, at some amateur level, except that it really is theology—and dangerous theology. The misguided character of the series becomes thoroughly warped especially in the last two books, with the portrayal of ultimate faithful discipleship as killing for Jesus' sake and the corollary depiction of Jesus as warrior. This makes the overall series dangerous spiritually, theologically, and politically."[67] Gorman goes on to argue that while eschatology is clearly a focus of the last book of the Bible, it is not the ultimate focus of Revelation at all. The book of the Revelation is intended to give hope to people in the midst of trying times, encouraging them to remain faithful to their commitment to God.[68] Imposing 19th-century "end times" ideas on a biblical text meant to speak to the church through the ages is the very height of cultural arrogance and a prime illustration of the damage that can be done when we insist on reading the Bible from our own narrow confines.

The overall theme of Scripture is not some escapist thriller where Christians wait around with bated breath to see if Christ and his angels can somehow overpower Satan and his minions and rescue us out of this world. The Bible is clear: our destiny involves a "new heaven and a new earth." Thus, the Bible is primarily a story of redemption and restoration. It is not a book designed for certain people to use to exclude others and to build walls between the insiders and outsiders. It is ultimately a book that tells us about a Creator God, whose love is so unending and steadfast that this God will go to unthinkable lengths to redeem and restore that creation. At the end of the day, the Bible is the consummate love story. Regardless of how badly Scripture has been interpreted or manipulated to serve questionable ends, it is a love letter from a God who has freely chosen to be known in a deeply redemptive relationship. The Bible is not a modern book by any stretch, but it has a message that encompasses all times, all cultures. God speaks! God makes Godself known. It is written in a book. A very, very, good book.

> The Bible is not about offering things like a biblical view of dating—but rather about how God the Father offered his Son, Jesus Christ, to death to redeem a rebellious world from the slavery and damnation of sin. The Bible is not about conveying divine principles for starting and managing a Christian business—but is instead about Christ on the cross triumphing over all principalities and powers and so radically transforming everything we consider to be our business. Scripture, this view helps us to see, is not about guiding Christian emotions management and conquering our anger problems—but is rather about Jesus Christ . . . . conquering the power of sin in his resurrection. Scripture then ceases to be about teaching about biblical manhood and womanhood or biblical motherhood and fatherhood—and becomes instead the story of how a covenant-making and promise-keeping God took on full human personhood in Jesus Christ in order to reconcile this alienated and wrecked world to the eternally gracious Father.[69]

This points us to what I consider to be the absolute hermeneutical key to Scripture—at the end of the day, it's all about Jesus Christ.

THE JESUS SEMINAR(Y)

In my Introduction to Christianity course, I used to tell students that in considering various theological and/or ethical issues, Christians ought always to remember that if all else fails, the answer is usually Jesus. Students tried that with me on exams, writing "Jesus" in when they didn't know the actual answer. I didn't bite, of course, but I did appreciate the fact that they were listening. I sometimes wonder if we truly grasp the extent to which Jesus indeed is the key, to virtually everything. As the Apostle said, writing about Christ, "in whom are hidden all the treasures of wisdom and knowledge" (Colossians 2:3). I would suggest that the Apostle's use of the word "all" certainly encompasses the content of the Bible. In their aforementioned essay "Rethinking the Bible," Rob Wall and Daniel Castello claim that "Scripture's substantive unity is located in its 'Christ-centered referent'. Scripture's unity is not a matter of proposing one particular portion of Scripture or one particular dogmatic theme that pulls all its parts together into a single but artificial unity. Scripture's oneness is rather a matter of interpreting its diverse parts by one Messiah whose work liberates the world from its slavery to sin and fear of death once for all."[70] They go on to speak about what they term Jesus' own "messianic hermeneutic" and cite the story of the Emmaus road and the words of the Great Commission as examples of what they mean.[71]

Hebrews 1:1–2 says, "In the past God spoke to our forefathers through the prophets at many times and in various ways, but in these last days he has spoken to us by his Son, whom he appointed heir of all things, and through whom he made the universe." This passage indicates that in Christ, things have come to a point of completion, in terms of what God will reveal of Godself via special revelation. In short, Jesus *is* the fullest, most complete revelation we have of God. There will be no new revelations that will supersede Jesus, so we absolutely must read the Bible with our "Jesus glasses" on. In this way, Scripture is authoritative, not in itself, but, as the Reformers insisted, as it "sets forth Christ," as it functions in the community of faith by the power of the Spirit to create a liberating and renewing relationship with God through Christ. This has deep significance for the way that we read and interpret the Bible. I suppose that most of us have had the experience of reading a novel where we found ourselves a bit lost or confused, only to come across a particular sentence or two that unlocked the whole book for us. This is what is called a "luminous sentence"; it illuminates everything behind it and onward from it. We can view the revelation of Jesus Christ as a kind of "luminous sentence," from which we can go forward and backward in Scripture to attain some understanding of the whole. In his *Church Dogmatics,* Karl Barth summed up Christ's significance in Scripture this way: "The Bible says all sorts of things, certainly; but in all this multiplicity and variety, it says in truth only one thing—just this: the name of Jesus Christ, concealed under the name Israel in the Old Testament, revealed under His own name in the New Testament . . . The Bible remains dark to us if we do not hear in it this sovereign name."[72] The Bible therefore is, in a manner of speaking, *the* Jesus Seminar! Or, as I prefer to say, the Bible is essentially a "seminary" in itself, which aims to teach us to grasp the most important thing God wants to say to us—Jesus. Jesus is not just an important *part* of what the Father has to say or even the *main thing* the Father has to say. As the one and only Word of God, Jesus is the *total content* of the Father's revelation to us.[73] This is why I have determined that Jesus will be my "hermeneutic." He will be the interpretive key as I read Scripture and try to discern its meaning. It's increasingly clear to me that Jesus must be the sole criterion by which we assess the rest of Scripture and how it is to be applied in our lives today. If people want to throw Bible verses around in some attempt to soften or even mitigate the teachings of Christ, we must be prepared to go back to the Mount of Transfiguration, where Jesus appeared alongside Moses and Elijah, the exemplars par excellence of biblical authority. In that surreal scene, God the Father unequivocally said, "This is my Son, listen to him!" Of course, we often don't listen; so much of what Jesus says constitutes things we don't much want to hear. As John Alexander put it, "Christians spend a lot of time and energy explaining why Jesus couldn't have meant what he said. This is understandable; Jesus was an extremist and we are all moderates. What's worse he was an extremist in his whole life—not just in the narrowly spiritual areas—but in everything, so we have to find ways to dilute his teachings."[74] Sadly, we've been pretty adept at that. But even when we try to use the Bible itself to debunk or dilute the teachings of Jesus, we have no authoritative leg on which to stand. N.T. Wright said, "In the Bible all authority belongs to God and is then delegated to Jesus. The risen Jesus doesn't say, 'All authority in heaven and earth is given to . . . the books you chaps are going to go and write,' He says, 'all authority has been given to me.' The phrase, 'authority of Scripture,' can only, at its best, be a shorthand for the authority of God in Jesus, mediated through Scripture."[75] Wright is joined in these sentiments by many, many other biblical scholars and theologians. Christian Smith cites Kevin Vanhoozer as saying, "The ground of Scripture's indispensable role in the economy of the gospel is ultimately Christological. The Bible—not only the Gospels but all of Scripture—is the (divinely) authorized version of the gospel, the necessary framework for understanding what God was doing in Jesus Christ. Scripture is the voice of God that articulates the Word of God: Jesus Christ."[76] Smith goes on to say, "Vanhoozer could not be more clear: The biblical stories, commands, promises, songs, prophecies, and didactic discourse all mediate God's communicative action, but not all in the same way. What they share, however, is the same basic orientation. The canon is a unique compass that points not to the north but to the church's North Star: Jesus Christ."[77]

So, here's what I've decided. I have decided that when it comes to interpreting the Bible, along with all the thorny issues that come at us these days, my bottom line is this: does it pass the "Jesus test?" If I can't reconcile what some biblical passage is claiming with the person, work, and teachings of Jesus, I am obligated to go back and figure out where I left the trail. The views I take throughout this book are my good-faith effort to allow Jesus to be my hermeneutic. The fact that these positions contribute to my status as an outlier is something that I find, at best, perplexing. But I take comfort in the fact that I find myself in some rather interesting company, and, I might add, our company is growing.

Chapter 4

Deciders or Disciples
Evangelism in a Post-Christian World

> What if leading people to Jesus wasn't about closing the deal with a magic prayer or getting them to come tearfully down a church aisle in the manufactured urgency of lights and crescendoing worship songs? What if sharing the gospel is really a matter of giving people a daily front-row seat to a life that looks like Christ? What if the way we BEST make disciples is by showing people the fullest incarnation of Jesus that we can manage and resting in that? ... The best evangelism is letting people know that we follow Jesus and then not being a complete jerk. It's a pretty low bar, really.
>
> —John Pavlovitz[78]

I suspect that I've been something of an outlier for much of my life, but I clearly recall when my outlier status became known in the church. At the completion of my first year as pastor at the Houghton church, I set about the task of filling out the dreaded "Annual Report" that all pastors so dearly love. I don't begrudge the denominational organization asking for such information, but completing those forms is not an enjoyable experience. I dutifully began my task, filling in the requested information for things like average Sunday morning worship attendance and church finances. No problem. But then came this question: "How many people were saved in the church during the past year?"

I didn't quite know what to make of that question, let alone what to put as an answer. Finally, I put an asterisk in the blank and printed the words "see reverse side" in the margin next to the response box. Then, I flipped that page over and wrote what I thought of that question. A couple of weeks later, I got a phone call from the district superintendent, requesting a meeting with me. At the meeting I had the opportunity to explain my response to that puzzling question. I don't recall exactly what I said, but my words likely outlined my discomfort with trying to quantify something so significant as the salvation of human persons, especially given that such knowledge is truly known only to God.

Later that summer, at our district conference, one of the denominational leaders was giving his annual report to our district. In his report, he referenced the number of conversions recorded in the denomination over the previous church year and then, glancing my way, said something to the effect that, "In our church, we are not opposed to counting conversions. After all, the early church in Acts counted the three thousand conversions on the day of Pentecost." I very much wanted to rise and say, "With all due respect, sir, the early church counted baptisms! I am more than happy to report the number of baptisms we did in our church. We actually know the correct number." It's probably a good thing I didn't make that statement, given that my outlier status was already confirmed.

As I look back on that experience, with many years gone by, I still believe that the question on the annual report form was, at best, poorly worded. I am confident that I do not have the "gift" of evangelism, however it is defined, but I believe in the call of the church to go and make disciples everywhere, and I know personally what that meant in my own life. I felt like the question on the annual report somehow trivialized a life-altering encounter, substituting something far less transforming, albeit more easily quantified. I fear that our modern notion of conversion is something less than what Scripture calls the "new birth," that we concentrate on the act of making a "decision" rather than a wholehearted submission to God and to the ethos of God's kingdom. If we are satisfied with people "making decisions," signing cards, raising their hands, or whatever, I fear that we have lost something of the very heart of evangelism. The adoption of this "decision" view has allowed us to claim thousands of "conversions" across the land with minimal visible effects. As one Houghton chapel speaker put it years ago when Time magazine claimed that a quarter of the U.S. population was born again, "if you put a quarter pound of salt into a pound of hamburger, it should make quite a difference." The minimal effect of huge numbers of "born again" people raises some difficult questions about how we conceive of evangelism and how we go about evangelizing.

Part of the issue lies in the fact that our understanding of conversion comes largely out of a revivalist culture, in which making a public "decision" for Christ has been the accepted milestone. Everything hinged on "closing the deal"—getting the person to sign off, pray the prayer, or whatever. This was illustrated by the widely used "Four Spiritual Laws" tract. Telling people that "God loves you and has a wonderful plan for your life" was the door-opener. But the tract offered nothing as to who this God was, what God was like, or what a relationship with God entailed. It was all about closing the deal. And it worked! At least, we told ourselves it did. But the salt isn't having much effect on the beef. Some evangelicals like to point to the growing megachurches and conclude that the overall decline of the church in America is just a "mainline" problem. A previous chapter in this book debunks that conclusion, even though the "decision" model of evangelism largely persists. Brian Zahnd's story could be the story of many an evangelical pastor in America.

> As a zealous American evangelical, I spent plenty of time peddling "the bus ride to heaven" reduced version of the gospel. I can tell you it's a pretty easy sell. You promise the moon (actually heaven) for the low one-time cost of a sinner's prayer. How hard is that? And since it mostly applies to the next life, why wouldn't you pray the prayer? If for no other reason than as a kind of afterlife insurance. Oh, yes, we did offer the optional discipleship package for those wanting to upgrade their Christian experience. But the important thing was to fill up the bus for the postmortem ride to heaven. That's largely how I understood and preached the gospel. And, yes, at times it did seem a little cheap. But plenty of people made decisions and prayed the prayer. As the saying goes, you can't argue with the numbers. (Actually you can argue with the numbers—that's what prophets do all the time.) [79]

What I'd like to do in this chapter is argue with the numbers, or more precisely, state some of the difficulties with this approach to evangelism and suggest some steps towards a more biblically centered and theologically informed understanding of the church's Great Commission task. The contemporary church, and especially the evangelical church, must be willing to look behind the curtain at this fundamentally important aspect of the church's life and mission. How do we address the growing number of people, some sitting in evangelical churches, who believe that sharing one's faith is inconsistent with religious tolerance? How do we account for the large numbers of people in the church's "spiritual nurseries" who seem unable or unwilling to go deeper into the faith? How do we address the post-colonial critiques of Western Christianity and the embarrassing hucksterism of some well-known evangelists? And how do we address the all-important fact that, in David Bosch's words, "much so-called evangelism aims at satisfying rather than transforming people."[80] Bosch, whose work and writings have transformed the way I think about evangelism, pulls no punches in his critique of the church's shortcomings in this crucial area of concern.

> Much "evangelism" leads to a conversion to the predominant culture, not to the Christ of the gospels. In much of the "electronic church" materialism is baptized. The Jesus of revivalism appears to have more in common with the Chamber of Commerce and the entertainment world than with a simple cave in Bethlehem or a rugged cross on a barren hill. Preachers steer clear of controversial social issues and concentrate on those personal sins of which most of their enthusiastic listeners are not guilty. However, what criterion decides that racism and structural injustice are social issues but pornography and abortion personal? Why is politics shunned and declared to fall outside the competence of the evangelist, except when it favors the position of the privileged in society? How is it that preachers who appear to have an interest only in the otherworldly destiny of their listeners can be so thoroughly worldly in their ethos and methods? ... Of course, to those who are experiencing personal tragedy, emptiness, loneliness, estrangement, and meaninglessness the gospel *does* come as peace, comfort, fullness, and joy. But the gospel offers this only within the context of it being a word about the lordship of Christ in all realms of life, an authoritative word of hope that the world as we know it will not always be the way it is.[81]

I hope to address the concerns Bosch raises here, along with others, not merely to scratch my outlier's itch, but to foster a much-needed conversation about the all-important task of evangelism in the modern world.

EVANGELISM EXPOSED

When I was a first-year student in Bible college I was required to take a course called Personal Evangelism. This course aimed to make the case for every Christian to be engaged in evangelism; it taught us a specific approach, or plan, to use to engage people we hoped to win to Christ. As you might be able to guess by now, putting me in a course that involved encountering total strangers and trying to engage them in the kind of conversation aimed at leading them to pray a prayer of repentance was doomed from the beginning. As a pronounced introvert, I didn't find talking to strangers easy at all. When I was younger in Arizona, my father sometimes would take me along with him as he went door to door talking to people about church, Jesus, heaven, etc. Honestly, I would rather have been horse-whipped. For me, it was torturous. So, years later, I find myself in a course requiring that I learn a "plan of salvation" by rote so that I can buttonhole strangers and "win" them to Christ. What could possibly go wrong?

Even if I could summon the fortitude to accost a stranger with the question, "If you died tonight, would you have the assurance of spending eternity in heaven?," I had to wonder how this person would react. I mean, who doesn't relish the idea of that question coming at them on a busy city street? I may be exaggerating a bit, but not by much. Packaging evangelism into predictable conversational sparring matches, where every possible response is anticipated and expertly parried, strikes me as much more descriptive of the methods of the Watchtower Society members who ring our doorbells than of the practices of the average evangelical believer.

Few want to talk about the dirty little secret that most Christians don't witness about their faith. Only about half of "born again" adults do it at all, and what they do they don't feel good about. "Studies show that spreading the gospel is one of the areas in which Christians have the lowest self-esteem and the least interest in self-improvement."[82] This is all the more concerning given that leading people to Christ has become an important way for Christians to gauge their personal faithfulness: "If you really love Jesus, you will do this." Evangelistic witnessing thus becomes something of a double-edged sword. If personal reticence can somehow be overcome, the danger becomes viewing relationships only, or primarily, in terms of their evangelistic potential. People resent this. No one wants to be viewed as a "project." Despite the centrality of evangelism in the church's mission, even within the church itself, evangelism has a negative connotation to it.

> The mental model that many church members have of doing evangelism is for them to act like tele-marketers. I mean, how popular are these people? Tele-marketers interrupt you with a marketing message about a product you haven't asked for and try to get their spiel out before you hang up on them. Then, if you do happen to buy what they're selling, they pass you along to some customer service person who may or may not be actually connected to the company the tele-marketer is pushing. Sound familiar yet? How many "evangelism programs" have you

encountered in which sharing the gospel assumes no relationship with the customer and Jesus is sold like soap?[83]

Numerous studies show that the most effective kind of evangelism is that which is done within the context of relationships, either familial or friendships. While familial relationships might understandably remain constant after someone makes a church commitment, the research shows that "within three to five years of a person becoming a Christian, they will have no meaningful relationships with anyone outside the church . . . Sever the relationships and we effectively stop the outward movement of the gospel into the broader culture. In other words, attractional evangelism results in extracting them from their previous relationships and cultural contexts."[84] Traditional approaches to evangelism yield the ironic consequences that even if people can be persuaded to engage in evangelism, it tends to gravitate toward the kind of encounter with strangers that we've already seen to be problematic in a variety of ways. Pursuing evangelism that depends on winning strangers reminds me of the religious sect called the Shakers who didn't believe in sex, which meant they had no natural way to sustain the colony!

Beyond the psychosocial issues raised by accosting strangers with questions like "if you died tonight, would you have the assurance of going to heaven?" we should also think deeply about some further ramifications of such approaches. For example, is the employment of fear or guilt a plausible way to engage people with what we claim to be "good news"? I grew up in a church that firmly believed in "evangelism by terrorism." When it came to scaring people, especially young people, into repentance, everything was considered fair game. I've sat through countless evangelistic or revival services where speakers told hair-raising stories of people being hit by trains on their way home from the revival service, where they dramatically counted off the seconds to eternity, or where they described the fires of hell in a way that would have done Jonathan Edwards proud. I guess they figured that the end justified the means. But that has never been a principle that finds traction in a Christian context, and frankly, it's no longer a viable methodology in our present world. Are these kinds of evangelistic tools at all faithful to the God who is revealed in Jesus Christ? I can remember, as a teen, pocketing a few of those infamous J.T. Chick tracts that always seemed to be available on the table in the back of our church. I used them as reading material during the service. I don't remember much of the actual content, except that God was portrayed as a vengeful judge who would examine me and my life, see my sin and imperfections and have none of it. The scars such approaches create in the lives of people like me take years to heal. I struggled with my view of

God for a long time, even following my conversion. John Pavlovitz wrote, "I know how disorienting it is to be compelled to cling to a loving Creator while simultaneously being taught to be terrified of what that Creator wants to do to you if you do not cling correctly"[85] Why do we think that teaching about God means stressing God's most austere attributes? Christians raised in this kind of spiritual environment tend to develop stunted and harmful understandings of God and how God relates to us as human persons.

What's more, the fact is that fewer and fewer people are susceptible to approaches that stress the fear of hell and the laying of guilt trips. Given the contingencies confronting today's citizens of the world, adding one more scary story about eternity isn't likely to gain an attentive ear. Kent Dobson, who found his way out of these evangelistic scare tactics, contends, "The message was always the same: we were born in sin and we had caused Jesus to suffer like this. If we didn't get right with God, we would end up being tortured forever . . . These are not benign messages. This is a kind of child abuse, and I'm not being flippant. The church I grew up in did tremendous damage to young people by telling them they're a problem to God from their first breath. The church wounded people with its low view of human beings and its narrow view of God."[86]

While many of us who grew up in such church environments have found ways to put this into some kind of context we can live with, multitudes of people in a post-Christian world hear this as the story of some petty, dictatorial God demanding satisfaction for every sin, or worse yet, some villain who creates a disaster and then shows up like a hero to save the day so he can feel good about himself.[87] Like the consummate insiders that we evangelicals tend to be, we need to think carefully about how what we say is being heard. As I've told my beginning preaching students over and again, "communication is not what's said, it's what's heard!" If we think through much of what we have historically said, why would anyone out there receive it as "good news"?

Well, we obscure the downside by going full speed ahead into selling Christian faith as a ticket to heaven. N.T. Wright laments that, "Western Christianity has allowed itself to embrace [a] dualism whereby the ultimate destiny of God's people is heaven, seen as a place detached from earth, so that the aim of Christianity as a whole, and of conversion, justification, sanctification, and salvation, is seen in terms of leaving earth behind and going home to a place called heaven."[88] This perspective has proven very user-friendly, but no amount of pragmatic evangelistic appeal can justify such an egregious misreading of Scripture. Interestingly, if we survey the eight gospel sermons recorded in the book of Acts, we find that none is based on the issue of the afterlife! Instead of promises of heaven, these sermons teach that the world has a new king, whose name is Jesus.[89] In the Bible, "eternal life" does not mean heaven. It means God sharing God's own eternal life with us, and we can have it right here, right now. Unfortunately, many people, including Christians, cannot divorce the idea of what Matthew's gospel calls the "kingdom of heaven" from some concept involving the afterlife. Richard Middleton describes the problem with this viewpoint:

> Not only is the term "heaven" never used in Scripture for the eternal destiny of the redeemed, but also continued use of "heaven" to name the Christian eschatological hope may well divert our attention from the legitimate expectation for the present transformation of our earthly life to conform to God's purposes. Indeed, to focus our expectation on an otherworldly salvation has the potential to dissipate our resistance to societal evil and the dedication needed to work for the redemptive transformation of this world. Therefore, for reasons exegetical, theological, and ethical, I have come to repent of using the term "heaven" to describe the future God has in store for the faithful.[90]

Given how much popular Christian writings, music, and even preaching seems centered around the notion of heaven, many will find Middleton's words unsettling. But as he goes on to point out, this understanding of salvation completely misses the biblical point—that heaven as the eternal hope of the righteous has no structural place in the biblical story of redemption. "Indeed, there is not one single reference in the entire biblical canon (Old and New Testaments) to heaven as the eternal destiny of the believer."[91] Despite the cherished place that heaven holds in the imaginations of so many, Scripture is not the source of the widespread contention that the destiny of believers is to live eternally in heaven. And when evangelism is built around a heavenly destination, we discover that many people will give their afterlife to Jesus, as long as they can keep their earthly lives for themselves.[92] It doesn't take a theology degree to see the problems inherent in an evangelistic approach that says, essentially, "Go tell others how to escape from Planet Earth." It hardly seems compelling to most modern people, even apart from its problems as an interpretive standpoint for Scripture. Selling Jesus as "fire insurance," or as a ticket to heaven, reduces evangelism to escapism rather than the kind of intentional engagement with the world that Christ himself demonstrated and to which all Christians are called. Brian McLaren argues that "framing Jesus in this [escapist] way relegates Jesus to practical irrelevance in relation to human social problems in history."[93] This view offers no real hope for human history in this life, and it easily becomes, according to McLaren, "an 'opiate of the masses', pacifying them with dreams of a better afterlife 'by and by' rather than motivating and mobilizing them to transform our world here and now"[94]

EVANGELISM EXPLAINED

If we're not trying to scare people away from hell, and we're not selling tickets to heaven, then what *are* we doing when we engage in evangelism? In short, what is evangelism? Elaine Heath reminds us that "real evangelism is never coercive, violent, or exploitive. Real evangelism is not colonialism, nationalism, or imperialism. Evangelism rightly understood is the holistic initiation of people into the reign of God as revealed in Jesus Christ."[95] Initiating people into the reign (or kingdom) of God as revealed in Jesus Christ. That's the goal we are attempting to reach in bringing someone into a "saving" relationship with God. So, rather than seeing salvation as "going to heaven when we die," or merely viewing it through the lens of justification (being forgiven of one's sins, which is surely a necessary beginning point), we must expand our understanding of what salvation entails. Richard Middleton puts it this way:

> In the Bible, salvation is a comprehensive reality, both future and present, and affects every aspect of existence. The most fundamental meaning of salvation in Scripture is twofold: it is God's deliverance of those in a situation of need from that which impedes their well-being, resulting in their restoration to wholeness. Wholeness or well-being is God's original intent for creation, and that which impedes wholeness—sin, evil, and death in all their forms—is fundamentally anti-creational. Both the deliverance of the needy and their full restoration to well-being (in relationship with God, others, and the world) are crucial to salvation, and the term may be used for either or for both together.[96]

Using Middleton's words as a stepping-off point, I'll offer a few observations on what Scripture tells us about the salvation of human persons.

1. *Salvation is both present and future.* Many Christians assume that "eternal life" refers to our afterlife in heaven, but that is a misreading of the phrase in terms of its biblical context. "Eternal life" (zoein aionian in Greek) is better translated as "life of the ages," or a life that *transcends* "life in the present age." In other words, eternal life refers to life in the kingdom of God.[97] Eternal life is less about time that starts when we die, and more about a quality of life lived here and now in

relationship to God. When Jesus says in John 10:10, "The thief comes only to steal and kill and destroy; I have come that they may have life, and have it to the full," he means a quality of life that starts here and now. Eternal life doesn't start when we die. It starts the moment we are born anew in Christ.

2. *Salvation is not static, but transformational.* Far too many people view salvation as something akin to getting their driver's license. You bone up on the rules, pass the test, and drive off on your merry way. Done. In a similar way, many see getting "saved" as praying a "sinner's prayer," getting your sins forgiven, and then going on with your life. Wrong. God's intention is not merely to save us *from* something, but to save us *to* something. God desires to restore in us His image, which has been defaced and hidden by sin and evil. This reality illustrates sharply how what many term "evangelism" remains miles away from what the Bible is calling "salvation." William Willimon rightly captures the disconnect between these two ideas relative to human salvation:

> Nothing so exposes the fashionable stoicism of American faith—faith in a vague God who, though generally approving of human projects, neither speaks nor acts—as the notion that our God means to change us. Conversion is a radical assault upon the conventional, officially sanctioned American faith that we are basically OK just as we are, and that this world, for any of its faults, is all there is. Conversion is a statement of faith that this God means to have us—all of us—that this God will have God's sovereign way with us. Whether or not one believes in even the possibility of conversion will relate in great part to one's conviction about what sort of God we have, or, more biblically, what sort of God has us. Conversion is one of God's most gracious, intrusive, demanding and sovereign acts.[98]

The notion of conversion implies change, and as Willimon points out, this change is radical in that God "means to have us—all of us." Thus, "salvation is about a certain way of being and becoming in this world . . . salvation is a metaphor for a life lived with greater and greater integration and wholeness."[99] Far beyond a simple adjustment of our state, or of our standing before God, biblical salvation involves the liberation of people so that they might be enlisted for the kingdom of God. This kind of liberation takes time.

3. *Salvation is not instant, it is a process.* I grew up in a church that stressed the instantaneous character of salvation. You were "born again." One

moment you were not alive (spiritually speaking) and the next moment you were, born as a child of God. Now, there's surely something right about that which should not be lost on us. There clearly must be a starting point to one's life in God. But, to continue to use this metaphor (which is merely one of many metaphors Scripture employs in this vein), if nothing happens after the baby is born, you will not have life, but death. Thus, salvation is something that is going to involve the rest of our lives after our initial spiritual awakening. As Diana Butler-Bass puts it, "Being a Christian is not a one-moment miracle of salvation. It takes practice. It is a process of faith and a continuing conversion. And it can be a long walk."[100] Indeed it can be. It really is, to borrow a phrase, "a long obedience in the same direction." What God intends to do in restoring us to God's original creational intent is not the kind of thing that happens overnight. That's why theologians use words like "sanctification" and "consecration," words which are shorthand for "Christlikeness," the end goal of God's salvific work in human persons. Becoming like Jesus doesn't happen overnight.

4. *Salvation is not individual, it is corporate.* I recall one occasion where I said to my students in an introductory theology class, "I have never, nor do I have any intentions to ask Jesus to be my personal savior." The looks on their faces ranged from puzzled to angry, although I took note that some wrote it down in case it showed up on the test! Why would I say such a thing? Because I wanted the students to grasp the truth that salvation is not individual but communal. As one of my faculty colleagues put it to me years ago, "salvation must be personal, but it must never be individualistic." The third-century church father, Cyprian, is famous for his words "extra ecclesiam nulla salus" (outside of the church, there is no salvation). Cyprian, sometimes called the father of the Roman Catholic Church, likely meant more than many Protestants want to accept, but it does emphasize that Christianity is intended to be a corporate, not individualistic, endeavor. Further, it reminds us that evangelism is an "initiatory" process, which is only complete when individuals are incorporated into the church, participating in the life and mission of the church.[101] Vincent Donovan uncovers the problematic nature of "individual" salvation when he says, "The salvation of one's own soul, or self-sanctification, or self-perfection, or self-fulfillment, may well be the goal of Buddhism or Greek philosophy or modern psychology. But it is not the goal of Christianity. For someone to embrace Christianity for the purpose of self-fulfillment or self-salvation is, I think, to betray or to misunderstand Christianity at

its deepest level."[102] The transformation God intends to effect in our lives as believers necessarily leads to involvement in the faith community. This is why I struggle so much with the concept of "churchless Christians" (see Chapter 2). Darrell Guder echoes this truth when he writes, "the reduction of the gospel to individual salvation, with all its surrounding and resulting implications, is the gravest and most influential expression of the human drive for control."[103] Ultimately, it is the church that is redeemed as Christ's bride, and by grace we are made members of this community of the redeemed.

5. *Salvation is best understood as dynamic rather than forensic.* When speaking of salvation as a "forensic" matter, we are essentially borrowing legal concepts. For example, salvation results in a forensic, juridical, or legal change in one's status before God. And, of course, this is true. But to leave matters there misses the point that salvation involves not only a change in our status *before* God, but also brings us into a new and dynamic relationship *with* God. Dennis Kinlaw addresses this element of salvation, saying, "Christ died to do more than get us past the judgment and help us escape hell. He became incarnate and died on Calvary's cross to remove any impediments that would hinder us from being comfortable in his presence and to change us so we can enjoy him in self-giving love now and forever. Any understanding of the atonement that does not make provision to get us ready for that intimacy with him is inadequate, incomplete, and only partially biblical."[104] Grasping the difference between a forensic and a dynamic redemption is crucially important for our evangelistic efforts. We are not selling tickets to eternal life; we are inviting people into a life-altering relationship with the God of this universe. I have often explained it as follows: I was married on a Friday evening in June many years ago in Wilmore, Kentucky. At the moment the minister pronounced us husband and wife, I was legally (forensically) married. In fact, from a legal point of view, I was as married as I ever would be. Legally, I couldn't be more married than I was in that moment. My status had changed. However, having now been married to my wife for more than forty years, I can tell you with no hesitation that I am *way* more married today than I was on that warm Friday night in Kentucky so many years ago. The reason is simple: while marriage clearly is a legal contract, a legal change in one's status, what marriage *really* involves is a living, breathing, changeable, deepening relationship with another person. Failure to grasp the significance of a relational dynamism

severely hampers one's appreciation of what the Bible is talking about when it speaks the language of salvation.

6. *Salvation is more addition than subtraction.* I get the whole vocabulary of God "taking our sins away," of that which separates from God being removed. But I can't help thinking that this imagery overlooks what is gained when we become followers of Christ and his kingdom. In the beginning, humankind is portrayed as being in a garden that is perfect in every way. In the infamous episode that we refer to as "the fall," something is lost—paradise, according to Milton. When we view salvation as God's initiative to restore humankind to what God originally intended (see the book of the Revelation to explore how this theme of restoration comes full circle), we can begin to understand how our redemption is indeed a gift, something that we receive. We are created in the very image of God, and that image remains in every human person, regardless of how defaced or defiled it has become through the consequences of sinful choices on our part. This image is what makes every human person intrinsically valuable. This is why the Bible tells us that we cannot claim to love God and hate our brother at the same time (1 John 4:20). Yes, we are forgiven, our sins are removed as far as the east is from the west (Psalm 103:12), but we are adopted into God's own family, invited to join the company of those who journey back to God's original home for humankind.

7. *Salvation is more mystical than transactional.* One of the main reasons I didn't, and don't, like the "canned" evangelism methods is that they come off as way too transactional to suit me. I do not resonate with any approach that makes accepting Christ as Lord and Savior seem like selling someone a car. As Jim Henderson puts it, "Modern-day evangelicalism has attempted to remove the mystery and wonder from the conversion process. It has attempted to reduce it to a transaction. But birth is always messy."[105] Beyond the unpredictable nature of a person's relationship with God, there is what I view as a "mystical" element to it all. The longer I live as a Christian the more I look on my life, and particularly on my salvation, as a thing of great mystery. I think this is akin to how the Apostle Paul viewed himself as an even greater sinner near the end of his life than he did at the beginning of his faith journey (1 Timothy 1:15). The agency of the Holy Spirit in redemption "reminds us that evangelism is not simply the transmission of information, it is a mysterious encounter between human beings and the Spirit of God, who loves, surrounds, and pursues them gently."[106] For

this reason, we ought to marvel that God entrusts human beings with a key role in such a mystery.

One day in the early days of my pastoral service in Houghton, the secretary said that there was a young man who wanted to speak with me. I asked her to show him in. I assumed he was a college student, but that wasn't the case. He told me that he was driving through Houghton on his way somewhere and just felt strongly impressed to stop at our church and speak to the pastor. He proceeded to share his story—a combination of bad choices, aimlessness, and despair. After listening to him, I began to tell him about God's love for him and how God wanted to be part of his life and so on. We conversed further until we reached a point where I asked him if he would be willing to invite God into his life. He agreed and we proceeded to pray together. He seemed genuinely peaceful and contented about what had happened there in my office. After he left, I never saw nor heard from him again. I have often thought about that young man. What really happened there in that office? Was he genuinely converted? Did he ever find his way into a community of faith? All I can do is rest in the mysterious ways in which God sometimes moves to make Godself known to people. At the end of the day, evangelism is not what *we* do, it is what God is doing, sometimes with us and sometimes without us.

God does, indeed, ask us to play a role in the mysterious working of the Father, Son, and Holy Spirit to bring the world God made back into proper relationship with its Creator. The call to be Christ's witnesses (Acts 1:8) is foundational to the Church's *raison d'etre*, and yet we often fall far short of what is required to fulfill such a monumental calling. I have come to believe that much of our trepidation and hesitancy to be witnesses is due to our misconstruing what a witness actually is or does. Many of us, me included, do not have the "gift" of evangelism. That there is such a gift, I have no doubt, but I'm just as convinced that I don't have it. What I do have is a story—a story of what God has done for me and how God has become the absolute anchor of life and reality for me. And if I can tell that story, then I am being a witness. Carol Howard Merritt is right on target in this regard. "When we think of the 'e' word, we might imagine tracts of 'Four Spiritual Laws,' wily street preachers, tacky Christian broadcasting, or uncomfortable family dinners. And yet, the heart of sharing the good news is simply telling one's story—letting friends know what happened in our life and how our community of faith helped. Reaching out begins with the practice of testimony, of sharing our lives with one another, and being fluent in talking about our spiritual journeys."[107] Maybe instead of trying to convince nervous believers to memorize mechanical plans that aren't likely to be well-received in these times, the church would be much better served by helping people get comfortable and more adept at telling their own stories.

EVANGELISM ENHANCED

Anyone who's been paying attention knows that evangelism has become something of a problem for the modern church. In a pluralistic society, some people question the appropriateness of even intimating that others should be approached with any evangelistic intent. Furthermore, the *results* of the church's evangelistic efforts are open to varied interpretations, often negative. But the call for Christian witness in the Scriptures is undeniable, so the question becomes "How do we proceed?" I would suggest the following five adjustments and new emphases aimed at enhancing evangelism in the twenty-first century church.

1. *Change the paradigm.* We must rethink our entire approach to evangelism. What "worked" in the past isn't likely to be tenable in today's world. First of all, we must move away from bait- and-switch tactics. Offering tickets to heaven or get-out-of-hell-free cards and then trying to bring these "converts" into a fuller understanding of discipleship is both unethical and mostly unsuccessful. Jesus never hid the hard truth from people ("You want to follow me? I don't have anywhere to sleep at night!") Jesus was quite willing to allow people to walk away. We can't hide the hard truth of discipleship somewhere in the evangelistic fine print.

    We must move away from evangelistic plans and canned approaches. You can't diagram the gospel or package it into four or five principles. You can't put it into a diagram. There is no definitive list of truths that people must embrace in order to be saved. David Bosch estimated that "there have been some 788 'global plans' to evangelize the world since the beginning of the Christian era, and most of these were intimately linked to eschatological expectations."[108] Obviously, such plans built around "go to heaven / avoid hell" themes haven't exactly bowled over the unbelieving world. It's time to let them go.

    We must leave behind event-based and decision-oriented approaches as remnants of our revivalistic pasts. Instead, we must reimagine evangelism as a more process-oriented endeavor, where relationships are cultivated and where sufficient time is allotted for people to thoughtfully consider the good news we are sharing.

Instantaneous decisions for Christ will increasingly be the exception rather than the rule.

Most of all, we must think about the persons with whom we share this good news. Who they are must determine what we say to them and how we say it. The one-size-fits-all approach that I was taught in Bible college is not only untenable in today's world, it's often thoughtless and unkind. William Willimon reminds us that, "There are many in our society who are in pain, but not because of some psychological malady or because of something bad that happened to them when they were five. There are hurting because they are wandering around like lost sheep in a desert. They are confused. It is not that they are sick; rather, they are ignorant. They simply have not taken the trouble, or had the opportunity, to think through the faith. They confront the complexity of life with bits and pieces of insight cobbled together from here or there. Or they try to live in an adult world with the faith they the received as a ten-year old or rejected as a fourteen-year old."[109]

2. *Expand the story.* We have too often presented the gospel as if it were merely a question of an individual person's eternal destiny. While that is not a small thing, the gospel is much larger than that. It is cosmic in its scope. What God is doing in this world involves not only human beings, but the entire creation as well. Scott Buetzow observes that "most presentations of the gospel start with the Fall and end with redemption."[110] He goes on to suggest that we expand the presentation to creation and restoration as the bookends of the story we want people to consider.[111] Such a cosmic understanding of redemption would keep us from overly "domesticating" the gospel, reducing it to the individual soul, the nuclear family, or a strictly personal scope. As Brian McLaren puts it, "we have in many ways responded to the big global crises of our day with an incredibly shrinking gospel. The world has said, 'no thanks.'"[112]

3. *All ministry (including evangelism) is now "cross-cultural."* Any Christian who aspires to evangelism is now, by definition, a cross-cultural missionary. Gone are the days in which we can assume much, if anything, about the ideological and cultural foundations of the person with whom we may be talking. I remember my culture shock after going to college and seminary in the Bible belt and then moving to western New York State, so accurately dubbed "The Burned-Over District" by religious historians. I was amazed and taken aback at how different these folks were from the average citizen of southern Ohio or central Kentucky. That's our world now. The idea of cultural literacy

takes on added significance. It is of paramount important that we culturally "exegete" people in order to be sure of what makes them tick spiritually and otherwise.

4. *Be the church!* In a post-Christian culture, where skepticism about metanarratives and the "hermeneutic of suspicion" is pervasive, learning canned gospel approaches that throw Bible verses at people isn't a promising approach. I have repeatedly contended that in today's world, the visible church actually incarnating the values of the kingdom of God is a far more powerful witness than any packaged evangelism plan. The power of a group of people who live the gospel in front of their communities is far preferable to any other evangelistic strategy.

    Churches must seriously consider outsiders' portals of entry into the church community. For centuries, churches have incorporated a "bounded set" approach, or a "believe, then you can belong" mentality. In other words, once you acknowledge Christ as savior, are baptized, or sign off on our belief system, then you can be part of the community. "Centered set" thinking, on the other hand, views the church as a community who welcomes people at different points in their journey towards commitment to Christ, including some who haven't even arrived there yet but who are moving in the right direction or who are simply interested in observing. They are not required to *believe* in order that they might *belong*. They are invited to come and *belong* in order that they might come to *believe*. This approach feels risky to many church members, and there may well be scenarios in which people fall short and otherwise disappoint, but truly *being* the church has always been a risk in a world that doesn't know God. The "centered set" approach is long overdue.

5. *Make disciples!* Dallas Willard is one of the people who has influenced me most. His thinking and writing have profoundly shaped my life and ministry, and nowhere is that more evident than on the topic of evangelism. He prioritizes making disciples over pursuing "deciders," and he has no qualms about it. He wrote, "It is, I gently suggest, a serious error to make 'outreach' a *primary* goal of the local congregation, and especially when those who are already 'with us' have not become clearheaded and devoted apprentices of Jesus, and are not, for the most part, solidly progressing along the path. Outreach is one essential task of Christ's people, and among them there will always be those especially gifted for evangelism. But the most successful work of outreach would be the work of *inreach* that turns people, wherever they are, into light in the darkened world."[113] Willard believed (rightly, in my

opinion) that the fundamental mistake of the conservative side of the American church is its primary goal of preparing as many people as possible to die and go to heaven, or aiming to "get people into heaven rather than to get heaven into people."[114] The result of such priorities is that the church's "spiritual nurseries" are full, but mature disciples are hard to find. David Kinnaman bluntly says "the Christian church in the United States has a shallow faith problem because we have a discipleship problem. Moreover, diagnosing and treating shallow faith among *young* adults is urgent because we have a shallow faith problem among *all* adults."[115] Taking disciple-making seriously means some significant changes to business as usual in the church. The mass production paradigms must be set aside for the time-consuming and often inglorious task of building disciples of Jesus Christ relationally, one at a time. Darrel Guder is on to something important when he talks about "the continuing conversion of the church." Evangelism isn't a one-off. And it cannot be solely addressed to non-believers. Guder writes, "The New Testament is, as I have stressed, addressed to believers from beginning to end, and it evangelizes at every turning. Evangelizing churches are churches that are being evangelized. For the sake of its evangelistic vocation, the continuing conversion of the church is essential."[116] Discipleship is precisely how a church is "continually being converted." Discipleship is a life-long journey; while initial evangelism necessarily brings a person to the door of the house, discipleship *is* the house itself that God desires to construct around the life of all who come to Him. Choosing to emphasize disciple-making will not likely be the route to the fastest growth in the district, but it has the best possible chance of creating a church capable of birthing and growing healthy Christians.

EVANGELISM EMBRACED

When it comes to evangelism in the local church, Jim Henderson describes the all-too-familiar response: "'I'm just a regular, ordinary person who loves God and would love to do something for his kingdom. Too bad I'm not unusual, extraordinary, or even consistently courageous. If that's what it takes to get evangelism done, I'll just write a check.' And that's what the majority of Jesus' followers do every Sunday. They listen to an extraordinary speaker, applaud when he or she is done, and write a check, the lowest form of commitment in any organization."[117] So how does the church resolve this common evangelistic impasse? And yes, despite the fruitful work of various para-church organizations, it is indeed the church itself that needs to find its way through the evangelistic reticence of its congregants and fully embrace its mission in the world. The church remains the key.

As I thought about this, I remembered the first course I took in graduate studies at St. Mary's University. It was called Doctrine of the Church, and it was taught by a wonderfully warm and charismatic priest who welcomed me into a class full of future Roman Catholic priests like I was their long-lost cousin. These were the days following Vatican II, and that made for exciting times in such classrooms as they explored the newly opened windows into their faith and the church's mission in the world. One of our textbooks was Cardinal Avery Dulles's *Models of the Church*. In this book Dulles suggests six different ways to construe the church in order to grasp the nature and purpose of Christ's body in the world. I've invoked Cardinal Dulles's categories through the years to help myself and others better understand the nature of the church. Dulles' sixth category speaks of the church as a "community of disciples." Here, we come full circle with what evangelism actually entails—the making of disciples, mature believers who have the ability to share their story with others in effective ways because their lives have put down deep spiritual roots. Dallas Willard noted that when Jesus commanded his followers to baptize disciples in the name of the Father, Son, and Holy Spirit (Matthew 28:19), he was asking us to do more than get them wet."[118] Willard's point is that we are not as effective at making disciples as we think we are. There is no greater need in today's evangelical church with respect to evangelism than to find and embrace more effective ways to take people into the spiritually deep waters of authentic discipleship. At the end of the day, evangelism boils down to cultivating a community of authentic lovers of God and neighbor and then seizing opportunities to be oneself and share your story. And, oh yeah, remember John Pavlovitz's words at the beginning of this chapter: don't be a jerk!

Chapter 5

Sex, Lies, and Flannelgraphs
Rethinking the Facts of Life
(Including Some We Learned at Church)

> We must get to the bottom of true Christian sexual morality. If the Christian standard is based on fear, it can be replaced by lessons in biology. If it is a pious trick to make sexual life more difficult for young people merely to teach them the virtue of self-discipline, the trick will not work. Sexual morality has to stand up on its own; the value of self-discipline can no longer support it. If Christian morality is a legalistic set of rules devised by anti-sexual ascetics, it could not possibly persuade Christian people in our sex-affirming time. If the prohibition of sexual intercourse for the unmarried is born of obsession with sheer genital virginity—as though penetration separated the chaste from the unchaste forever—it will be a weak moral stance indeed. And, finally, if Christian morality has no compassionate sense of the differences between people and their motives for engaging in sexual intercourse—no feel at all for the moral differences between sheer physical exploitation and a genuine act of love, or between two irresponsible people acting in a fit of passion and two mature adults acting in tender responsibility toward each other—it will seem insensitive and indifferent to the facts of real life.
>
> —Lewis Smedes[119]

I'VE SPENT MOST OF my adult life around college students. Whether as a pastor in a Christian college community or a faculty member at the college itself, I loved being around these young adults. As one who often addressed students either in church or college chapel, I learned that with college-aged people there are two can't-miss topics: God's will and sex! Given their ages and faith commitments, it was only natural that they were keen to discover God's plan for their lives. Also given their ages and circumstances, it was only natural that they had a keen interest in sex! It occurred to me on more than one occasion that if I could craft a talk on "God's will for your sex life," I would hit the ball out of the park. This chapter is my attempt at combining these two topics, in a certain sense. I won't presume or suggest that I accurately know God's will in all the matters under discussion, but I do think that Scripture and the traditions of the church give us good guidance to at least begin the conversation. And I want to honestly and candidly reflect on my experiences with young people, mostly of the evangelical church, who are red-blooded sexual beings and who are (at least many of them) vitally interested in honoring God in this very complicated dimension of their lives. In short, we need to rethink some of what we have taken for granted about the so-called facts of life, and in particular, some facts of life that we likely learned at church.

In his comprehensive study of the relationship between religious commitment and sex in young people, Mark Regnerus cites a young man named Butch Hancock as saying, "Life in Lubbock, Texas, taught me . . . that sex is the most awful, filthy thing on Earth and you should save it for someone you love."[120] Surely that is an exaggerated example of the mixed messages that the church has sent to our youth about sex. Let's hope so. But, given this and similar statements, it appears that talking about sex within the walls of the church building hasn't exactly clarified matters. Something is being garbled in transmission.

It is a gross understatement to say that sexuality is a powerful force in our world, one that can be an extremely beautiful dimension of human existence. But it is also the height of understatement to assert that the church has not always done a good job of communicating about sex. Many of us can recall torturous experiences like having a well-meaning church official attempt to give "the talk," or hearing preachers try to explain the Song of Solomon, all the while clearly uncomfortable. Stanley Hauerwas pointedly observed, "Current reflection about sexual ethics by Christian ethicists is a mess. That may seem an odd state of affairs, for it is generally thought that while the church may often be confused about issues of war or politics, we can surely count on Christians to have a clear view about sex. It has been assumed that the church and her theologians have seldom spoken ambiguously about sex and most of what they had to say took the form of a negative. 'No,' you should not have sexual intercourse before marriage. 'No,' you should not commit adultery. 'No,' you should not practice contraception. And so on."[121]

What strikes me about Hauerwas' assessment is that it was written nearly forty years ago! If anything, matters have deteriorated since then. I think the way the church typically "helps" younger people deal with this topic should be re-examined and, in some cases, jettisoned. The traditional approaches often seem naive, overly idealistic, and theologically debatable. In a world where the average age of "sexual debut" for evangelical youth is 16.3 years,[122] one can make the case that however well-intentioned the church's efforts have been, there is a lot of room for improvement. Today's young people get a lot of slack from me in these matters. I'm willing to err on the side of empathy. I came of age in the 1960s, the days of the sexual revolution. In the aftermath of "free love," Haight-Ashbury, and Woodstock, all of the sexual horses were out of the barn, so to speak. But my sexually liberated friends and I never experienced anything remotely as unrelenting as the 24/7 sexual siren that plays in the ears of kids today. Regnerus puts it like this, "If there is a developmental trajectory for anything during adolescence, it is sex. Nothing—not smoking, drinking, drug use, nor any form of delinquency—compares to the rapid commencement of paired sexual practices during the latter half of adolescence."[123] Given this reality, evangelicals have been understandably concerned with establishing acceptable sexual boundaries, but too often this comes across to young people, obviously intrigued by sexuality, as "anti-sex." But at least the church is surely correct in thinking that it should be addressing sex. Regnerus points out that "Religion and sexuality tap basic drives. Sex concerns the pursuit of an intimate connection with another human being . . . Religion concerns the need to make sense and meaning out of life. . . In short, both religion and sex are *elemental* life pursuits, not mere window dressing but close to the heart of what it means to be human."[124] What the church must do, in my opinion, is find an informed and charitable voice in speaking clearly, candidly, and unapologetically to these elemental life pursuits. Allow me to initiate this discussion.

JESUS YAWNED

It would be a mistake to assume that I intend to question most of the church's traditional stances on sex, particularly as they relate to youth and unmarried people. For this group, much of what the church has taught about sexual activity remains significant and well-reasoned. Despite all the advances in contraception, sex can still lead to unplanned pregnancies, which bring a plethora of complications and issues. Sex prior to marriage or extra-marital sex can expose all manner of difficulties and can carry destructive consequences. So our discussion isn't about jettisoning "traditional" morality—it's more about presenting the church's viewpoints in a manner that takes the realities of young lives and the historical context seriously, and about inspecting what the Bible actually says (or doesn't say) about sex.

First, we must understand that adolescence itself is a new cultural invention. There were no "teenagers" identified in the Bible. Children became adults, got married and moved on with their lives. But today, teen culture is a major aspect of life and economics in our world. And the teen years are a longer span than ever before. The average age of puberty's onset is creeping ever downward. Circumstances are elongating the wait between childhood and adulthood. As impossible at it may sound, adolescence can begin as early as ten years of age, yet assuming the responsibilities of "adulthood" may not happen until that young person's mid-twenties or even later. That's anywhere from eight to fifteen-plus years of "just saying no!" The phenomenon of "extended adolescence" can also include deferring marriage for additional years, which can easily postpone the debut into "adulthood" to age 30 or beyond. The net result: a huge number of young people living in developmental limbo, where sexual interest is at its peak but the adult capacities, financial and otherwise, to assume parental responsibility is lacking. These changing physiological and social facts of life have moved the developmental goalposts, and I'm not at all certain that the church is fully aware of just how far.

Historically, most of these changes only became apparent in the 20th century. Pre-marital sex between people planning to marry became much more common in the 1920s, while the sexual revolution of the 1960s saw great increases in sexual activity between people without any long-term commitments whatsoever. Today, the church struggles to find its way through "friends with benefits," "sexting," and the Internet pornography sites carried around in teenagers' smartphones. Rethinking the "facts of life" will require a robust recalibration of precisely what today's adolescents confront when it comes to sex and their participation in it. And unfortunately, the Bible isn't as immediately helpful here as we might wish it to be.

Again, when the Bible was written it was a product of its cultural milieus and social understandings. Children who reached puberty were considered adults. In most cases, marriage followed—marriage very different in conception from our modern romanticized notions. The New Testament generally, and Jesus specifically, say very little about sex and marriage. OK, maybe Jesus didn't exactly "yawn" in response to questions about sex, but he didn't seem anywhere near as interested in it as one might expect, if sex is as big a deal as many seem to think. Furthermore, what is said on the topic, by Jesus and others in the New Testament, does not easily translate into the cultural and sexual understandings of the 21st century. Lewis Smedes summarizes what we might make of Scripture in this regard.

> The Bible does not spell out divine theories of sexuality. Nor is it a book with only one response to sexuality: its several writers always write in response to the needs and conditions of their situations. Many Old Testament writers have one eye slanted toward the pagan religions, and their warnings against certain sexual practices are often a warning against a religion that turns worship into a sex orgy. Jesus talks amid legalistic Jews, reminding them that sexual chastity is not bought simply by avoiding illegal acts. Further, he sees marriage as rooted in creation and thus evidently thinks very highly of it. Paul, on the other hand, expecting Christ to return soon, at first sees no great value in marriage, except as a way to cabin and control sexual drives.[125]

Smedes is not warning us that the Bible won't be of much help, but he is suggesting that Scripture doesn't *immediately* address the issues of sexual behavior as overtly and authoritatively as we might have hoped. Instead, we will need to dig deeper to uncover an overall biblical ethos towards human life, sexuality, the role of the body, and how the faith community and the mission of the church inform teachings about sexual attitudes and behaviors. The biblical authors didn't major on sexual themes because they were concerned with other, more urgent matters for their own day and times. We can hardly fault Scripture in this regard. We need to construct a viable sexual ethic using Jesus as our primary hermeneutical tool (as I've discussed in an early chapter on the Bible). Yes, Jesus was single and showed little to no discernible interest in matters of human sexuality, but he is the incarnation of what human wholeness is supposed to look like. Martin Luther called the Bible "the cradle that holds Christ." If we can speak to the issues of human sexuality within the broader parameters of Jesus' life and teachings, we will be headed down a more productive path.

NAKED AND AFRAID

Fear, shame, and guilt characterize the way conservative Christians have viewed sex through the years. It's not so much that we have been "naked and afraid"; rather, we've been "afraid to be naked." It may seem that we have closeted our sexuality, at times almost ignoring it, in the hopes that it might go away.

Part of why many are so afraid of sex is that we have bought into the notion that sexual sins are at the top of the heap in a "hierarchy" of sin. Ask any group of evangelical believers to name which category of sin will get one rapidly voted off the ecclesial island—sexual sin will win, hands down. In fact, whatever comes in second isn't within hollering distance, as they say in some parts. But this is a mistake, one that has had ongoing consequences for the church, and nowhere is that more evident than in today's youth culture.

C. S. Lewis was right to chastise the Christian world for suggesting that illicit sex is the unforgivable sin. Lewis said, "If anyone thinks that Christians regard unchastity as the supreme vice, he is quite wrong. The sins of the flesh are bad, but they are the least bad of all sins. All the worst pleasures are purely spiritual: the pleasure of putting other people in the wrong, of bossing and patronizing and spoiling sport, and back-biting; the pleasure of power, and hatred ... [Thus] a cold, self-righteous prig who goes regularly to church may be far nearer to hell than a prostitute."[126] The fact that Jesus told the Pharisees that prostitutes would get into the kingdom ahead of them (Matthew 21:31) should dampen any enthusiasm for establishing hierarchies of sin that are primarily used to condemn and exclude. On the other hand, even though I owe many unpayable debts to C.S. Lewis for opening my eyes to so much in my Christian life, I'd like us all to rethink one way in which we have traditionally read him on the topic of sex. In *Mere Christianity*, a compilation of radio talks that Lewis gave during World War II, Lewis suggests that while some said that "sex has become a mess because it was hushed up," he contends that humankind rightly "hushed up" about sex precisely because it had become such a mess (Book III, Chapter 5). Whatever the motives for the hushing up, our silence has not improved matters in the sexual arena. In fact, it has only exacerbated the deleterious effects of the reigning sexual anarchy.

Sex has become, in the words of one, "relentlessly consuming in our society in no small part because, for many, orgasm is the only way they experience self-transcendence. Sex gives them not just pleasure and release, but the closest approximation they have to an encounter with the mystical. With the decline of significant roles for religion and the arts in our culture, sexual ecstasy fills the hole vacated by the sublime."[127] Given the ubiquitous nature of sex in this culture, it behooves the church to overcome the understandable desire to hush things up, and instead find ways to get comfortable talking about being naked! David Fitch and Geoffrey Holsclaw suggest that "Christians have become a people with whom it is unsafe to talk about any sexual issues. Amid the sexualized cultures of North America, we have become an inhospitable and dysfunctional people."[128]

My own experiences as a pastor bear this out. I remember a time when a man spoke publicly about his struggle with pornography, demonstrating an openness that I wanted to encourage. Instead, a noticeable chill came over those in attendance, and I know that some found it more convenient to isolate this person than to embrace him. This must end. We have to move away from *shame* as our default setting when we deal with sexual behavior and attitudes in the people who seek the church's help. Pretending that such issues do not exist only make them worse. And the church is supposed to be the one place where it is safe to "confess our faults" to one another. It's way too easy to become Pharisaical—pretend that we have it all together while standing in judgment of those who are being honest about their struggles. Actually, one of the most pressing problems in Christian ministry today are ministers who have so sublimated their sexuality that it resurfaces in improper emotional attachments, pornography addictions, or extra-marital affairs. Years in ministry have taught me to be a bit uncomfortable around the "morality crusaders" because I have seen far too many instances in which the crusade was a way to hide or compensate for something going on where no one could see.

Hushing up about these issues is a completely misguided approach in the world we currently encounter. The only thing keeping silent accomplishes is allowing other voices to fill the void. Think of the classic parental dilemma: do they overcome their reticence and talk candidly with their children about sex, or do they leave it to the older kids on the school bus or the bathroom-wall poets to fill the informational void? Even the discomfort parents may have with school-based sex education must be weighed against the ubiquity of sex talk and sexual information all around our kids. Regnerus reminds us, "Whether or not Jane Q. Teacher is allowed to talk about condoms pales in significance and gravity to the democratized ability of the so-called sexual education that is available in the mass media, especially on the Internet . . . Debates about whether educators will or will not address oral sex or anal sex or condoms or gay or lesbian sex are quickly becoming utterly irrelevant, since a few clicks of a mouse will bring any of us to a demonstration of exactly how each is performed and "experienced."[129] Regnerus cites a column in which a British writer recounts his interview with a seventeen-year-old boy who is lamenting how far sex education lags behind electronic media. The young man said that "the school sex education we got was something from another age. We were told in class what a vulva was when I was 14, but by that time I had been inspecting them in detail on my computer screen for years, and so had every other lad in the room."[130] While this may seem a bit graphic to some readers, it's routine reality for kids living in our sexualized culture. The church must not abdicate its moral responsibility in this regard. I remember teaching on the spiritual discipline of chastity in my Spiritual Formation course. I deliberately talked very openly and candidly about human sexuality and all that goes with it. A young woman, a pastor's kid who was among the most brilliant students in the class, asked with noticeable anger in her voice, "why have we never heard this at church?" I had no answer for her. Why, indeed?

The church must find its voice in these matters, lest we surrender our children to those who view them as "walking hormones" with money to spend. Among other things, this means being willing to move away from some of the historical nonsense that infiltrated the church's teachings about sex. Augustine was surely right when he said that the "desire to love and be loved is one of the deepest and most profound markers of the fact that we belong to God and exist for relationship with God,"[131] But for Augustine and for many other theologians in the church, sex was a problem. Many believed that "procreation was not only the central purpose of marriage; it was the only God-ordained reason for married people to have sexual relations as all. Saint Ambrose, for example, rejected sexual intercourse as immoral even between husband and wife while the wife is pregnant, since such an act cannot be procreative."[132] The church must be clear; sex is about much, much more than biology. It is even more than satisfying "desire." James Brownson correctly observes that "sexual desire is . . . radically different from other bodily desires, such as hunger, for example. If I am hungry, I can find food on my own and satisfy my hunger. Sexual desire . . . requires another person, and if sex is to achieve what the body must deeply longs for, one must enter into deep communion with the other—the kind of communion that the Bible speaks of as a one-flesh union."[133] This deeper view is what must become the centerpiece of our teachings on human sexuality and how it is best expressed in our lives.

And we must, at all costs, not set our commitment to God against our sexual drives. The fact that the human sex drive needs careful control can easily lead to the idea that sexuality itself is a threat to our Christian lives. Throughout the centuries, there have been many examples of this happening: an incipient Gnosticism that disparages the body: a hyper-ascetical suspicion of pleasure; or blatant sexism that viewed women in unwholesome and unworthy ways.

We must be prepared to speak to the connection between sexuality and spirituality. Yes, you heard that right. Lewis Smedes was right when he said that sexuality is a deep dimension of God-likeness.[134] Not that God is a sexual being, but that our sexuality "is our deeply human drive toward and our means of discovering human communion at its intimate peak."[135] This is not to say that we somehow find our way to God through the ecstasy of the flesh; that's what the prophets of Baal claimed. But even there, it is important to note that Old Testament pagan religions understood that there was *some* relationship between sexual fulfillment and the ecstasy of religious experience. Rob Bell writes, "The word sex is related to the Latin word, *secare*, which means to sever, to amputate, or to disconnect from the whole. This is where we get words like sect, section, dissect, bisect. Our sexuality, then, has two dimensions. First, our sexuality is our awareness of how profoundly we're severed and cut off and disconnected. Second, our sexuality is all of the ways we go about trying to re-connect."[136] Ironic as it may sound, those ancient Canaanite religious orgies were a misguided and destructive way of trying to scratch a real itch! But they confused sexual ecstasy with something even deeper and more primal—our need to be one with our Creator. Our speaking of human sexuality must be contextualized within the creational purpose of our being in communion with God. As human beings, Lewis Smedes reminds us, we have deep desires to for personal, intimate involvement with another person.

> The glandular urge, it turns out, is the undercurrent of a need for sharing ourselves with another person. Sexuality throbs within us as movement toward relationship, intimacy, companionship. The desire is more than a wish for somebody's fingers to play with our bodies, though it is that also; it is an exciting desire, sometimes a melancholy longing, to give ourselves in trust to another. We want to expose our whole selves to another and to be trusted with another person's self-exposure to us; we want to stretch out and reach into another person so that the other can add himself to what we are; we want to probe into the mystery of another person's being. It is also a feeling that we cannot be complete until we give ourselves to another person.[137]

This gets to the heart of the viable sexual ethic that Christians need to formulate and talk about. Sex is clearly about more than bodily pleasure or procreation. Engaging in sex binds people together in ways that far transcend the physical. I've had more than enough college students sit in my office and tell me how intensely they realize, after the fact, that having sex was much more than just "hooking up" with another. Sex created an emotional connection they hadn't counted on. Unlike other species, humans are "embodied selves who bring those selves into sexual encounters and do not leave such encounters unchanged."[138] This is what no one writes on the bathroom walls—that sex has the capacity to affect us more profoundly than we expect. All the more reason for the church to talk about what really happens when we are naked.

MASTERING OUR DOMAIN

Earlier I mentioned my Spiritual Formation course for Houghton students. I created it in the 1990s, and it quickly became my favorite course to teach because it scratched my "pastoral itch." I felt like I was being paid to disciple later adolescents! One component of the course was to ask students to "try on" a variety of classical spiritual disciplines, in the hope that they would find practices that would help them in their current lives as students as well as later in life. One such practice was that of spiritual journaling. Learning how to write one's spiritual thoughts and experiences has proven to be an invaluable tool to many Christians through the centuries.

One day in my office, I began reading through a stack of student journals that had been turned in a day or so before. The journals of two students particularly got my attention—angered me, in fact. Both journals were from male students who were among the finest young men on our campus. But both journals revealed a deeply distraught struggle these young men were having with masturbation. That they were sincere about their desire to live in a way that pleased God was without question. But they also manifested a kind of despair that all of their aspirations for their faith journey were undermined by this particular behavior. It tortured them. I was angry that such exemplary young men were so distraught over something that is very common in early to late adolescence. (Even an evangelical psychologist as conservative as James Dobson of *Focus on the Family* has suggested that "tolerating adolescent masturbation is less harmful than its condemnation and may provide an outlet for 'normal' sexual energy that might otherwise be channeled toward more clearly immoral paired sexual activity.")[139] But I was even more irritated given what had happened earlier that day in college chapel. Chapel that day had been devoted to hearing a children's choir from Uganda, all of whom had been orphaned by the scourge of HIV-AIDS. As I listened to those beautiful children sing so joyfully, I contemplated how sexual activity indeed has a very dark side to it. The juxtaposition of the visible consequences of a sexually transmitted disease with the despair of a couple of college students doing their best to manage their sexuality made my frustration with how the church communicates on these issues boil over. And beyond my momentary irritation, I wondered about the messages these two students had picked up through the years regarding the human body and role it plays in our spiritual formation. One of the least-understood dimensions of spirituality in the Christian world, especially among conservative Protestants, is the role of the physical body in the spiritual life.

I was raised in a tradition that didn't have much of anything good to say about the body. Galatians 5:17 was something we heard often: "For the flesh lusteth against the Spirit, and the Spirit against the flesh; and these are contrary the one to the other, so that ye cannot do the things that ye would." I deliberately chose the King James Version here, because that's what we used and particularly because it uses the word "flesh." I grew up convinced that there was something inherently amiss, even evil, with the flesh, which I assumed meant "skin." And this verse became a kind of final verdict on what human life must be until we can somehow escape the body through death. I remember hymns that seemed to celebrate the day when we could join the happy, ethereal angel band in heaven, finally liberated from the "prison" of these blasted bodies. I was well into my seminary years before I realized that such thinking had much more in common with Plato than it did with Jesus Christ. We were created as bodily beings and our eternal hope lies in the resurrection of those bodies. The fact is that when we deny the physical, and yes, the sexual dimension of our existence, we end up living in a manner contrary to God's creative and redemptive purposes. In the book, *The Altars Where We Worship*, the authors plainly summarize the side-effects of bodily denial in the church.

> Since many traditional expressions of religion seek to save souls, often ignoring or losing bodies in the process, congregants as consumers are today tending to look elsewhere to address their human cravings or to come to grips with understanding the meaning associated with embodied sexuality. Purveyors of body and sex promise an overflowing wellspring of pleasure and desire: "whoever drinks of the water that (we) will give . . . shall never thirst." While churches and other religious communities may be in a crisis over mind-body dualism, gender roles, sex in general, and sexual orientation in particular, this altar of body and sex communicates a clear message. Whosoever will may come.[140]

The church cannot afford to cede the physical dimension of human life over to the cultural "purveyors of body and sex" while it contentedly deals with matters of the soul. Bodies are not neutral; they are not matters of indifference—they matter, profoundly. But if all we have to say about the body comes across as a kind of happy anticipation of being released from our fleshly prisons, we will continue to see the type of spiritual frustration and defeat that I read in those student journals.

The picture of the body and flesh found in the Apostle Paul's writings stands in sharp contrast to the "hopeless" picture of the body so commonly presented in some Christian churches. Paul presents the body as a "temple of the Holy Spirit" meant to be "for the Lord" (I Cor. 6:13–20). Paul wants his readers to understand that the body is important. Some in the Corinthian community evidently viewed that bodily functions like eating and sex were matters of indifference to Christians. When Paul quotes what appears to be a Corinthian slogan in verse 13 of 1 Corinthians 6 ("Food is meant for the stomach and the stomach for food, and God will destroy both one and the other"), he pointedly disagrees. What we do with our bodies illustrates our hope of bodily resurrection. It is part of how we rightly worship God. Paul goes on to summarize that "You are not your own; you were bought with a price. Therefore honor God with your body" (I Cor. 6:19b-20). In Romans 12, Paul indicates that the offering of our *bodies* as living, breathing sacrifices is a quintessential part of our worship of God. Any form of bodily denial, or underestimating the significance of our bodily existence, has taken a modern gnostic offramp into the kinds of problems that the New Testament epistles confront quite aggressively. The early church had to fight against the mind/body or soul/body dualisms that Gnostics proposed, lest Christianity become little more than a "head trip." The modern church does well to continue these understandings.

We have to differentiate between the body as it was created by God and pronounced "good," and what Paul terms the "flesh," or the human body formed or de-formed in ways that make it an obstacle to the redemptive designs of God. The body is not evil, but we know that a body shaped by that which is fundamentally opposed to God can create unbelievable chaos. My major problem with how the church approaches the phenomenon of embodied life is that it suggests that simple conversion fixes the problem. But as my young male students attested in their journals, that was hardly the case. And as so often happens, the perfect becomes the enemy of the good. The ideal is a kind of pristine purity that never fails a test, but since no one can attain that, we fall into despair and frustration. This is where thoughtful discipleship in the form of spiritual practices becomes irreplaceable. As I've often told students, the body is the playing field on which we live out our spiritual existence. But that body needs to be properly formed (actually re-formed, or re-habituated) so that instead of thoughtlessly doing what is displeasing to God, we can begin, with the aid of God's Spirit, to gain some sense of control over our bodies and move them onto a path where we can actually respond in such a way that God is honored. It's actually possible to direct our bodies so that our actions are headed in a positive direction for spiritual growth. What we must do is teach our young people that it's not a zero-sum game. It's a process. Not every instance is predictably victorious. There will be setbacks. There may even be seasons of life where we seem to regress, but we can master the domain of the body over time, with patient practice in spiritual skills that have served Christians well through the ages, and with the support of an honest and loving community around us.

TRUE LOVE WAITS, BUT NOT FOR LONG!

In response to what some evangelical leaders termed the "condom culture" of the 1990s, campaigns emerged that were aimed at teaching teenagers abstinence. This movement flew in the face of a hypersexualized culture that viewed abstinence as unrealistic, that seemed resigned to the inevitability of teenage sex. While several distinct versions of this abstinence-only approach emerged, by far the largest and most visible was "True Love Waits." This movement featured large rallies at which young people pledged to remain sexually "pure" until marriage. This approach aimed to counter much of the sex education being done in public schools where, in the minds of many pastors and parents, abstinence did not get a fair hearing. There is no doubt that some young people found the abstinence-only approach helpful, so the efforts of "True Love Waits" deserve appreciation. But the limited "success" of this approach serves as a wake-up call to the realities of such unrelenting pressure to become sexually active. Christine Gardner summarized these findings.

> The impact of the pledge on delaying sexual debut is "substantial and robust," however the abstinence pledge delays sexual debut among fifteen- and sixteen-year-olds by only eighteen months (which is a third longer than those who do not make a pledge). Also, those who pledge are less likely to use contraception when they have their first sexual experience. A 2009 study published in *Pediatrics* uses the same data to compare pledgers and nonpledgers who share similar characteristics such as church attendance and religiosity. After five years the pledgers were just as likely to have had sex as non-pledgers.[141]

Further, Gardner noted that by the time pledgers reached the age of twenty-one, they are just as likely to have had sex as those who never pledged abstinence.[142] In his study of American youth's religious and sexual practices, Mark Regnerus found that on average, evangelical teens lose their virginity slightly younger (16.3 years of age) than mainline Protestant and Catholic teens (16.7 years of age) and are much more likely (13.7 percent) to have three or more sexual partners by age seventeen than mainline teens (8.9 percent).[143] Finally, "in a study published in the June 2017 *Journal of Pediatrics*, researchers found that teen pregnancy rates are 40–50 percent higher than the national average in areas of Texas where abstinence[-]only education is the law."[144] To reiterate, this is not meant to show that "True Love Waits" was a failure, but only to suggest that abstinence-only" approaches to teen sexuality are not, in themselves, adequate to address the issue of teenage sexual activity.

Gardner suggests that one reason for the mixed results of "True Love Waits" is that too often "American evangelicals seem to be persuading teenagers to avoid sex by making abstinence 'sexy.' Evangelicals are using sex to 'sell' abstinence, shifting from a negative focus on 'just say no' to sex before marriage to a positive focus on 'just say yes' to great sex within marriage."[145] David Kinnaman echoes this criticism, arguing that "abstinence teaching can focus too much on the personal, individualist benefits of delaying sex until marriage. 'Save yourself for marriage and have fantastic sex with one partner, the way it's meant to be. Sex as God intended will blow your mind. Be safe; avoid the risks of STD's and an unwanted pregnancy. Think about your future.' Much of the abstinence messaging, however well-intended, capitulates to culturally cultivated individualism: *sex is about me.*"[146] Perhaps the most unsettling long-range consequence of this type of approach is how it can lead an understanding of marriage as primarily about personal fulfillment instead of giving oneself to another. Moreover, in his study of youth sexuality, Mark Regnerus identifies a "middle-class sexual morality" among religious young people, where the higher rewards of vaginal sex are bypassed in favor of lower-risk substitutes such as oral sex, masturbation and pornography.[147] Sociologists at Columbia and Yale found that "students who broke the pledge were less likely than their non-pledging peers to use birth control—presumably in part because the use of birth control implies that one thought about sex beforehand."[148] In summary, although well-intentioned, and likely helpful to some teens, the abstinence-only approach looks to be inadequate *by itself*, to address the challenge of youth sexual practices. And with the average age of marriage creeping ever older, abstinence-only approaches will not likely retain and sustain even those who found them helpful earlier. As Lauren Winner put it, "'True love waits' is not that compelling when you're twenty-nine and have been waiting, and wonder what, really, you're waiting for?"[149]

SIX BIG LITTLE LIES ABOUT SEX

Outside of politics, it's hard to imagine any area of human life that is so fraught with misinformation and, let's face it, outright lies, than sex. Given the limitations of abstinence education, I believe that the church must adopt an informed practice of effectively exposing the untruths that are trotted out daily and fed into the information universe, many of them crafted particularly with young people in mind. De-constructing sexual nonsense is the task of every pastor, youth pastor, and tuned-in church member. Here are some "big little lies" that I consider prime candidates for some good old-fashioned truth-telling.

1. *Sex is everything.* Or, at least close to everything. The way sex is portrayed in the media one might easily conclude that it is right up there with breathing and good car insurance as indispensable for human life. In some quarters of the media, we're led to believe that if you're not "getting laid" regularly, with multiple partners, you've been deprived of a worthwhile life. The ironic thing about our obsession with this unreality called sex is that, in the words of Lewis Smedes, "it makes us prisoners of a myth. Perhaps this is why sex dominates so much of modern life: it is an abstraction promoted to the status of reality, and unreality turned into a myth tends to become a dominating force in life. And so we can seriously speak of our age as being demonized: we have come to worship at the shrine of a non-thing.[150] That word "demonized" should not be thrown around carelessly, and yet, because sex has so many bound up, even "possessed," it may well be accurate much of the time. Christ intends to liberate us from such bondage, but liberation begins when we acknowledge that it is absurd and dangerously misguided to regard sexual passion as the real point of human life.

   There's another equally problematic dimension to this "little lie." It is the notion, prevalent within the church, that sex before marriage must be avoided at all costs, as if this alone is the secret to a happy adult (married?) life. At the risk of undermining all of my previous agreement with traditional church teachings on sex, I think we need to take a few deep breaths and back away from the belief that one's sexual behavior will essentially write the story of their lives. I'm not minimizing or underestimating the potential problems that can come with behavioral choices around sex, but let's be honest, human beings have been sexually active for a long time. How many of us have encountered instances of family marriages where babies arrived a bit too soon after the wedding? Sex happens! It's part of life. But it isn't everything. Is waiting until marriage the best approach? I believe it is. Does falling short of that disqualify a person from any hope of a good, resourceful life? Not at all. Thankfully, the grace of God is exceedingly resourceful.

2. *Sex is mere biology.* In 1928, American composer Cole Porter musically suggested that because birds and bees and all living things "do it," we might as well also, crooning "let's fall in love." Of course, no one talks like that these days, because we know full well that birds and bees don't fall in love—they have sex! So what Porter was saying in the polite euphemisms of the Roaring Twenties was, in essence, all animals and living creatures do this, why should we be any different? It's the nature of things, so let's do it! Such thinking suggests that sex is nothing more than basic biology. While some have embraced this half-truth, it is hardly the whole story when it comes to human sexuality. In fact, such thinking exemplifies the most banal sort of reductionism. Yes, sexual behavior is part and parcel of virtually every form of biological life, but in the case of human beings, sexual intimacy is hardly mere biology. Behavioral science assures us that sex between people has consequences at "every level of our existence: neurological, psychological, social and spiritual. And given that each one of us is a bio-psycho-socio-spiritual entity, it is no surprise that our sexual nature and how we express that nature has such wide-reaching implications."[151] I've yet to hear a song extolling sex written by any love-bitten mammal other than *homo sapiens*!

3. *Love is enough.* If music can champion the view of sex as mere biology, it can also prevalently declare love being the reason and justification for sex, virtually regardless of the circumstances, and peddle the assumption that all sexual relationships can be sustained over the long haul. Clearly, falling in love is a wonderful and desirable experience, but before you use it as a sort of justification for all things pertaining to human sexuality, it turns out that you may actually need a bit more than love, whatever the Beatles said. As Caroline Simon puts it, "Falling in love is a delicious, astonishing experience, but it has very little connection to the feelings and abilities two people need in order to build a life together and sustain a family. Falling in love is a wonderful, addictive, obsessive experience that usually lasts less than twenty months."[152] Besides, the difficulty of separating love from the kind of heat and passion that often ends up as the justification for sexual intimacy is a lesson in how easily we can be convinced that sexual

lust is actually true love. The infamous morning-after "walk of shame" reminds us that after passion recedes, realism remains.

4. *Casual sex*. Whether it goes by the name of "hooking up," or "friends with benefits," or even more crudely, "gettin' laid," the idea that sex can be casual is one of the most impressive lies pervading our sexually intoxicated culture. Casual sex is the idea is that some consensual sex amounts to little more than a kind of "mutual use pact," where no one is overly invested and each partner walks away at the end "no harm, no foul." Casual sex attempts to limit intercourse to the physical act itself, justifying it on the basis of its pleasure potential and mutual agreement that "it's just sex." Problem! In sexual union, as Scripture views it, a person is known fully. In Genesis, when we're told that Adam *knew* his wife, Eve (*"yada"* in Hebrew), we're not being presented with some prudish euphemism, but rather with a profound theological insight into how sexual intercourse was intended to be. This kind of all-encompassing self-revealing is precisely why the Apostle Paul is so outraged at the "casual sex" going on in the Corinthian church. "Do you not know that he who unites himself with a prostitute is one with her in body? For it is said, 'the two will become one flesh'" (1 Corinthians 6:16).[153] Sexual intercourse by unmarried people is wrong because it ignores the "one flesh" reality of the act; it is wrong because unmarried people thereby engage in a life-uniting act without any life-uniting intentions. Rob Bell captures the essence of why "casual sex" is not real sex at all.

> It's easy to take off your clothes and have sex. People do it all the time. But opening up your soul to someone, letting them into your spirit and thoughts and fears and future and hopes and dreams, that is being naked. This is why when people sleep together after they've just met, they're raising the chances significantly that the relationship will not survive. Racing ahead in the progression always costs something. When there is no common mission, no shared task, no sense of bone of bone and flesh of flesh, no bonds that take years to develop, many end up moving from relationship to relationship, having sex but never really being naked.[154]

There you go. The real problem with "casual sex" is that there's no way get naked enough!

5. *Safe Sex*. This is one of my favorite oxymorons. Safe sex? What could possibly be safe about sex? A huge reason why sex is interesting is that

it is so inherently risky! As was mentioned above, getting naked, completely undressed, physically and beyond, in the presence of another person is the relational equivalent to lighting a match in a fireworks factory. The discarding of restraint and reserve is what gives sex the capacity to be what Smedes termed "the epitome of communion, precisely because it involves the greatest amount of personal risk."[155] When we speak of sexual ecstasy, we are talking about a realm of vulnerability that requires the safety of a covenantal pledge of marriage to make it a risk worth taking. The word *ecstasy* comes from the Latin word, *ecstasis* which means "to step outside oneself." In sexual ecstasy, we are literally "stepping outside ourselves," relinquishing all control. By way of illustration, look at William M. Struthers's description of male orgasm:

> What happens in ejaculation? Usually there's some sort of stimulation coming from the spinal cord, which goes up to the hypothalamus. It also goes to the VTA, because when there's ejaculation, there's a release of dopamine. All this shuts down the amygdala. Why is that important? The amygdala is our emotional center and primarily our fear center in the brain. The amygdala shuts down at the moment of ejaculation. Thus an orgasm is associated with an absence of fear. Men experience a sort of emotional hovering, a transcendent freedom from all worry.[156]

Struthers's description serves to demonstrate that sexual ecstasy moves a person, in this case, a male, to a point of extreme vulnerability. To be rendered essentially helpless while naked in the presence of another, suggests that such behavior should be covered by the protection of a covenant, not just a condom. If sex were safe, it wouldn't be nearly as interesting.

6. *Sex is private business.* It should surprise no one that in the hyper-individualism of contemporary Western culture, one's sexual behavior is considered to be the exclusive concern of that individual. Sexual ethics boils down to "as long as I'm not hurting anyone, I can do what I want." Sexuality, then, becomes almost solely a matter of personal satisfaction. Stanley Hauerwas argues that "any attempt to reclaim an authentic Christian ethic of sex must begin by challenging the assumption that sex is a 'private matter.'"[157] The reasons for this should be clear by now: sex has consequences, consequences that extend far beyond the person or persons engaging in it. We live in a culture ravaged by

how much and how often the sexual activity between individuals eventually affects the lives of many others. Lauren Winner contends that "sex is communal because it is real . . . Sex is dangerous and delightful and elemental, and it matters. What we do with our bodies, what we do sexually, shapes our persons. If we believe that sex forms us, then it goes without saying that is public business, because how we build the persons we are—persons who are social and communal and political and economic beings—is itself a matter of social concern."[158]

Contrary to those who contend that what they do is their own business, the church replies, "no, sex is everybody's business!" But the church must find its collective voice in matters of human sexuality, must move beyond our traditional hesitancy to address matters which have often been assigned to the confessional, or closeted and ignored. The church must enter this conversation fully confident that it has something of great import to say, mostly because it rings true.

JUST SAY NO?

Hopefully by now it's obvious that asking young people to "just say no" to sex without giving them a fuller account of *why* we would do so is to leave them virtually defenseless against the force of our hypersexualized culture. We must help youth to grasp that while desire is a good thing, surrendering to any and all desire is a recipe for disaster.

All sorts of studies demonstrate the positive impact of "delayed gratification," helping us see that nature has to be controlled lest it negatively impact our lives. Anyone in athletics, music—any field requiring discipline—can see that. That we don't seem to grasp this when it comes to sex is part of the larger problem we face. The results are in, and they underscore both the size of the task before us and the futility of thinking that we can simply continue to do what we've been doing. One survey concludes that four out of five unmarried evangelicals between the ages of eighteen and twenty-nine have had sex.[159] We must take a step back from the quick fix of "just say no" and begin to put sexual ethics into a much larger perspective. Hauerwas is right: "What the 'conservatives' must recognize is that prior to the issue of whether premarital or extramarital sexual intercourse is wrong is the question of character: What kind of people do you want to encourage? Hidden in the question of 'What ought we to do' is always the prior question 'What ought we to be?'"[160] Furthermore, the question of sexual behavior must be subsumed into the larger question of the church and its mission in the world. When we adopt an ecclesiological context for this discussion, sexual behavior becomes "subservient to the demanding business of maintaining a revolutionary community in a world that often uses sex as a means of momentarily anesthetizing or distracting people from the basic vacuity of their lives."[161] The church is an alternative view of life in the world, and nowhere is that more evident than in the way it approaches the topic of sex.

An important next step is for us to recover and/or encourage the widespread practice of the virtue of chastity. As a spiritual discipline, chastity first appears in church history in the monastic tradition, where it flourishes even today. Chastity seeks to reinforce our very basic conviction regarding the interplay between will and body. Until our bodies can be "trained in righteousness" (read: brought into proper condition), we will find it difficult to parry the permissiveness that pervades our sexualized culture. How to go about this? I think David Kinnaman is on the right track when he says, "We need to reconsider doing 'sexual formation' on a mass-scale. Our research leads me to be skeptical of the long-term transformational power of events and rallies. I'm not saying we should never have large-scale worship events or that proclaiming the gospel in public places is pointless. It is not, and doing so is clearly a biblical pattern. Yet if we measure our impact solely by the number of students making pledges or raising their hands, I think we have to wonder if we are really committed to making disciples."[162] Moving away from "sexual formation on a mass scale" comes down to the church taking its disciple-making task seriously, ensuring that sexuality has its proper place in the discussion. The church must be a place where people can openly and honestly deal with the issues of sexuality. The worst aspect of traditionalism in this regard has been the church's reticence about sex. Cultivating faith environments that invite such conversations is a huge step in the right direction. If Christians want to demonstrate the possibility of a life that is not dominated by a disorderly and destructive brand of sexuality, it has to be done openly, in full view of others, with all of us always ready to give an answer as to why we choose to live in this manner. Hauerwas is surely right to say, "There is no 'ethic' in itself, which can solve all the problems involved in [teenagers in the back seat of a car]. Rather, what the young properly demand is an account of life and the initiation into a community that makes intelligible why their interest in sex should be subordinate to other interests."[163] While the "back seat of a car" may no longer apply (studies show that sex between teens most often happens these days in the home, while parents are sleeping!), the basic point remains. Once again, in the end, it all comes down to the church.

Chapter 6

The Body Politic

> Theology is political language. What people think about God, Jesus Christ, and the Church cannot be separated from their own social and political status in a given society
>
> —James Cone[164]

It was the week following the 1992 presidential election. The couple walked into my office and wordlessly sat down. They were not members of the church, but they had been regular Sunday-morning attendees for some time. He was a highly visible long-time member of our small community and although I didn't know him well, I had always found him friendly and helpful. After a few pleasantries, he got right down to business.

"Who did you vote for in the presidential election?" he asked.

I was taken aback by this unexpected question, but after an uncomfortable pause I said, "Well, you know, they put curtains on those voting booths for a reason; voting is supposed to be a private matter. Why do you want to know something like that?"

He looked at me and said, "Well, we heard you voted for Clinton and we wanted to know if that's true."

By that time, I had been a pastor in small college community for ten years. My politics weren't exactly a secret. So I replied, "That's right, I did vote for Bill Clinton."

He proceeded to tell me why Clinton was morally unfit for office and that, because of my vote, he and his wife could no longer "sit under my ministry." After they left, I wished I'd said, "Well, I voted for Mondale and Dukakis as well, but you didn't seem to have a problem with that. I guess it only counts if your candidate loses." It's probably best I didn't get the chance.

Yes, it's true I was a registered Democrat, mostly because of Jimmy Carter. I was raised in a Republican family, but I can't recall much being made of that. I didn't give politics much thought until Barry Goldwater ran for President in 1964. He was from Arizona, after all, and his "AU-H2o" bumper stickers were way cooler than "All the Way with LBJ," so I was all in.

I went off to Bible college in 1968—my first-ever plane flight—on the day of the riots at the Democratic National Convention in Chicago. At O'Hare, I missed my connecting flight to Columbus and thus spent hours wandering around the airport. Although people seemed on edge and lots of police were on hand, I was blissfully unaware of what was happening that day in national politics. I'm a bit embarrassed to admit that, politically speaking, my clueless bliss continued through Bible college, where we were taught to care mostly about "heavenly" matters. I cast my first-ever vote for Richard Nixon a couple of months into my seminary education. Only then did I begin the process of pondering, for the first time, the political implications of what I professed to believe as a Christian. That's why Jimmy Carter caught my imagination. I re-registered as a Democrat because I thought he was the first authentically Christian politician I had ever seen.

But the truth is, neither the Democratic nor the Republican Party adequately represents my allegiances as a Christian. In recent years I've been thinking about that a great deal, and I actually changed my voter registration to "independent." Since seminary, I have endeavored to align my political viewpoints with my theological commitments and my understanding of Scripture. Given the fact that I'm a white male in America who is considered wealthy by the standards of most of the world, I have concluded that I'll be just fine, regardless of who is President. So, I cast my vote for whoever I believe will do the most for the poor. It's a pretty simple approach. Some would call it simplistic, but I sleep well. I deliberately stay away from the kind of one-issue voting that has come to characterize much of American evangelicalism the past forty-plus years. I find such an approach far too subject to manipulation by political machines that care only about one thing: power. A few years ago, I brought the well-known American religious historian Randall Balmer to Houghton for a lecture series sponsored by our department. His lecture, which basically appears intact in his book *Evangelicalism in America* (Waco: Baylor University Press, 2016), essentially covered the story of how Republican political operatives devised the strategy of employing abortion as a wedge issue in the 1980 election, to guarantee the loyalty of evangelical voters. I'm no fan of abortion, but I have grown increasingly skeptical of political parties having "come-to-Jesus" moments so they can turn out the vote.

I remember reading Charles Colson's book, *Born Again*, where he recalls his days in the Nixon White House. They laughed among themselves at how easy it was to ensure the support of conservative Christians, simply by giving them a bit of public attention. As a Christian who votes, I am going to do my best not to be co-opted politically like that in any way. The denomination in which I was raised held the prohibition of "partisan political preaching" as one of their cardinal principles. As with most things of that nature, it's easy to say but hard to do. I've observed far too many evangelical churches that seem quite willing to accommodate themselves to partisan politics in the belief that this is somehow consistent with what it means to be the church in America. But that's precisely the problem; I sense that large numbers of American Christians are far more interested in being "American" than they are in being "Christian." For me, that's a bridge too far, and if that is part of the burden I bear as an outlier, I am more than happy to bear it. James Cone is right; theological language is by nature "political." If being Christian necessitates a brand of political activism of some sort, it behooves all of us who claim the label to carefully investigate the substance and direction of that activism.

Which brings me to Donald J. Trump. I can't even pretend to have words sufficient to describe my distress and disappointment at the widespread evangelical embrace of Donald Trump. As a long-time New Yorker, I have watched his celebrity circus act more closely than many, and so I foolishly discounted his candidacy; it was as unlikely as the cow jumping over the moon. What I did not count on was the willingness of white evangelical Christians to completely relativize many of their faith commitments in order to justify their votes for this man. It seems that his "pro-life" stance was the determining factor for many, and that vividly demonstrates my antipathy for one-issue voting. Honestly, how does one rationalize that an administration enacting policy that tears children out of the arms of their parents and puts them in cages is even remotely "pro-life"? How is it possible that we look the other way when the person who would lead our nation insults women, the physically challenged, and people of different races or religions, and what's more, seeks to undermine, at every opportunity, any effort by the press or the government to hold him to account? John Pavlovitz vividly summarizes the disconnect of supporting Trump.

And yet, despite the vitriol he dispensed and the divisiveness he generated and the violence his campaign yielded at rallies and in rising hate crimes, Trump was somehow embraced by large numbers of (mainly white, conservative) Christians who looked at the candidate's body of work, littered with vile words and moral failings and unscrupulous business dealings—-and deemed it all acceptable. As the race wound into the fall, high-profile preachers began aligning themselves with the GOP candidate, leveraging their pulpits and platforms to champion his cause. Local church leaders became less apprehensive about injecting themselves into the political process and more vocal in their support of him. Otherwise strictly sin-intolerant Christians engaged in all manner of theological gymnastics in order to justify Trump as somehow the "lesser of two evil" options. And with each pastor's public endorsement and with every social media sanctioning, the disconnect between American Christianity and the Jesus of the Gospels became more noticeable to those of us looking closely and grieving it all.[165]

I recently gathered with a group of men, all Christians, to listen to a presentation by a political science colleague of mine. In his talk on "The New Politics," my colleague noted the unacceptability of "the end justifies the means" arguments for Christians. And yet, when questions and dialogue began around the table, several voiced this sentiment: "Well, I don't agree with his methods, but I like what he's doing." Did they not hear the same talk I heard? Has the Christian church in America become so overcome with tunnel vision on the issue of abortion that we are blind to anything else? Are we willing, essentially, to say to the millions of young people who observe our hypocrisy, "But he appoints 'pro-life' judges?" Do we even begin to recognize how far the mission of the church has been set back by evangelical Christianity's embrace of Donald Trump? I fear that we may well have lost a generation.

In their book, *Resident Aliens: Life in the Christian Colony*, Stanley Hauerwas and William Willimon state that "Christianity is mostly a matter of politics—politics as defined by the gospel. The challenge of Jesus is the political dilemma of how to be faithful to a strange community, which is shaped by a story of how God is with us."[166] As Christians, there is no way to avoid political involvement because our way of being in the world is summed up in the words: Jesus is Lord! That is a blatantly political assertion, because if Jesus is Lord, then, by definition, Caesar is not. So the idea that the church ought to stay out of politics is a non-starter unless one shifts the church's existence in this world solely toward the "soul saving" business.

This is precisely where some churches have planted their flag, and it's precisely where, by the way, most of the Caesars of this world would prefer the church to stay. But when the church adopts such a non-participatory position, it forfeits its saltiness and an important vehicle for pursuing its mission in the world.

In the early fifth century, the world seemed to be in chaos. The Roman Empire was teetering on the brink of collapse. St. Augustine wrote a book which typically bears the English title, *City of God*. The basic premise of the book is his view of reality as two cities, the earthly city of man and the heavenly city of God. Augustine reminds us that although Christians inhabit both cities, their ultimate loyalty must be to God's city. Nevertheless, they must "seek the good" of the earthly city, and work for its flourishing, without ever forgetting that they belong to the other city. As Christians, we live somewhere between the kingdom's inaugural coming to earth and the kingdom's consummation, its unquestioned reign on this earth. We live, as it were, life in the meantime, and this requires our active involvement as citizens of two cities. In light of this, our participation in politics is meant to provide a way for us to "seek the good" of our earthly city. There are a host of ways in which Christians might lend their voices in support of the welfare of fellow earthly citizens. David Gushee suggests that Christians should advocate for certain basic reforms of the current functioning of our democracy:

> Congressional districts should be drawn up by nonpartisan commissions, not self-interested politicians and parties. Senate rules should be altered so that more legislation can pass with a simple majority. Our political parties need the more active participation of centrist and moderate voters so that they are not constantly pulled to the right or left. The creaky old Electoral College system needs reconsideration so that every voter matters in a presidential election, not just those in six or eight "swing states." Voting needs to be made easier, not harder, for all American citizens to ensure the greatest participation. The financing of our political campaigns needs to be as transparent as possible, and the power of big corporate money needs to be reined in. The quasi-official role of the Republican and Democratic parties needs to be fought. A strong, free, independent press must be protected and so on.[167]

I could add several more items to this list. For example, making health care more accessible, addressing the issue of hunger in the richest nation on earth, and adopting more earth-friendly policies. I realize that some will take issue with any number of these recommendations, if not all of them, because that's the nature of politics. Political discourse has virtually no end. But at the end of the day, what we discover is that politics itself has built-in limitations for which we must account if we are to sustain civil society, and even more importantly for my immediate interests, to allow the flourishing of the church's witness in the world.

POLITICAL LIMITATIONS

In thinking about how politics has certain built-in limitations, especially for Christians, we must begin by considering the "power paradigm" within which politics operates. If one pays attention to national politics in particular, one immediately sees that much of what is attempted or proposed by elected officials is driven by gaining or preserving power. This flies in the face of a Christianity which takes as its symbol a cross. Our hero as Christians was the One who willingly laid aside power and became a servant. Where do we see that in our political leaders? Could they even get elected if they proposed such an approach? But this is God's way in the world. God did not "come into the world to win an argument but to incarnationally engage a lost and fallen world by inviting all peoples to be reconciled and renewed in Christ."[168] This is the mission of God, and God will accomplish it in God's own way, which involves the "foolishness" of the cross. When we begin to recognize the ongoing power plays employed by our politicians, we begin to see that everyone is playing the same game, albeit from slightly different perspectives, all designed to win the power struggle. Brian McLaren unmasks the so-called "political divide" saying,

> I'm suggesting that if we go deep enough, we will realize that Democrats and Republicans, left and right, even "terrorists" and "free world" are generally playing by the same rules and part of the same system—in much the same way as in Jesus' day, complacent Herodians and Sadducees and activist Pharisees and Zealots were, for all their squabbles, playing with the same system: defining their lives in relation to Caesar . . . Which side wins—Democrats or Republicans, East or West, elite or bourgeois or proletariat, Herodian or Zealot—may be considered *news* within the system, but until someone brings into the system resources from outside it, unless someone kicks a hole in the wall of the system so we aren't trapped within it, there is no real *good news*.[169]

When Christians profess Jesus as Lord, they are introducing a revolutionary truth into the systemic status quo of the political machine. Christians don't play the power games of Caesar and of those who see imperial placation as the only means of instituting change.

This calls into the question the whole notion of political labels. I freely admit that I do not like labels. I don't even like having to wear nametags at conferences, but that's most likely owing to a personal pathology or two. By and large, our culture loves labels and the judgments that such labels bring with them. But, again, this serves to demonstrate the limitations of politics for those of us who willingly accept the label "Christian." Was Jesus a liberal or conservative? Well, that depends on the issue and how it is presented, which shows that the modern categories—labels—of liberal or conservative don't work very well when describing Jesus. Maybe we shouldn't apply them to Christ's followers or the Christian church. Even as I say that, I suspect I've violated it multiple times in the course of writing this book because it's become so much of a part of our daily discourse. Categorizing everyone has a way of excluding people and preventing the growth of genuine community. When we start looking at one another as "conservative" or "liberal" we are growing the logs in our own eyes, becoming less able to see things for what and how they truly are. Will there be disagreements about how best to approach specific issues? Absolutely! But the church must be able to demonstrate the ability to speak the truth to one another, as we see it, in loving ways, eschewing the harsh partisanship that so characterizes today's political landscape in America.

Civility is all the more necessary because, as Christians, we know that there are not political fixes to all that ails us. Despite the best intentions of our elected leaders, there are no "easy button" solutions to many of the problems that plague our world. James Davison Hunter reveals the inherent limitations of politics, writing,

> There are no comprehensive political solutions to the deterioration of "family values," the desire for equity, or the challenge of achieving consensus and solidarity in a cultural context of fragmentation and polarization. There are no real political solutions to the absence of decency or the spread of vulgarity. But because the state is a clumsy instrument and finally rooted in coercion, it will always fail to adequately or directly address the human elements of these problems; the elements that make them poignant in the first place. As a rule, when the state does become involved in such matters, its actions can often create more problems through unintended consequences, not fewer.[170]

While politics can be a most noble venture, and Christians ought to wholeheartedly support well-intentioned efforts to make our world better, we must always remember that we live in a world that, even if it is not all it should be, will be set aright in God's own time and choosing, according to His own promise. That's not a convenient Christian cop-out, and should never be employed as such, but it is part and parcel of what Christians mean when we say, "even so, come, Lord Jesus."

Politics done well needs character, or, as some would put it, virtue. Character matters! It's one of the more frustrating realities of the limitations shaping political discourse and activism. I think that's what makes Donald Trump's elevation to the Presidency so mind-boggling to many of us. We are learning that democracy is a fairly fragile thing. It is premised on the basis that elected officials adhere to certain boundaries in their use of power, their understanding of accountability, and their upholding of the accepted norms of governance. We are witnessing what can happen in the absence of such virtues. Can anyone really contend that the swamp is being drained? But it goes well beyond any one elected official. American-style democracy involves an entire citizenry of character and virtue.

> It is clear that America's founders understood that the freedom-maximizing government they were creating required a citizenry of sound character to go along with it. Government could stay small and limited if, and only if, people could regulate their own actions in virtuous ways. You don't need a whole lot of police in a town in which 99.9 percent of the citizenry on a given day are choosing not to break the laws that their representatives have established. Virtuous business owners don't cheat their customers or mistreat their employees, so government does not need to get involved in that arena very much. Spouses of sound mind and character do not physically harm their children or each other, so again, government can remain minimally involved in the affairs of most families.[171]

What's underscored here is that no matter how enlightened the politics of a time may be, well-intentioned political activism can never overcome the moral deficits of a community lacking in virtue or lacking a widely held consensus with regards to its moral vison. To continue trying to fix such a community through political means alone is doomed to fall far short. Neglecting to consider this reality contributes mightily to the current frustrations of American citizens with their government and exposes some of the dangers of politics that lack a sufficient moral context. It's like hiking in the wilderness without a map.

POLITICAL DANGERS

"Politics ain't beanbag." This well-known phrase dates back to 1895, when a writer named Finley Peter Dunne put it in the mouth of a fictional character who pontificated on the issues of the day from a Chicago pub. It still fits our times. Politics can indeed be a rough and unsavory business, but beyond that, politics can be dangerous—especially for Christians. This is doubly the case when Christians do not reflectively consider the nature of political involvements and fail to see how this influences, or even compromises, their theological commitments.

If you haven't noticed, politics is a 24/7, around-the-clock business. The proliferation of cable news shows, talk radio, and social media all promote the idea that politics is reality's epicenter. It isn't. Just ask the Amish. Here in western New York, the Amish have established multiple communities where they farm, run small businesses, and quietly go about their lives. I'll wager they don't have much of a clue about what's happening on the political front. Curiously, they don't seem deprived in any way at this lack of knowledge. Sometimes, I envy them and wonder what it might be like to live off the political grid. But that sort of political innocence comes at a price heavier than most of us are willing to pay. So we need to exercise discernment as we navigate the body politic.

The primary danger of politics, in my view, is buying into the idea that politics is the primary way of changing the world. Such thinking reasons that if bad law is the outcome of bad choices made by politicians and judges, then the solution is as simple as voting into office those who hold proper values and have a worldview that is more consistent with Christian faith. Oh, if it were only that easy! A number of "professing Christians" have been elected to office; obviously something isn't working. James Davison Hunter regrets that "politics is the tactic of choice for many Christians as they think about changing the world. This has been most conspicuously true for Evangelicals . . . It is not an exaggeration to say that the *dominant public witness of the Christian churches in America since the early 1980s has been a political witness.*"[172] But Hunter suggests that rather than being a viable way of the church helping to solve society's problems, "Contemporary Christian understandings of power and politics are a very large part of what has made contemporary Christianity in America appalling, irrelevant, and ineffective—part and parcel of the worst elements of our late-modern culture today, rather than a healthy alternative to it."[173] That's a painful indictment, but it is a fair assessment of how things are. Before Christians throw themselves into the political arena, they should remember how Jesus carefully negotiated his own relationship to the politics of his day. He refused to buy into the accommodating strategies of the Sadducees, the extreme separatism of the Pharisees, or the outright rebelliousness of the Zealots. When Christians put too much hope into political solutions, it betrays the intoxicating allure that raw power can hold over us, despite our faith commitments to the contrary. Hunter contends that "Nietzsche was mostly right; that while the will to power has always been present, American democracy increasingly operates within a political culture . . . that sanctions a will to domination."[174] A quick perusal of a daily newspaper or some time in front of an evening newscast bears out Hunter's fear that American politics has become a frighteningly predictable power play. And Christians ought to be wary of such tactics. As Hunter notes, "The tragedy is that in the name of resisting the internal deterioration of faith and the corruption of the world around them, many Christians—and Christian conservatives most significantly—unwittingly embrace some of the most corrosive aspects of the cultural disintegration they decry. By nurturing its resentments, sustaining them through a discourse of negation toward outsiders, and in cases, pursuing their will to power, they become functional Nietzscheans, participating in the very cultural breakdown they so ardently strive to resist."[175]

Popular news outlets offer a constant drumbeat of fear and resentment along with subtle and not-so-subtle calls to resist. Any policy not to the liking of these media sources is mocked and undermined. During the Coronavirus pandemic, we've seen photos of heavily armed protesters (some waving Confederate flags or swastikas) storming state capitol buildings, demanding that state ordinances aimed at preserving the health of the community be lifted to allow individual choice. Getting into bed with power, coercive power, and even legitimate forms of political power, is laden with difficulties for those of us who have chosen to be followers of "The Way." While much good can be accomplished through political processes, Christians must be aware of the dangerous side-effects of embracing power politics as the only or even the best way to foster change in our world. In his book, *Jesus Wants to Save Christians*, Rob Bell points out the church's aversion to "politics as usual":

> The authority that the church has in culture does not come from how right, cool, or loud it is, or how convinced it is of its doctrinal superiority. As Paul says, "We don't' fight with those weapons." A church's authority comes from somewhere else—it comes from how we've been broken open and poured out, not from how well we've pursued power and lobbied and organized ourselves to triumph. This is why when Christians organize politically and start flexing that muscle, making threats about how they are going to impose their way on others, so many people

turn away from Jesus. Jesus' followers at that point are claiming to be the voice of God, but they are speaking the language of Caesar and using the methods of Rome, and for millions of us it has the stench of Solomon.[176]

One troubling method for ensuring Christian cooperation in political power plays is the questionable use of Scripture to coerce Christians' consent and support for whatever the powers-that-be might desire to do. We've ceded too much power to those who control governmental and political processes. In particular, Romans 13:1–7 has been used to bring about compliance within the Christian community for everything from government taxation, to capital punishment, to declarations of war. These verses from the Apostle Paul have been used like a hammer to squelch dissent and to virtually compel Christians to accede to the desires of earthly authority. But these verses trigger substantial dissonance in the minds of many Christians, myself included, who refuse to believe that Paul is admonishing us to blindly obey authority. For example, David Gushee says that Romans 13, read uncritically, makes total sense if you are a white citizen of the middle or upper classes. It makes less sense if you are someone whose race and social position are not so favorable."[177] I can easily imagine the discomfort that many African-American Christians would have with taking these verses at face value. And make no mistake, participants in the Black Lives Matter protests have more than likely had these Scriptures thrown in their faces. The real problem is that Romans 13:1–7 has been terribly misinterpreted to allow it to be used for coercive purposes. Sylvia Keesmaat and Brian Walsh write,

> . . . it is particularly when governments call themselves Christian while engaging in oppressive and violent behavior that Romans 13:1–7 is appealed to as the summation of Paul's political ethic. For example, under the rule of Hitler this passage was used to legitimate allegiance to the Nazi regime . . . Similarly, under the apartheid regime in South Africa, Allan Boesak described how Romans 13 was used as a stick to demand obedience to the state. The same appeal to Romans 13 was used by church leaders in Rwanda to justify their uncritical support of a genocidal government. And in the United States it doesn't matter how weak the evidence for war or how despicable the character of the commander in chief, Christians (especially white, evangelical Christians) continue to use Romans 13 as a tool of ideological legitimation.[178]

I can well remember how Romans 13 became a club with which to hammer young people of my generation questioning the war in Vietnam, or of my own children's generation questioning war in Iraq. How ironic that powers who would defy biblical authority in virtually every way are so quick to wield that very authority to manipulate the Christian community into subservience.

The hard truth is that the traditional reading of the Romans 13 passage is very much divorced from the prophetic traditions of Israel, which railed against such deceptive use of religion. And it is completely disconnected from what we see in Jesus, who himself died, unjustly, at the hands of an oppressive governmental authority. Perhaps, most importantly, it "fails to take seriously the context of Romans 13 in relation to Romans 12 or to the whole of the epistle."[179] The authority so often appealed to as that which must be obeyed is not inherent in Rome's imperial government. Neither has it been conferred by Rome's gods. Christians must be clear on this point: "all authority is rooted in the God of Jesus Christ—the very God that Rome rejects in its persecution of [Jews] and Christians alike. Far from providing sanction for Rome's rule, this is a relativization of imperial authority. As a result Romans 13 constitutes a severe demotion of arrogant and self-divinizing rulers. It is an undermining of totalitarianism, not a reinforcement of it."[180] Christians should, of course, pursue peace and good citizenship, but they must never bow to the imperial pretenders of this world, whether they employ coercive laws as their means of compliance or the subtle appeals of patriotism and love of the flag to seduce the faith community into blind obedience.

The current political strategy (employed by both major parties, by the way) seems to be framing ideological commitments in ways that reduce all issues to binary choices. For example, in America these days, you are either "pro-life" or "pro-choice." I disagree. Both of those labels are overly simplistic and deceptive in their claims. The reason abortion is such an intractable issue is that it involves complicated moral dilemmas which defy slogans and easy solutions. Support of the government as patriotism is yet another example of trying to oversimplify complicated issues. Even a cursory reading of history shows that there have been moments where the truly patriotic thing was standing in opposition to governmental authority. The world is complicated, and we must be wary of those who would render everything black or white.

Another dangerous outcome of our overly politicized culture is what I would term "political fecundity." Fecundity simply means the ability to produce an abundance of offspring. Political "solutions" often bring unintended consequences. In America, we have seen how fertile the political atmosphere has become at producing class-based inequality and conflict. Gar Alperovitz urges us to examine,

> the Supreme Court's 2010 Citizens United decision, which has added enormously to the corporate-dominated system's capacity to block solutions to a number of critical social, economic, and environmental problems. The court's finding that unrestricted amounts of money can be contributed by corporate "persons" to affect politics, and its clarification that money spent on advertising by such "persons" is "speech" protected by the Constitution, opened powerful new flows of highly conservative political funding. A recent study tracking money in politics by the Center for Responsive Politics found that "business interests dominate, with an overall advantage over organized labor of about 15-to-1." Between 2009 and 2010 contributions by corporations and other businesses totaled $1.36 billion compared with a modest $96 million from labor groups.[181]

This type of law puts a legislative thumb on the scales of political justice and undermines foundational assumptions about fair play within a democratic society. Large corporate interests should not be permitted to dominate the electoral process in the way the Citizens United decision seems to permit and even encourage. Daily, we see how class-based inequalities are creating growing geographical divides in our country, pitting red states against blue states and undermining the *E Pluribus Unum* (out of the many one) ideal of America.

Perhaps the single most troubling offspring produced by the American approach to politics is the rampant individualism that has been fostered and set loose in American culture. Recently I was part of a group of emeriti faculty who read *Why Liberalism Failed*, a book by Notre Dame political scientist Patrick J. Deneen. "Liberalism" here refers not to the hard left of the Democratic party, but rather, to the broader sense of that approach to governance that seeks the liberty of its citizens. In the foreword to Deneen's book, James Davison Hunter writes, "The problem is not that liberalism has been hijacked, but that its elevation of individual autonomy was wrong from the start, and the passage of decades has only made its error more evident."[182] Hunter is arguing that the American democratic system has been overly successful in its liberation of individuals—to the point where the entire system is faltering due to the complexities of sustaining a nation of autonomous individuals. Again, the picture of Americans protesting the violation of their individual rights in the Coronavirus pandemic, refusing to wear masks, etc., illustrates Hunter's point. If *my* rights trump the rights of the greater community's right to be protected from a potentially deadly disease, it's hard to see where all this ends up other than a point where "what we call 'freedom' becomes the tyranny of our own desires. We are kept detached, strangers to one another, as we go about fulfilling our needs and asserting our rights."[183] Again, a properly conceived ecclesiology and the only possible antidote to this particular progeny of American politics, is one in which the church exists "for others."

But in the absence of such faith communities, the more likely result to emerge from the failure of "liberal democracy" is that of populism. Populism is reactive, the populace's gut-level responses to and interpretations of what they see happening around them. Donald Trump is said to have ridden a wave of populist anger into the White House. Whatever one thinks of Trump, he found a way to tap into the widespread discontent and fear gripping American citizens who felt left behind in the latest edition of the American dream. Personally, I have my doubts that these good folk will look back on his election as any sort of real solution to their dissatisfactions, but I also believe that historians will regard this moment in our history with a mixture of both fascination and unease. In *Why Liberalism Failed*, Patrick Deneen wrote these prescient words regarding the virtually inevitable rising of the citizens in our current "liberal" order:

> The successes of this order generate the pathologies of a citizenry that finds itself powerless before forces of government, economy, technology, and globalizing forces. Yet once degraded, such a citizenry would be unlikely to insist upon Tocquevillian self-command; its response would predictably take the form of inarticulate cries for a strongman to rein in the power of a distant and ungovernable state and market. Liberalism itself seems likely to generate demotic demands for an illiberal autocrat who promises to protect the people against the vagaries of liberalism itself. Liberals are right to fear this eventuality, but persist in willful obliviousness of their own complicity in the birth of the illiberal progeny of the liberal order itself.[184]

The last part of this quote haunts me. We are "right to fear this eventuality, but persist in willful obliviousness of [our] own complicity in the birth of the illiberal progeny of the liberal order itself." I'm not enough of a political thinker to declare our current political reality the ultimate case of "chickens coming home to roost," but it seems that forewarned is forearmed—that something sinister has been loosed in our country and we need to address it before it is too late.

Perhaps much of today's political angst comes from a widespread feeling that, yes, something is amiss and we need to try to fix it. But as understandable as such sentiments may be, I can take little comfort in how a majority of evangelical Christians have chosen to respond. Rather than doubling down on our common faith commitments to be an alternative community, a "body of Christ politic" that shows a different way to shape the community around us, evangelicals too often wind up forgoing those basic commitments and finding refuge in the latest attempt to "make American great again." Invariably, the "good old days" were never quite as good as some would have us believe. And I find it baffling that so many American Christians are willing to join in this kind of nostalgic distraction rather than press on in the power of the Spirit towards a better vision, a just society. Recently, I saw a sign in a front yard that read: TRUMP: God, Guns, and Country! "Where would one come up with such a combination as that?" I wondered. As someone who has read the entire Bible several times, I can tell you with confidence that they didn't get it from Scripture! I don't know if that homeowner claims to be a Christian, but I know that in these strange days in America it's very, very possible that he does.

Patrick Deneen observes that "democracy is the most demanding regime, given its demands for civic *virtue*. The cultivation of virtue requires the thick presence of virtue-forming and virtue-supporting institutions, but these are precisely the institutions and practices that liberalism aims to hollow and eviscerate in the name of individual liberty."[185] I'm not at all certain that present-day America has the "thick presence of virtue-forming and virtue-supporting institutions" necessary to combat the out-of-control individualism plaguing our democracy. But I am sure that the church has a crucial part of play in how the end of America's story will be written. The question is whether the American church, specifically the evangelical church, is willing to forgo power politics in order to show a more excellent way?

BEYOND RED OR BLUE

Earlier in this chapter, I mentioned my decision to re-register as a political independent. There are no circumstances under which I would consider aligning with the current Republican Party, which has become, effectively, "the party of Trump." And I have been put off by the incessant political calculations of the Democratic Party, making every decision based on what enables them to gain political advantage over the opposition. I cannot accept that either of these parties, nor any other party, adequately speaks for me as a follower of Christ. As Colin Morris put it so long ago, "To follow Jesus in our day is to stand within that tradition for political radicalism that makes the most extreme political party seem pale pink."[186] In light of this, I have concluded that Ched Myers is right, that Christians are wise to adopt what he terms "non-aligned radicalism."[187] The choice American Christians must make politically is whether they will be the modern-day equivalent of those Old Testament "prophets of the court," who told the kings what they wanted to hear, or true patriots, whose love of country compels them to speak truth to power. The American church must not hide behind some form of comfortable, individualistic approach to salvation and neglect the powerful truth that biblical faith is always shaped in the shadow of empire. "Personal piety may be fulfilling and rewarding, but it is unfaithful to the radical call to submit to Jesus as the Lord of all life."[188]

The primary way to do this is for the church to actually *be* the church in its witness to the world. Kevin Vanhoozer aptly describes the effect of this witness.

> When the people of God fulfill their vocation, the church becomes not a sign of the times-this way lies cultural conformism-but rather a sign of the end time: a work and world of evangelical meaning. The church's life thus becomes an "apocalypse"—a revelation, an unveiling-that unmasks the powers that be and reminds us that they will not, contra appearances, be dominant forever. The church is to be a glimpse of the new world in the midst of the old, a reminder that the old order is passing away and a standing witness to the new. Accordingly, it is charged with the task of being a permanent revolution to prevailing plausibility structures. To "do church" is to engage in a different kind of politics, the "art of the impossible," an art that challenges our tired conceptions of what is possible. For "with God all things are possible."[189]

This doesn't mean that the church becomes a "no-politics zone," but rather that the politics of the church have been re-imagined—that its witness is not primarily about new laws or increased funding for social programs, as good as those things may be. The church should offer the world "a manner of life the world can never achieve through social coercion or governmental action. We serve the world by showing it something that it is not: namely, a place where God is forming a family out of strangers."[190] Rather than throwing the weight of the "Christian vote" around in ways that give Christians some assurance of power in the political process, Christians must attend to the life-changing and virtue-forming practices of worship, fellowship, hospitality, and mission as the "civics" of the kingdom of God on this earth, because these are the heart of the "inescapably 'political' vision of a people called as a *royal* priesthood and sent as ambassadors of the King above all kings."[191] This is, in truth, the essence of what it means for the church to be "leaven" in the culture, or to properly retain its saltiness. As Peter Leithart reminds us, "So long as the Church preaches the gospel and functions as a properly 'political' reality, a polity of her own, the kings of the earth have a problem on their hands . . . As soon as the church appears, it becomes clear to any alert politician that worldly politics is no longer the only game in town. The introduction of the church into *any* city means that the city has a challenger within its walls."[192] I love the possibility of the church once again being a "threat" to the Caesars of this world. But it will not become so by gaining some sort of "Christian majority" in the halls of governmental power, it will become that "threat" through what James Davison Hunter terms, "faithful presence, the recognition that the vocation of the church is to bear witness to and to be the embodiment of the coming Kingdom of God."[193]

I well know that my "outlier politics" sometimes make my friends and family uncomfortable, even irate. But, as God is my witness, I have been endeavoring to allow the substance of my faith to dictate the direction of my political viewpoints and convictions. I do not claim, in any respect, to be a finished product. I continue to reflect on what it means to actually live out my faith in world that believes itself to be in control. I want to live beyond red and blue in a manner that demonstrates that Jesus is Lord. My ardent hope is that the church can adopt this as the summation of its political strategy in the world. Diana Butler-Bass ably summarizes this aspiration:

> Purple is more than a blend of red and blue, a kind of right-left political hybrid. Purple is an ancient Christian symbol. Early Christians borrowed purple, the color of imperial power, from their Roman persecutors and inverted its symbolism. For Christians, purple symbolized God as ruler and God's reign. Yet, that kingdom was not one of imperial power—it was birthed from the martyred church, unified around a crucified savior, and formed by the spiritual authority of the baptized in a community of humility and forgiveness. For Christians, purple is more than a blending of political extremes. Purple is about power that comes through loving service, laying down one's life for others, and following Jesus' path.[194]

As James Cone insisted, theological language is inescapably political language. There is no way to speak meaningfully of a personally transformative faith without that faith producing a particular kind of vision for the surrounding world. God grant that a church who has transformed the symbolism of imperial purple might find creative ways to rightly embody its political life in the world by emulating the One who came not to be served, but to serve.

Chapter 7

American Idol(s)

Religion is important to Americans. But the religion we practice is often not the religion we confess... Let's be honest with ourselves. Even though some Americans claim the country's population is deeply divided, often described as engaged in a "culture war," most Americans tend to worship at similar altars.
—Juan Floyd-Thomas, Stacey M. Floyd-Thomas, and Mark G. Toulouse.[195]

One day I was the guest speaker at a large evangelical church in a small city in central Ohio, close to where I lived at the time. I had been at this church several times before, so I was familiar with the congregation and the details of the building. Normally, the sanctuary featured a large wooden cross suspended against the front wall of the building behind the pulpit. It was ten to twelve feet in height, the dominant visual point in the sanctuary. But as I walked in that day, I immediately noticed a change. The large cross was virtually covered by an equally large American flag. I recall stopping in my tracks when I saw this. I knew that this congregation was very conservative theologically and politically, but I was genuinely taken aback. It's not just that the flag struck me as aesthetically tacky, but even more so, it offended me. I found it idolatrous!

The dictionary defines idolatry as the "worship of a physical object as god." A secondary definition reads "an immoderate attachment or devotion to something." The Bible is uncompromising in its condemnation of idolatry in all forms. The first commandment, which prohibits placing anything above or ahead of the God of this universe, is unequivocal. And yet idolatry was a persistent issue throughout the pages of the Old Testament, and it continued into New Testament times, albeit in more subtle expressions. It would be a grave mistake to assume that idolatry is an ancient sin that we've left behind. As that evangelical church sanctuary demonstrated, idolatry is still all around us. Jesus said, "Where your treasure is, there your heart will be also," (Matthew 621). In other words, what you truly value captures your hearts. One reason why I view myself as an evangelical outlier is that I believe the American church has been subtly co-opted by institutions, values, and ideological commitments in ways which are idolatrous at their core and which jeopardize the church's witness and vitality. In his *Large Catechism*, Martin Luther said, "Whatever your heart clings to and confides in, that is really your god."[196] I once heard someone paraphrase Luther's words this way: "Whatever you would sacrifice your daughter for, that is really your God." When we look at idolatry in that light, it feels more intelligible and more costly. We see children effectively being sacrificed in the pursuit of money, sex, and power—and sacrificed through our willing participation in some of *America*'s values and practices. Idolatry stalks the American landscape in our worship of sports, entertainment, and "the good life," all of which can exact a devastating price on children. There is a long list of American enticements that substitute other "gods" for God, but I want to discuss four particularly troublesome affections that I believe to be idolatrous and dangerously costly to our country, to its children, and to the church.

AMERICA FIRST

I herded the twenty or so American college students, who were part of our study abroad program in Australia, into their seats at the hallowed Melbourne Cricket Ground. They were visibly excited, anticipating their first look at the madness of Australian Rules Football, locally known as "footy." The students had just finished their first week in Australia and were keen to experience the culture of sports-mad Aussies. The referees came to the middle of the field and blew their whistles signaling the players to gather around the center circle. Then one official bounced the ball high off the ground, and they were off. A couple of the students turned to me in puzzlement and asked, "What? No national anthem?" Strange as it may sound, that footy game had no symbolism attached to its opening other than two long-time rivals hoping to win the match. The fact that American students noticed the absence of such ceremonial trappings was, I thought, a good introduction to the cultural lessons of that night (although it may now be the case that at least some Aussie sporting events feature the Australian anthem). These students would come to observe that few, if any, of the Aussie churches we visited had Australian flags prominently displayed. What our students learned was not so much the absence of civil religion in Australia as the virtual omnipresence of civil religion in America, expressed in a forceful kind of American nationalism. When the national anthem marks the beginning of sporting events across our country, Americans are ritualistically embodying and expressing their hopes for the country and its politics. What may appear to be a simple act of patriotism is, in truth, the affirmation and acceptance of a uniquely American kind of syncretism between God and country.

Michael Gorman says, "I would contend, in fact, that the most alluring and dangerous deity in the United States is the omnipresent, syncretistic god of nationalism mixed with Christianity lite: religious beliefs, language, and practices that are superficially Christian but infused with national myths and habits. Sadly, most of this civil religion's practitioners belong to Christian churches, which is precisely why Revelation is addressed to the seven churches (not to Babylon), to all Christians tempted by the civil cult."[197] Oddly, many American Christians don't see any tension at all between the gospel according to America and the gospel of Jesus Christ. They have been so shaped by the liturgies of American nationalism that they essentially read the Bible through a red, white, and blue lens. Perhaps the most disturbing side-effect of our allegiance to civil religion is the notion of "American exceptionalism." This idea defends the belief that the U.S.A. is so special, so superior to other nations, that it should be immune to criticism with regard to our national policies and relationships with the rest of the world. The problems with such thinking are legion, but chief among them is this salient biblical point: God doesn't have nations, God has a people! America is not especially chosen by God in any sense over the other nations of our world. This extreme kind of ethnocentrism is so mistaken theologically that it would be laughable if it didn't have such harmful consequences. And what makes American nationalism so seductive is the way it borrows so freely from Christianity. This is what caused Martin Luther King jr. to claim that "if America's original sin vis-a-vis others is racism, then its original sin vis-a-vis God is civil religion."[198]

Any congregation with an American flag standing somewhere in its sanctuary needs, at some point, to hold a discussion about the relationship of church and state. And take it from me, that discussion will generate a lot of heat! Such discussions almost invariably end up with some reference to

America's founding and how that founding was made possible by America's Christian commitments. Evangelical Christians, in particular, seem most interested in extolling America's Christian heritage. Media preachers trumpet the nation's Christian past. Conservative groups produce textbooks that claim God's special providence in the discovery of America and that generally write a version of history that implies any questioning of America's Christian foundations is utterly out of touch with the facts. Such revisionist histories "portray our Founders as saints, personally inspired and directed by God, while ignoring national evils like slavery, the genocide of native peoples, the persecution of non-Protestants and violence against women and children."[199] In Michael Gorman's view, this "evangelical version of American history is not just a divine drama, however; it is a morality play. Spectators are asked to do more than watch. Believers become heirs and actors, people required to follow the script as revealed to the Founding Fathers by God in Jesus Christ."[200] The immediate problem with such views is that they run counter to actual history in a variety of ways. In his book *Was America Founded as a Christian Nation?* historian John Fea states that one of his goals in writing was to "get Christians to see the danger of cherry-picking from the past as a means of promoting a political or cultural agenda in the present."[201] As Fea puts it, "words ripped from their cultural and chronological contexts provide useful material for compilers of quotation books, but they are useless to the historian. The words of the founders, for example, must always be interpreted from the perspective of the eighteenth-century world in which they were uttered or written."[202] Historians have periodically discovered instances in which evangelical sources attribute words to the founders that, in fact, they never uttered.[203] While there is no denying that America's past is very much intertwined with religion, the jump from there to claiming a Christian America is simply not justified historically. Yes, the ideals that shaped the origins and early years of the American nation are almost wholly owing to Christendom and its influence in Europe and the American colonies. But as significant as this was, and is, we are not free to assume a historical narrative that justifies any sort of smug nationalism.

When such nationalistic attitudes prevail, everything takes on a "red, white, and blue" tinge, including Scripture itself. American politicians are savvy, and they have become experts at appropriating Scripture to support all kinds of policies designed to serve narrow national interests. Biblical phrases like "a city on a hill," "the new Israel," "a light to the nations," the "servant of the Lord," and "the chosen people" are applied wholesale to our nation, demonstrating the willingness of politicians to co-opt the Bible for their own purposes. Even Rainn Wilson, who played Dwight on TV's *The Office*, can call out a "red, white, and blue" Jesus when he sees one: "The metamorphosis of Jesus Christ from a humble servant of the abject poor to a symbol that stands for gun rights, prosperity theology, anti-science, limited government (that neglects the destitute) and fierce nationalism is truly the strangest transformation in human history."[204] Rather than embracing an "American Jesus," the church must understand its God-ordained role as a prophetic voice to the nation. Unfortunately, the American church often reflects pagan American culture in almost every respect. Jesus and his kingdom have been appropriated with the goals of political gain and the preservation of the vitality of civil religion. And, far beyond the damage this kind of dalliance with civil religion does to the vitality and character of the church, it also deeply affects the church's witness and mission in the world.

In my travels to other nations, the eye rolls in response to Americans referring to their country as a "Christian nation" are unmistakable. And the cynicism engendered by that claim spills over onto Jesus and the entire Christian faith. As a consequence, people around the world associate Christianity with many less-than-flattering aspects of American life. This is why Christians should be very wary when the flag and the Bible start holding hands. Rob Bell is right: "this is not a romance we want to encourage."[205] The church must regain its prophetic voice to counteract this dangerous form of idolatry. The church must confidently proclaim that there are no "Christian nations" in the political sense. The only "nation" Christ has is that of his baptized body.[206] America is my country, and I dearly love it, but it is *not* the church. As Augustine would remind us, it is the "city of God" that has our first and foremost allegiance. Keeping this allegiance clear is, not coincidentally, the best way for American Christians to best express their love of country. "Conscripting Jesus to a nationalistic agenda creates a grotesque caricature of Christ that the church must reject—now more than ever! Understanding Jesus as the Prince of Peace who transcends idolatrous nationalism . . . is an imperative the church must at last begin to take seriously."[207] As hard as it is for some to hear, God has no special plan for America to rule the world. That is reserved for God's Son. To confess that Jesus is Lord—not Caesar, not even the President—is a political act that precludes Christian participation in any form of nationalistic chest-thumping.

In my opinion, nationalism provides convenient cover for Americans to profess their love of country, when what they really love most is the luxury of pursuing autonomous lives of consumption. I find it difficult to interpret as "patriotic," in any sense of the word, pandemic protests against community-health restrictions on freedom of movement. And yet protesters wave the flag (and brandish their weapons) and claim to represent the best interests of their country, while loudly demanding their freedom to do as they like. Of course, some of them are justifiably worried about their economic well-being, but clearly, others simply don't want anyone telling them what to do. I suspect the uneasy truth is that fierce American nationalism exists as long, and only as long, as the aspirations of individual Americans can be realized. "America first" nationalism provides a seemingly patriotic mechanism to preserve the autonomous status quo allowing Americans to "do their own thing." If the pandemic has shown us anything, it's that a lot of America's most ardent God-and-country patriots will turn on governmental authority the moment it begins to cramp their style. The source of much of America's nationalistic fervor lies not in some super-patriotism but in our love of pursuing personal happiness on our own terms. And that pursuit brings us face to face with another "American idol" that flourishes parasitically off our nationalistic impulses: Consumer Capitalism.

I SHOP THEREFORE I AM

One day a certain board I sat on was preparing to meet. I walked into the room and nodded greetings to several fellow pastors and board members. The church official about to chair the meeting was huddled in a corner with a couple of others. He was showing these pastors his wristwatch, which I found a bit strange, until one of the onlookers asked, "Is that a Rolex?"

"No," the chair answered triumphantly. "It's a knock-off, but you can't even tell the difference. I can get you one, at a real good price!"

I watched all this in mild disbelief. This happened around the time when the "What Would Jesus Do?" craze was in full flower. That had spun off into a variety of issue-oriented questions such as, "Would Jesus drive a Hummer?" one of those gas-guzzling monstrosities that had recently hit the market. Suddenly that day in the boardroom, I recalled seeing an article entitled "Would Jesus wear a Rolex?" It tried to show the pointlessness of out-of-control consumerism and finding one's self-worth in possessions. But, now, I was faced with a different question altogether: "Would Jesus wear a *fake* Rolex?" The idea of trying to project an illusion of affluence by wearing counterfeit jewelry struck me as odd in itself; the fact that it was an officer of the church caused me to wonder how the church had become so susceptible to the lure of consumer capitalism.

Augustine called it "covetousness," an inordinate desire for *more*. Covetousness keeps us restless as we focus on what we lack and ignore all we possess. We end up trading away our tranquility for the newest trinkets of the day. Without a doubt, Western culture, and particularly the U.S.A., are consumers out of control. Luxuries easily become "needs," and extravagances become "rights." No one seems to be able to predict anything but a chaotic and tragic endgame for it all. Ironically, "consumption" was the name given to a disease that took so many lives prior to the 20th century. It was a disease that slowly decreased lung capacity in people until they suffocated. Thankfully, that disease was largely tamed by antibiotics, but in its own way, present-day consumption is proving just as deadly and resistant to control. Consumption is indeed suffocating. We face the distressing reality that "the average American Christian is just as drunk on consumerism as the non-Christian at the other end of the bar."[208] The idolatry of consumer capitalism lies in the fact that anxiety and insecurity drives us to try to make ourselves secure, substituting devotion to something temporal rather than God. This is why Paul connected greed with idolatry (Colossians 3:5). It is idolatrous because it shifts the worship of God to the worship of mammon. In breaking the tenth commandment ("thou shalt not covet") we end up breaking the first commandment as well.

Keesmaat and Walsh maintain that in our shop-till-you-drop culture, "North American Christians have bowed the knee to Caesar and to his predatory economy in their daily economic lives, while still confessing Jesus as Lord at church and in personal piety."[209] This kind of dual allegiance is precisely what Jesus warned about in Matthew 6 when he said "you cannot serve both God and money" (6:24c). As clear as Christ's words are here, however, many Christians interpret Jesus to mean "just be careful about money." That's obviously good counsel, but it proves spectacularly inadequate in the face of every patriotic American's duty to do one's part to support the national economy. Jamie Smith contends that this economic imperative teaches us to "both overvalue and undervalue things: we're being trained to invest them with a meaning and significance as objects of love and desire in which we place disproportionate hopes while at the same time treating them as easily discarded."[210] Our throwaway culture of planned obsolescence subordinates all other consequences to the continual rise of the gross national product. The economy becomes the insatiable god which must, at all costs, be appeased. Consumer capitalism elevates the economic dimension of life into the pantheon of the gods. Should you doubt that, just consider the boisterous pandemic debate over defeating a horrific disease versus "opening up the economy," allowing Americans the freedom and opportunity to spend the money necessary to "get the country back on track." When we reach the frightening point where we are crafting rational arguments that put profit margins ahead of human welfare, even life itself, it's safe to say that we have added yet one more "god" to the national pantheon.

The mission of the church is not to sustain the GNP, but to represent and incarnate a kingdom defined by very different values. But if the church is hurrying off to the mall with the rest of America, how can this ever happen? Please don't misunderstand. This is not a veiled appeal for vows of poverty. Goodness knows, that ship sailed from American Christianity long ago. But I do mean to remind us that we cannot submit to the gods of this age without serious consequences to the church's health and mission. Christians must understand the power of the market to shape and *misshape* those who enter in. Richard Foster puts it this way:

> Because we lack a divine center, our need for security has led us into an insane attachment to things. We really must understand that the lust for affluence in contemporary society is psychotic. It is psychotic because it has completely lost touch with reality. We crave things we neither need nor enjoy. We buy things we do not want to impress people we do not like. Where planned obsolesence leaves off, psychological obsolesence takes over. We are made to feel ashamed to wear old clothes or drive cars until they wear out. The mass media has convinced us that to be out of fashion is to be out of step with reality. It is time we awaken to the fact that to be in conformity with a sick society is to be sick.[211]

Far beyond the destructive power of consumer capitalism to damage the lives of individual Christians, there is the hard reality of how it damages others in our world, and the world itself. The desires created by a life of consumption creates desires that are destructive to creation, and in essence they create a culture of national privilege that can't extend to much of the rest of the world. Scott Bessenecker observes that "if the entire planet lived like North Americans, we'd need two more earths just to keep the supply of lattes, Lexuses and other luxury items flowing in order to accommodate our voracious environmental appetite."[212] Our addiction to the wealth generated by the exploitation of our planet is an indicator of what some term "covenantal amnesia," where people forget who their God is and embrace idols that can only bring about the bitter fruit of economic oppression and injustice.[213] But that is not the Christian story. Our story speaks of creation's stewardship and justice for all people, not just those whose economic resources can afford the entry fee to the party. Wendell Berry, who embodies this alternative story as well as anyone, warns the church against the siren call of the consumeristic narrative:

> The church has, for the most part, stood silently by while a predatory economy has ravaged the world, destroyed its natural beauty and health, divided and plundered its human communities and households. It has flown the flag and chanted the slogans of empire. It has assumed with the economists that "economic

forces" automatically work for good and has assumed with the industrialists and militarists that technology determines history. It has assumed with almost everybody that "progress" is good, that it is good to be modern and up with the times. It has admired Caesar and comforted him in his depredations and defaults. But in its de facto alliance with Caesar, Christianity connives directly in the murder of creation. "Christianity and the Survival of Creation," in *Sex, Economy Freedom and Community*, (New York Pantheon, 1993).[214]

Berry's words should awaken us to the cost of this particular idolatry in terms of how it so visibly compromises the church and its witness in the world. Our idolatrous pursuit of *more* inescapably throws our children and grandchildren into the jaws of this economic beast. Remember the paraphrase to Luther's catechism, "Whatever you would sacrifice your daughter for that is your God." Are we prepared to sacrifice our children and grandchildren to the gross national product? If we allow ourselves to be reduced to competitive consumers, then, as Keesmaat and Walsh put it, "future generations end up being little more than competitors, people who would strip us of our entitlement to prosperity now. Let's not mince words here. This is a praxis of child sacrifice."[215] Surely, the church would never knowingly choose such a path, but it must not be deceived about the ultimate consequences of unbridled consumerism, either for its children, or for the planet.

ENDLESS WAR

I'm not an overly emotional person. I am not cold or unfeeling, not at all; inwardly, I feel things acutely. I just tend to suppress such feelings from showing on the outside. This is why I so vividly remember my one and only visit to the Vietnam memorial in Washington D.C. For my generation, pre-9/11, pre-"war on terror," and pre-Coronavirus, the war in Vietnam was our defining crisis. It stands, to this day, as the historical event that most overshadows the baby boomers' transition into adulthood. That day in our capital, as I placed my hands on those black stone panels inscribed with the names of the war dead who included some of my high school classmates, the tears flowed openly; I could not stop them. My emotions that day were a mix of frustration, anger, and deep sadness. It's the nearest to what the Bible terms "lament" that I've ever experienced.

Looking back on that day at the wall helps me understand why I approach this particular American idol with such apprehension. I am fearful that some readers might interpret my words as disrespecting, in some way, the service and sacrifice of men and women who have worn the uniform of the United States military. I honestly do not have adequate words to articulate the gratitude I have for those who put themselves in harm's way for people like me. As I consider the heroism and sacrificial acts that are called for and played out in times of war, I desperately want to avoid casting any aspersions on the lives and actions of America's veterans. And I would quickly add that for the same government who sent service veterans into harm's way to enact policies and laws denying them proper care and support is the most underhanded, most despicable kind of betrayal. Politicians who send soldiers to war are obligated to care for these honorable men and women when they return home—for the rest of their lives! Failure to do so disqualifies such politicians from further roles in leadership.

But . . ! America has a problem with militarism, which I define as a kind of overconfidence, or *faith,* if you will, in military power. We see it in the constant saber-rattling at sporting events, as fighter jets and stealth bombers fly over cheering crowds. We see it in the constant TV ads extolling the glamour and adventure of military service. We see it in the not-so-subtle attempts to glorify war, using violent video games to recruit a new generation of warriors. We see it in the constant prioritization of military expenditures over virtually all other kinds of government spending. The U.S. has a military budget higher than the next-highest fifteen nations combined. We spend billions of dollars per day on the military. And this is while children in America go hungry, and millions of our citizens do not have adequate access to health care. So, I'm sorry, but as a Christian, I can't look at that and pronounce it "good." In "The Afghanistan Papers" published by the *Washington Post* under the headline "Afghanistan—the endless war," the war was summarized: "Nearly 1 trillion dollars in military spending. Death of more than 100,000 Afghans, 2300 U.S. soldiers, 133 billion in development spending 'creating mostly just a toxic mix of corruption and opium.'"[216] And the spending and the dying in Afghanistan continues, with no apparent end in sight. Sylvia Keesmaat and Brian Walsh raise the obvious question in response to such matters by asking, "When taxes are decreased in order to benefit the rich, but military expenditures dramatically increase in order to fund imperial expansion, the only possible result will be skyrocketing national debt. And so the economic question becomes, how long can the world's biggest borrower remain the world's leading power?[217] The words "imperial expansion" used here ought to give Christians pause. Some might object that America does not seek expansion in Afghanistan. Hopefully, that's true. But in fighting "endless wars" we perpetuate the myth of American power as the solution to the world's problems.

Deep historical lessons are to be found in such accumulation and projection of power. In the Bible, particularly in the book of Revelation, Scripture is clear that God's judgment is especially focused on the phenomenon of "empire." Whether one reads of Assyria, Babylon, or Rome, the Bible clearly condemns imperial ambitions on the part of any nation as being on an inevitable collision course with a kingdom where Jesus, and Jesus alone, is Lord. It seems obvious, as we observe today's nations, that the primary route by which they would reach imperialistic goals is a military one. Military power is the proverbial "big stick" that achieves and maintains one's standing as "king of the mountain." Recalling the faltering of imperial Rome under the burden of financing what was then the world's largest military, Keesmaat and Walsh rightly question the long-term viability of repeating such a strategy in our world today. But even laying aside the fiscal folly of such policies, Christians must question a world view that effectively sees conducting "endless war" as part of the price of being the world's only superpower.

In his book *Washington Rules: America's Path to Permanent War*, Andrew Bacevich, a retired army officer, contends that it has been an understood, if unwritten, policy of the U.S. since the end of World War II that the primary means of establishing and continuing American dominance in the world will be through the resources of the military-industrial complex.[218] Bacevich reminds us that "the burden of paying for the disaster concocted by the national security establishment falls most savagely on the majority of Americans with incomes under $20,000, the people whose pocketbooks do the paying and whose sons tend to do the dying for foreign policy but whose voices are largely absent in its making."[219] He cites President Dwight Eisenhower's well-known words, "Every gun that is made, every warship launched, every rocket fired signifies, in the final sense, a theft from those who hunger and are not fed, those who are cold and are not clothed."[220]

I freely admit that I would prefer Bacevich to be wrong in his claims, yet he lays out a compelling case of how the power of the military-industrial complex has stymied one U.S. president after another (regardless of party affiliation) in any attempt to institute significant change in this state of affairs. And more often than not, America's presidents have willingly participated in these policies for fear of appearing "weak." But the pursuit of such militant ideology yields confused and uncomfortable conclusions.

> Not even the most hawkish proponent of American global leadership . . . had ever proposed committing the United States to a policy of war without foreseeable end. Yet over the course of George W. Bush's presidency, open-ended war became accepted

> policy, hardly more controversial than the practices of stationing U.S. troops abroad[221]. . . . When presidents use phrases like *fighting for freedom, eliminating tyranny,* and, *liberating the oppressed*, they speak in code. Their real meaning, easily deciphered by their listeners, is this: Safeguarding the American way of life requires that others conform to American values. Military victory offers the medium through which American warriors impose that conformity.[222]

I'm confident that some readers will think this far too conspiratorial, somewhat like how recent and current talk about the "deep state" points to the Pentagon and to corporations that supply America's military. But as Bacevich and others have pointed out, the money to be had in the continuation of American military presence around the world has made a lot of people, including politicians, very wealthy. Bacevich urges the American public to gain some sense of perspective when it comes to the *true* costs of implementing and maintaining such policies:

> At one level, we can with little difficulty calculate the cost of these efforts: The untold billions of dollars added annually to the national debt and the mounting toll of dead and wounded U.S. troops provide one gauge. At a deeper level, the costs of adhering to the Washington consensus defy measurement: families shattered by loss; veterans bearing the physical or psychological scars of combat; the perpetuation of ponderous bureaucracies subsisting in a climate of secrecy, dissembling, and outright deceptions; the distortion of national priorities as the military-industrial-complex siphons off scarce resources; environmentally devastating by-products of war and the preparation for war; the evisceration of civic culture that results when a small praetorian guard shoulders the burden of waging perpetual war, while the great majority of citizens purport to revere its members, even as they ignore or profit from their service.[223]

As harmful as the costs of bowing to the idol of militarism are, we must rigorously question its effectiveness as policy. It's a heavy lift, indeed, to argue that America's love affair with all things military has made our world demonstrably safer, even as we continue to pour arms and troops into unstable areas of the globe hoping to maintain our position atop the nations of the world. For decades, we've armed Middle Eastern nations; we want to influence them toward "keeping the peace"—so long as that benefits U.S. interests, economic and otherwise. How's that working out for us? The Middle East is a tinderbox that threatens to explode almost any moment, bringing about a conflagration that will engulf most of the world. The Einstein-attributed definition of "insanity" comes to mind here, as we continue to do the same thing year in and year out, expecting different results.

Beyond the questionable wisdom of allowing policies to be defined and directed by militarism, the sheer injustice of economic inequities in our "national defense" must be considered. How are hunger, and health care, and deeply flawed infrastructure not part of what we mean when we speak about "defending" the lives and well-being of American citizens? How does the Lordship of Christ impact the phrasing of such questions, and, more importantly, the answers we might expect from His followers? There are few issues that are so fraught with peril for Christians in America today as questioning the militarism of the U.S. If we question it, we will be called "unpatriotic" or even "traitorous." War has taken on an iconic role in America's story. To critique it amounts to blasphemy. But, even at the cost of being labeled unpatriotic outliers, we must bear witness to the peaceable kingdom that Christ has brought to us. We are obligated, in turn, to proclaim that peaceable kingdom to the world, and especially to our own beloved country. Richard Middleton reminds us that, "we live in a world that glorifies violence and makes an ideal of conquest and military supremacy. Whereas God wants the cloud of his Glory-presence to fill and cover the earth (as it did the tabernacle), we, by our violent misuse of the power entrusted to us, have covered the earth with a cloud of pollution, both physical and moral, thus shutting earth off from God's full presence."[224] I'm not naive enough to think that we can alter the course of U.S. militarism overnight, but the story of Maximillianus comes to mind as instructive. He was a young Roman Christian, who in 295 refused to be inducted into the Roman army and was sentenced to death, causing some to view him as the first conscientious objector.[225] This reminds us that Christians throughout history have freely chosen their citizenship in Christ's peaceable kingdom over the drumbeats of war, even at great personal cost. Can evangelical Americans demonstrate such fidelity to God's kingdom today?

GUNS R US!

"Our beloved country is wonderful in many respects, troubled in others, but on no other issue do we seem as completely out of our minds as on the issue of guns and the control of guns."[226] These words from David Gushee express so vividly my exasperation with America's love affair with guns and violence. Gushee adds, "Our paralysis, our inability to do anything to address this problem is one of the greatest examples of national dysfunction that we currently see."²²⁷ I couldn't agree more, though I confess I never look forward to having a dialogue on the topic. Honestly, I think I'd rather have a root canal than attempt a reasonable conversation with a Second Amendment fanatic. Typically, in such "conversations," rationality is about as rare as a unicorn sighting. The fact that so many evangelical Christians clearly align themselves with the "guns for everyone" crowd both astonishes and disheartens me. I cannot figure how they correlate these views on guns with anything resembling Jesus' teachings. How is it possible that so many American Christians appear to value the Second Amendment over the Great Commandment? As the updated Luther paraphrase reminds us, "whatever you'd sacrifice your daughter for, that is your God." Looking around at the gun violence in America's schools forces us draw a rather obvious conclusion.

Stanley Hauerwas and William Willimon note that "Luther called security the ultimate idol. And [Americans] have shown, time and again, our willingness to exchange anything—family, health, church, truth—for a taste of security. We are vulnerable animals who seek to secure and to establish our lives in improper ways, living by our wits rather than by faith."²²⁸ In our rush to secure ourselves against any number of threats, real or imagined, we have latched onto guns as our best hope of keeping all the societal "beasts" at bay. But in so doing we exchange our hope in God and God's peaceable kingdom for a false security, one making promises of well-being that it is unable to keep. In his book, *American and Its Guns: A Theological Expose'*, James Atwood defines America's gun idolatry as "a confrontational belief system based on acquiring power over others. The system is buttressed by a fascination for and devotion to the violence guns provide. [They] believe they need guns to prove to themselves and others that they are in control, to protect them from harm, and to give them a sense of security."²²⁹ As is always the case with idolatry, the necessary exchange brings consequences that no one would actually choose. Consider some of the realities of America's gun culture:

- They are more gun dealers in America than McDonald's restaurants, more gun dealers than gas stations. A dealer's license costs ten dollars and most do business out of the trunks of their cars.²³⁰
- Children in the U.S. are twelve times more likely to die from firearms injury than children in twenty-five other industrialized nations. Gun murder rates in the U.S. per 100,000 people are more than 17 times higher than those in Australia, 35 times higher than Germany, 37 times higher than in Spain, and 355 times higher than in Japan.²³¹

- Domestically, we possess more than 300 million guns with another three million coming off assembly lines each year.[232]
- The United States began keeping records of gun deaths in 1933. Since then, over 1.7 million Americans have died from guns. More American citizens (651,697) were killed with guns in the eighteen-year period between 1979 and 1997 than all servicemen and -women killed in all of the United States' wars since 1775 (650,858).[233]
- Of all civilian murders in all the developed countries of the world, 86 percent of them occur in the United States.[234]

Unfortunately, this grim statistical litany could go on for several pages. The fact that so many Americans, especially Christians, are not shamed or outraged by this data is the primary reason that I contend that something idolatrous, something sinister, is afoot in America's love of guns.

I grew up with guns. My family took hunting very seriously. I ate venison, pheasant, rabbit, and even squirrel shot by my father or by other members of my family. I looked forward to joining the men of the family on the annual Thanksgiving-morning pheasant hunt. Unfortunately, we moved to Arizona before I was old enough to qualify for that rite of passage. In Arizona, hunting was much more expensive and way more complicated than roaming the woods of Southern Ohio, so I never graduated into the hunter's guild that I had imagined. So let me be clear, I am not arguing in any way against hunting, sport shooting, or even having a firearm close by for emergencies. I am asking America's churches to consider the broader implications of their support for the gun violence culture in this country, whether that support is overt or tacit. To defend our current approach to gun violence as part of the "cost of freedom" is even more callous than it is absurd. Whose freedom? Certainly not the school children, or movie-goers, or worshipers gunned down by men (almost invariably, white men) armed with military-grade weapons. The NRA wants us to believe that it's all about patriotism. The leaders of the NRA wrap themselves in the flag and portray the gun lobby as only interested in preserving America's way of life. But, if you listen carefully to the rhetoric, there is the implied threat of pursing this agenda through violent means if necessary. How can the gun culture boast of its American values and yet hint at insurrection and threaten the overthrow of a democratically elected government?[235] Why is it that every public protest involving the right wing always produces large numbers of gun-wielding men who brandish their weapons in menacing fashion, using their guns to intimidate and make their point? More importantly, why is the church so silent about this? Jesus drew an unmistakable line between thought and action. Why is it acceptable to threaten people with automatic weapons? The NRA would have us believe that a "bad guy's worst nightmare is a good guy with a gun." How are we to know who the "good guys" really are? And there are far too many examples of people being shot and killed by men who, seconds before they pulled the trigger mirror every criterion of the NRA's "good guy with a gun."

A while back I was watching *Sportscenter* on ESPN. They were reporting on the growing popularity of bare-knuckle boxing. As you might guess, this involves men (and women) in a boxing ring without boxing gloves. It is now legal in five states. They showed a clip of two men beating each other to bloody pulps, with frequent cutaways showing the spectators (many of whom were women) jumping and screaming with delight. Ancient Rome and the gladiators had nothing on modern America! Theologian Walter Wink says,

> Violence is the ethos of our times. It is the spirituality of the modern world. It has been accorded the status of a religion, demanding from its devotees an absolute obedience to death. Its followers are not aware, however, that the devotion they pay to violence is a form of religious piety. Violence is successful as a myth precisely because it does not seem to be mythic in the least. Violence simply appears to be the nature of things. It is what works. It is inevitable, the last, and often, the first resort in conflicts. It is embraced with equal alacrity by people on the left and on the right, by religious liberals and religious conservatives. The threat of violence, it is believed, alone can deter aggressors. Some would argue the threat of nuclear annihilation has bought the world sixty-six years of peace. Violence is thriving as never before in every sector of American popular culture, civil religion, nationalism, and foreign policy. Violence, not Christianity, is the real religion of America.[236]

I am not convinced that Americans are inherently more violent than are the people of other modern nations. In these days of globalism, media offerings from movies to TV, sports broadcasts to video games, are found in virtually every corner of the world. The one glaring difference appears to be that Americans can acquire guns more easily than anywhere else on earth. America's fierce protection of the gun culture brings me back to Wink's contention that in America, violence "has been accorded the status of a religion." Americans embrace this idolatrous notion because we assume that it works! But I am suspicious that something deeper and darker is at work here. According to the Apostle Paul, "our struggle is not against flesh and blood, but against the rulers, against the authorities, against the powers of this dark world and against the spiritual forces of evil in the heavenly realms" (Eph. 6:12). James Davison Hunter explains,

> The concept refers to the institutional or systemic patterns of thought, behavior, and relationship that govern our lives and the spiritual realm that animates them. They were originally part of the created order and as such, were good. They were intended to mediate the creative purposes of God in the world, but like us they are now fallen. Rather than reflecting truth, they became adversaries of the truth. Rather than serving the aim of human flourishing, they came to dominate, coerce, and enslave humankind by claiming for themselves absolute power. They are "the rulers of this age" (1 Cor. 2:6). The power they wield is, at its source and in its consequences, demonic in character.[237]

However this may brand me, I am increasingly of the mind that America's culture of violence can be traced back to these "principalities and powers" which resist any and all efforts to break the hold of violence on this society and which is most evident in the power and influence of the gun culture. As a Christian, I believe that a cosmic battle is being waged between the powers of darkness and the peaceable kingdom of God. I have every confidence that Christ will triumph in the end, but in the meantime, great battles are being fought. The battle over a culture of violence is one that rages in this country I love and call home. I realize how easy it would be assume that I've simply gone off the rails here, but think it through. When 74% of NRA members and 84% of gun owners in America support ending the private sales loophole that permits gun "dealers" to sell military-style weapons out of the trunks of their cars, and 95% of all Americans support background checks for gun purchases, and yet no votes or actions have been taken by our elected representatives, how do we explain that? It defies all reason. Personally, I'm not at all optimistic that we can solve the problem of gun violence in this country legislatively, even though I support all efforts to do so. The reason for my pessimism is my belief that there are forces at work, human and spiritual, that ardently seek to perpetuate our violent culture. As much as gun violence is a political and social problem, I argue that it is more specifically a spiritual problem. That means that the church must not abdicate its role in speaking truth to power, even to the powers of darkness. Brian McLaren is right: "To follow Jesus is to become an atheist in regard to all bloodthirsty, tribal warrior gods, and to become a believer in the living God of grace and peace, who, in Christ, sheds God's own blood in a manifestation of amnesty and reconciliation."[238]

The hope of the world lies in a kingdom that is not of this world. And it is a kingdom that is not symbolized by any of the modern-day idols that have so captured the hearts of American Christians. Greg Boyd asserts that, "the evangelical church in America has, to a large extent, been co-opted by an American, religious version of the kingdom of the world. We have come to trust the power of the sword more than the power of the cross. We have become intoxicated with the Constantinian, nationalistic, violent mind set of imperialistic Christendom."[239] We dare not baptize our county or elements of our culture into the church in the false assumption that they become part of the will of God. Idolatry is never an accident. It is the result of our continued attempts to bend deity to our own ends. Such attempts always yield "bad fruit." The American church must find a way to emphasize its being the authentic church rather than succumb to being just one more example of American civil religion and culture. Biblically, we are confronted with a stark choice when it comes to idolatry. There is no middle ground. As Brian Zahnd prophetically writes, "In Revelation, John's vision is clear: Either we follow the Lamb into the shalom of New Jerusalem, or we follow the Beast into the horrors of Armageddon. We either listen to the Lamb or we listen to the frogs. The frogs know the way to another Armageddon. The Lamb leads the way to the beautiful city of peace."[240]

Chapter 8

Dinosaurs on the Ark

> Unfortunately, many Christians cannot fully appreciate how science enriches our understanding of God's creation. They have been robbed of this experience by an unfortunate misunderstanding that the scientific picture of the world is not compatible with their belief that God created that world. For various reasons they have come to fear and even reject science.
>
> —Karl W. Gibberson and Francis S. Collins[241]

Early in the winter of 2020, I began laying out the chapters in this book. When I settled on the title "Dinosaurs on the Ark" for the chapter on church and science, I determined to make a spring road trip to northern Kentucky to visit The Ark Encounter, an exhibit billed as a full-size replica of Noah's ark and supplemented with information and commentary based in Young Earth creationism. Unfortunately, a shelter-in-place order from my governor derailed my best intentions for journalistic integrity, so I have had to content myself with websites and articles about this very large boat residing in Kentucky.

The Ark Encounter draws huge numbers of visitors each year—not all that surprising, given that upwards of 45% of Americans believe that the earth is less than 10,000 years old.[242] This belief runs counter to virtually all scientific data, and nowhere is this more clearly demonstrated than by the presence of dinosaurs on the Kentucky ark. Science contends that dinosaurs went extinct some sixty-five million years before human beings arrived on the scene.[243] My first thought upon hearing about the inclusion of dinosaurs on the ark was, "Did those people not see *Jurassic Park*?" The questions raised by trying to fit dinosaurs into this timeframe are legion; they lead to graphic mental images of dinosaurs eating other animals and of eight people struggling to deal with an estimated five to twelve *tons* of manure each day? To their credit, the folks at The Ark Encounter have carefully prepared answers to such questions, but the main question still goes begging. *Why?* What's the point of a multimillion-dollar, high-tech reproduction of a Bible story that was first written to people for whom the word "dinosaur" meant absolutely nothing? Why is it considered necessary to find ways to reconcile scientific information with a biblical story that doesn't seem the least bit interested in addressing such issues?

The Ark Encounter is just one of many well-intentioned attempts to show that the Bible, along with being a guide to knowing God, is also a first-rate source for science. I can't buy into Young Earth creationism myself, but in the long run it doesn't undermine the Christian commitments of those who believe in such a reading of Scripture. In the same way that pre-tribulation, mid-tribulation, or post-tribulation views of eschatology do not ultimately matter in terms of one's standing with God, neither does one's cosmological viewpoints on things like the age of the earth. Nevertheless, I still have a twofold problem with this approach. First, it originates from the very same modernity these folks profess to reject. They use scientific categories to question scientific conclusions. They are applying modern principles to ancient documents and asking questions of Scripture that the Bible shows no interest at all in answering. Massaging Scripture exegetically and historically in the name of defending the Bible is self-defeating in the long run. People who claim to love the Bible should stop abusing the Bible. Second, and more importantly, while it might not make much difference if adult Christians choose to believe that things like The Ark Encounter are an accurate response to science, what about the children, the all-important next generation who is the core of the church's mission? If young people are forced into thinking that they have to make a choice between Christian faith and science, some may choose Christianity, but many won't, and sadly, they will have been presented with a false dilemma, a completely bogus choice. There are no substantive contradictions between science and the message of the Bible.

Francis Collins is a committed man of faith who headed up the Human Genome Project and who has gone on to play a major role in the government's response to the pandemic. He contends that,

> ... it is not science that suffers most here. Young Earth Creationism does even more damage to faith, by demanding that belief in God requires assent to fundamentally flawed claims about the natural world. Young people brought up in homes and churches that insist on [this form of] Creationism sooner or later encounter the overwhelming scientific evidence in favor of an ancient universe and the relatedness of all living things through the process of evolution and natural selection. What a terrible and unnecessary choice they then face! To adhere to the faith of their childhood, they are required to reject a broad and rigorous body of scientific data, effectively committing intellectual suicide. Presented with no other alternative than [Young Earth] Creationism, is it any wonder that many of these young people turn away from faith, concluding that they simply cannot believe in a God who would ask them to reject what science has so compellingly taught us about the natural world?[244]

I remember well, as a first-year biology student in a large state university, being presented with evolution as science's answer to how life on earth began and progressed. Although I had been raised in a conservative Christian home, the material from my biology class made sense to me. I began to wonder if this might mean that everything I had been taught had to be revisited, if not jettisoned? After I began to prepare for Christian ministry, I spent a few years in the "Bible as science text" camp, but I soon began to understand what Collins and many other scientists and theologians have concluded: science and religion are not mortal enemies, they are different ways of knowing, of dealing with different kinds of knowledge.

I make no claim to scientific competence. People in my discipline (theology) tend to avoid science courses like mice avoid cats. Our ministry students were required to take a lab science course as part of their liberal arts curriculum, and typically they were not usually keen on taking biology, chemistry, or physics. If I had a dollar for every ministry student I enrolled in Introduction to Nutrition, I'm guessing I could have paid for the coffee in our faculty lounge for a whole semester. All this just to underscore that I'm a bit out of my element here. But, as Collins points out, the stakes in the science-and-religion discussion are so high and so long-range that the church must find its way through it, in a manner that honors both faith and science.

CHURCH AND SCIENCE

For those of us who take the Bible seriously, it has sometimes seemed as if science has declared war on biblical faith. This has understandably led to some Christians becoming antagonistic towards science and its claims. But Christians must recognize that we not only affirm special revelation (the Bible) but also general revelation (the world as God's handiwork). As stewards of creation, we should welcome the attempts of science to help us understand the world in which we live. But when science is largely perceived as claiming that the process of creation is undirected and essentially meaningless, it is little wonder that many Christians take offense. These claims violate not only Christian faith, but, as I will argue later, also undermine the true nature of science itself. The damage has been done, however, and it's no secret that the church has had a very complicated relationship with science. But this rocky relationship is hardly the whole story.

Gibberson and Collins argue that the "works of many of the first Christian theologians and philosophers actually reveal an interpretation of Genesis surprisingly compatible with both the great age of the earth and Darwin's theory of evolution."[245] They go on to note that St. Augustine (late 4th, early 5th centuries) claimed that "the first two chapters of Genesis are written to suit the understanding of the people of that time."[246] Oxford University scholar William Carroll writes that, "Thomas Aquinas did not think that the opening of Genesis presented any difficulties for the natural sciences, for the Bible is not a textbook in the sciences. What is essential to Christian faith, according to Aquinas, is the 'fact of creation,' not the manner or mode of the formation of the world."[247] John Wesley, the founder of Methodism, agreed with Augustine, that Scriptures were written in terms suitable for their audience. "The inspired penman in this history (Genesis) . . . [wrote] for the Jews first and, calculating his narratives for the infant state of the church, describes things by their outward sensible appearances, and leaves us, by further discoveries of the divine light, to be led into the understanding of the mysteries couched under them."[248] Gibberson and Collins share the example of B.B. Warfield (1851–1912), the Princeton theologian who championed biblical inerrancy and is often cited by many conservatives, including young-earth advocates. Warfield wrote, "I am free to say, for myself, that I do not think that there is any general statement in the Bible or any part of the account of creation, either as given in Gen. I & II (sic) or elsewhere alluded to, that need be opposed to evolution."[249] Theodosius Dobzhansky (1900–1975), a prominent scientist who subscribed to the Russian Orthodox faith and to theistic evolution, said: "Creation is not an event that happened in 4004 BC; it is a process that began some 10 billion years ago and is still underway . . . Does the evolutionary doctrine clash with religious faith? It does not. It is a blunder to mistake the Holy Scriptures for elementary textbooks of astronomy, geology, biology, and anthropology. Only if symbols are construed to mean what they are not intended to mean can there arise imaginary, insoluble conflicts."[250] The overall truth is this: not discounting the well-documented conflicts with Galileo and others, the church's views on scientific advancement have been anything but uniformly negative. Furthermore, the antagonism that many Christians today have towards science is largely a reactive carry-over from the so-called Fundamentalist/Modernist controversy of the early to middle 20th century.

Apart from evolution itself, the major source of continued antagonism centers on the age of the earth. Science contends that the universe is extremely old (around 13 billion years) and that the earth itself is less than half that old, human life younger still. Karl Gibberson suggests that "if the history of earth is the Eiffel Tower, human history is the paint on the very top."[251] This has proven to be a flash point for many conservative Christians, who have mounted efforts to restrict the teaching of earth's antiquity and evolution in public schools and to adopt textbooks written from a "creationist" perspective. "Creationist" here refers to those who argue for a literal reading of Genesis 1 and 2 to explain the origins of the universe and the formation of life on earth. Reading Genesis literally, according to those who subscribe to Young Earth creationism, makes the earth around 6,000 years old. That presents quite a stark contrast with scientific findings. And there is a lot of evidence that flies in the face of a young earth.

A few years ago, my wife and I sat in a cave in Kakadu National Park in the Northern Territory of Australia, looking at cave paintings dated to nearly 10,000 years ago. Evidence suggests that aboriginal dwellers in Australia lived as long ago as 40,000 years ago. Little wonder, then, that scientists regard using "literal" readings of the Bible to establish the age of the earth as problematic, as something that completely undermines most of the natural sciences as we know them. Scientists are understandably defensive about their disciplines, and at the same time many Christians view science as inherently threatening. They rush to defend their beliefs against "godless scientists," bent on "destroying" the Bible. But I happily resist joining this particular battle. It's unwinnable, for one thing, but I question whether it needs to be fought at all. Why do we believe that God needs to be defended at all around this issue? If God is the Creator of the universe, why should anyone devoted to discovering truth about the universe be considered a threat to God and God's creation? But apparently the work of science haunts a lot of Christians, who willingly engage in all manner of biblical gymnastics to debunk scientific claims and "prove" the scientific accuracy of Scripture.

Nowhere does the Bible make any claims about the age of the earth. Establishing the age of the earth is, by definition, an empirical claim; Scripture simply does not go there. The biblical text has much to tell us about God and God's nature, and the purpose of creation, but when it comes to matters of natural science, the biblical text is "thoroughly ancient and communicates in that context."[252] Christians should be extremely wary about using the Bible as a science text. Our understanding of the world today differs markedly from what biblical writers knew, but that in no way undermines the truth that those authors were trying to communicate about God and the world. The information in the Bible is "non-scientific," simply because the Bible isn't trying to teach science. Genesis 1 and 2 does not offer a competing claim to the scientific account of human origins. As John Walton states, "That does not mean the science is right; it means only that the Bible does not offer a competing claim. The Bible's claim is that whatever happened, God did it. He is the one responsible for our human existence and our human identity regardless of the mechanisms or the time period. The Bible does not say clearly how he did it. Consequently, the Bible does not necessarily make a de novo claim for human origins, though it does make a claim that God is the ultimate cause of human origins."[253]

Walton goes on to note that, "in our culture, we think 'scientifically.' We are primarily concerned with causation, composition and systematization. In the ancient world they are more likely to think of the world in terms of symbols and to express their understanding by means of imagery. We are primarily interested in events and material reality whereas they are more interested in ideas and their representations."[254] This failure to account for the fundamental differences in aims, interests, and thought processes creates much of the conflict between the Bible and science. Part of reverencing Scripture is resisting efforts to make the Bible into something it isn't and has no interest in becoming. The Bible is theology, not science. To treat the Bible with respect means listening to the text in its ancient voice, refusing to impose questions on it that its authors would not even understand, because they were addressing issues that were of importance to them, in their own times and places. Peter Enns rightly reminds us that, "the final form of the creation story in Genesis (along with the rest of the Pentateuch) reflects the concerns of the community that produced it: post-exilic Israelites who had experienced God's rejection in Babylon. The Genesis creation narrative we have in our Bibles today, although surely rooted in much older material, was shaped as a theological response to Israel's national crisis of exile. These stories were not written to speak of 'origins' as we might think of them today (in a natural-science sense). They were written to say something of God and Israel's place in the world as God's chosen people."[255] This becomes clear when we look at the overall structure of the book of Genesis. Ask virtually any group of Christians what the book of Genesis is about and the immediate answer will be "creation." Yet in a book of fifty chapters, only two are devoted to origins, while thirteen tell the story of Abraham, thirteen chapters tell the story of Jacob, and thirteen chapters tell the story of Joseph. Reading Genesis through the eyes of an exiled Israelite is surely more compelling and faithful to the text than trying to push it forward as a scientific account of the beginning of the earth and human origins. I have found that allowing the Bible to be itself, rather than imposing modern categories on it (notably empirical science), allows these ancient texts to come alive with relevance and meaning for our own times and places. The true value of Scripture is that words written thousands of years ago can indeed, inspire, instruct, and transform us if we let go of modern notions and categories and surrender ourselves to the timeless truth that it brings to us.

Along with applying sound hermeneutical and exegetical principles to Scripture, we need to be clear in our understanding of what science is and how it necessarily differs from religion. Science subscribes to the methodologies of empiricism, which basically means that truth claims must be verifiable. Scientific truth is not a matter of getting the most votes or winning a debate. It's all about evidence. And science does not stand still—consider the shifts from Newtonian physics to the work of Einstein and quantum theory, and on into wherever this body of knowledge is headed next. It often discovers new evidence that refutes older evidence. In that respect, science is self-correcting. I've heard some Christians suggest that some kind of scientific conspiracy is afoot to take down the Bible and undermine religious faith. Such thinking betrays a woefully inadequate understanding of both science and scientists. Francis Collins describes scientists thusly, "One of the most cherished hopes of a scientist is to make an observation that shakes up a field of research. Scientists have a streak of closeted anarchism, hoping that someday they will turn up some unexpected fact that will force a disruption of the framework of the day. That's what Nobel Prizes are given for. In that regard, any assumption that a conspiracy could exist among scientists to keep a widely current theory alive when it actually contains serious flaws is completely antithetical to the restless mind-set of the profession."[256]

So, if scientists are empirical "anarchists," how does their work relate to the world of religion and the language of faith? Sir John C. Polkinghorne is an English theoretical physicist, theologian, writer, and Anglican priest. He served as Professor of Mathematical Physics at Cambridge University for eleven years, after which he resigned his professorial chair to study for the priesthood. He was knighted in 1997. Polkinghorne walks in both the world of science and religion. He suggests that "One could summarize the difference between science and religion by saying that they are asking different questions about the nature of reality. Science is concerned with the question, How?—by what process do things happen? Theology is concerned with the question, Why?—is there a meaning and purpose behind what is happening?"[257] Francis Collins contends that "Science's domain is to explore nature. God's domain is in the spiritual world, a realm not possible to explore with the tools and language of science. It must be examined with the heart, the mind, and the soul—and the mind must find a way to embrace both realms."[258] In his book, *The Great Partnership: God, Science and the Search for Meaning*, Rabbi Jonathan Sacks reiterates that "science takes things apart to see how they work, but religion puts things together to see what they mean."[259]

I once had a rather extraordinary student in my introductory theology course. He sat all by himself in the front row, a mere six feet or so from my lectern. He never once took a note in class, yet he made very high grades on every exam. He also claimed he was an atheist, which was fairly surprising at a Christian liberal arts college. One day he asked me if science threatened me as a Christian.

"Not at all," I said, "as long they do science and refrain from becoming philosophers or theologians."

I told him (along with the rest of the class) that I was quite happy to cheer on my scientific colleagues doing whatever they do in their labs, but that I would have issues with them if they began to detour away from empirical claims and try to assert "truths" that cannot be empirically verified. As long as scientists practice real science, I say, "Have at it." But leave the metaphysical questions to philosophers and theologians, because that's what we do best. As Collins reminds us, "Science is powerless to answer questions such as 'Why did the universe come into being?' 'What is the meaning of human existence?' 'What happens after we die?'"[260]

This essential epistemological boundary between science and religion must be observed. We need not try to make empirical claims based on ancient texts that have little or no empirical interests. On the other hand, science must refrain from making metaphysical claims that are outside the purview of empirical methodology. At the end of the day, I ardently believe that it is simply wrong to assume that church and science are mortal enemies. Although a controversy-seeking media often paints them as such, the chasm between them is, in today's parlance, "fake news." Science is typically portrayed as challenging religion, while religion is portrayed as defensive and reactionary. Both are exaggerations of how things truly are. The real tragedy here is that the deleterious consequences of this conflict are borne, virtually unilaterally, by the church. Mark Knoll argues that,

> Creationism at root is a religion. It has become politics because of the overweening metaphysical pretensions of elitist pundits exploiting the "prestige" of science. But it is only marginally a way of studying the world. In their enthusiasm for reading the world in light of Scripture, evangelicals forget the proposition that the Western world's early modern scientists had so successfully taken to heart as a product of their own deep Christian convictions—to understand something, one must look at that something.
>
> The result is a twofold tragedy. First, millions of evangelicals think they are defending the bible by defending creation science, but in reality they are giving ultimate authority to the merely temporal, situated, and contextualized interpretations of the Bible that arose from the mania for science in the early nineteenth century. Second, with that predisposition, evangelicals lost the ability to look at nature as it was and so lost out on the opportunity to understand more about nature as it is. By holding on so determinedly to our beliefs concerning how we concluded God had made nature, we evangelicals forfeited the opportunity to glorify God for the way he had made nature. In a mirror reaction to the zealous secularists of the twentieth century, evangelicals have gone back to thinking that we must shut up one of God's books if we want to read the other one.[261]

As has been said often, God has given humankind two books—the book of Scripture and the book of creation—and we need to read both of them. Far too many evangelical Christians fail to grasp that God's two books are actually complementary if only we have the willingness to read them both.

SCIENCE AS THE ALLY OF FAITH

Once we cease picking fights with science and accept the fact that scientists are in the "truth" business, it becomes possible to see science as an ally of faith rather than its mortal enemy. Despite my limited knowledge of science, I have found it reassuring to read the work of scientists who are also men and women of great faith. Their effort to merge the findings of science with theological understandings is remarkably helpful. When we accept that science is investigating a genuine part of God's revelation, we can take encouragement from inquiries and discoveries, rather than constructing arguments to counter them. For example, John Polkinghorne explains creation from the perspective of a scientist who also understands the theological ramifications of such claims.

> The universe started in an extremely simple way. Following the big bang it was just an expanding ball of energy. Now, after 13.7 billion years, it is rich and complex, the home of saints and scientists. This fact in itself might suggest something significant has been going on in cosmic history. But there is much more to say. As we have come to understand many of the processes by which this great fertility has come about, we have come to see that their possibility had to be built into the given physical fabric of the world from the start. The laws of physics (which science assumes but does not explain) had to take a very precise "finely tuned" form if anything as complex as carbon-based life was to be possible. For example, the only place in the universe where carbon is made is in the nuclear furnaces of the stars. Every atom of carbon in our bodies was once inside a star—we are literally people of stardust. The process by which this happens is delicate, and if the laws of nuclear physics had been even a little bit different, there would have been no carbon, and thus no you and me. Many more examples of such fine tuning have been identified. What are we to make of them? It would be far too intellectually lazy just to say it was all a happy accident. So remarkable a fact surely calls for an adequate explanation. Some scientists have suggested that there are trillions of different universes, all different and all separate from one another. If there were such a vast multiverse, then maybe one of those universes might by chance be suitable for carbon-based life—a kind of winning ticket in a multiversal lottery, you might say—and that, of course, would be ours since we are carbon-based life. Such a prodigal suggestion is not science, since we have no knowledge of, or access to, any universe other than our own. The mulitverse is a metaphysical guess. A much more economic suggestion is that there is only one universe that is the way it is, in its fine-tuned fruitfulness, precisely because it is not just "any old world" but a creation endowed by its Creator with the potentialities that have given it so remarkable a history.[262]

What I love about Polkinghorne's statement is that he gives the straight scientific facts but he also fully understands the inherent limitations of science when it comes to making metaphysical claims. Science can't really explain the "fine-tuning" that makes life possible. Polkinghorne goes on to quote the work of a British colleague who said that "the accuracy of just one of [the life enabling] parameters is comparable to getting the mix of flour and sugar right to within one grain of sugar in a cake ten times the mass of the sun."[263] The requirement of that kind of accuracy is mind-boggling. Our "finely-tuned" universe defies the capacity of science to fully explain it. Even Steven Hawking, in his book *A Brief History of Time*, admitted that "the odds against a universe like ours emerging out of something like the Big Bang are enormous. I think there are clearly religious implications. It would be very difficult to explain why the universe should have begun this way, except as the act of a God who intended to create beings like us."[264] Hawking suggests that the multiverse hypothesis is really the only way to get around the implication that our universe has been fine-tuned.[265] Awe and wonder would be much more suitable responses than a sense of being under threat, when it comes to what science is trying to tell us about the antiquity of the universe and the earth. Ironically, at least some scientists have been trying to tell us this for a good while. As far back as the 1950s, a Cambridge University astronomer named Fred Hoyle became enthralled with the precision of the energy matchup in the universe. He claimed, "A commonsense interpretation of the facts suggests that a super-intellect has monkeyed with physics as well as with chemistry and biology, and that there are no blind forces worth speaking about in nature."[266] Gibberson and Collins contend that any change made to "gravity by even a tiny fraction of a percent—enough so that you would be, say, one billionth of a gram heavier or lighter when you get on the bathroom scale—the universe becomes so different that there are no stars, galaxies or planets. And no planets implies no life."[267] All this fine-tuning strongly suggests that our universe is "curiously bio-friendly."[268] So, science is able to tell us with remarkable clarity just how improbable our universe is, but cannot tell us why, apart from either speculating about "multiverses" and infinitesimal matters of chance, or turning to theologians and philosophers who can actually address the "why."

In my limited reading of scientific materials, I stumbled onto a couple of other items which I found most interesting from a theological perspective. On January 11, 2013, the discovery of the "Large Quasar Group" (LQG) was announced by the University of Central Lancashire in the U.K. The LQG was heralded as the largest known structure in the universe by far. It comprises seventy-three quasars with a minimum diameter of 1.4 billion light years, but spanning over four billion light years at its widest point. The existence of structures of the magnitude of large quasar clusters was believed theoretically impossible. Cosmological structures had been believed to have a size limit of approximately 1.2 billion light-years.[269] If you recall that a "light year" is the distance that light, traveling at a speed of just under 300,000 kilometers per second, would cover in a year's time, it's dizzying to contemplate a structure so immense. Four billion light years to traverse it! But evidently, this universe is significantly larger than we thought! In the eighth Psalm we read these words: "When I consider your heavens, the work of your fingers, the moon and the stars, which you have set in place, what is humankind that you are mindful of them, human beings that you care for them?" (Psalm 8: 3–4) The unbelievable vastness of creation, as verified to us by the world of science, causes us to catch our breath and bow our heads as we attempt to get our minds around the magnitude of what God has created.

I also read about what is called "The Circumstellar Habitable Zone" (CHZ), sometimes referred to as the "Goldilocks Zone" because it is neither too hot nor too cold for life to be at least theoretically possible. On November 4, 2013, Kepler Space Data reported that there could be as many as 40 billion earth-like planets in this galaxy alone![270] Even apart from all the resulting speculation about *what* might be out there—the "We told you so" comments from *Star Trek* and *Star Wars* fanatics—we are again staggered at the magnitude of God's creation. And, without inferring anything or attempting explanation, I recall Jesus' words in John 14:2, "In my Father's house, there are many rooms."

FINDING COMMON GROUND

In the musical *Oklahoma* there's a song called "The Farmer and the Cowman Should Be Friends." The chorus advises, "territory folk should stick together," reminding all "Okies" that their futures are inextricably bound up together, so they might as well figure out how to get along. Christians and scientists should be friends because whether they like it or not, they are on this earth together, and as I've tried to show, their mutual interests actually overlap in more ways than they have commonly imagined. This is not to say that there are no speed bumps in such a friendship. Christians are justifiably suspicious of some of the more grandiose claims of science where some (not all) scientists seem to ascribe omnipotence to natural science with a corresponding denigration of all other forms of knowledge as inferior by comparison. This is what is known as "scientism," and it promises way more than it can deliver. We must rightly keep in mind the parameters of empirical method and be prepared to remind scientists of the limitations of pure rationality and of their fields' boundaries with regard to metaphysics. David Bosch wrote that "The problem with scientism is that it fetters human thought as cruelly as any authoritarian belief system has ever done, that it 'offers no scope for our most vital beliefs and . . . forces us to disguise them in farcically inadequate terms' (Polanyi)."[271] So, our friendship with science must be one of *mutual* respect and understanding. Currently, I find that the interface of science and the Christian concern for earth stewardship presents us with an almost ideal platform for modeling common ground. The confluence of climate science and a growing and committed sense of creation-care on the part of many contemporary Christians holds the promise of demonstrating what a true partnership between faith and science might entail.

I've never quite understood the widespread suspicion that evangelical Christians have towards ecological concerns. It just doesn't make any sense to me at all. I'm well aware of how certain theological ideas seem to permit, if not encourage, an attitude of indifference towards the creation. If we believe that our destiny is to escape this earth and spend eternity in a place we commonly call "heaven," then it's easy to see why some might not be all that invested in creation stewardship. N.T. Wright is correct, "Why wallpaper the house if it's going to be knocked down tomorrow?"[272] The problem is that this is hardly a sound interpretation of what the Bible is trying to tell us about our destiny. That humans have been assigned stewardship of the earth is, biblically speaking, undebatable (Genesis 2:15), so to plunder and trash the earth is a fundamental failure to accept our reason for being here in the first place. As Wright reminds us, "to deny a Christian passion for ecological work, for putting the world to rights insofar as we can right now, is to deny either the goodness of creation or the power of God in the resurrection and the Spirit, and quite possibly both."[273] But denial has indeed become the "weapon of choice" for those who prefer to exploit the earth for economic gain, no matter how short-sighted a strategy that is. The fact that so many conservative Christians trumpet their reverence for Scripture, while at the same time resisting the truth about the ecological crisis that is upon us, is positively puzzling. As Charles Eisenstein put it, "Socialism failed because it couldn't tell the economic truth; capitalism may fail because it couldn't tell the ecological truth."[274] In a February 3, 2020 article prepared for the Australian Broadcast Company (ABC), Zoology professor Michael Clarke wrote,

> In the midst of unprecedented bushfires in Australia in the early weeks of 2020, Australian " Liberal" (think: conservative) politician and former Prime Minister, Tony Abbot criticized scientists for getting "religious" by arguing that there are links between global emissions, record-breaking drought, mega-fires and climate change. This was closely followed by Donald Trump, speaking in Davos, Switzerland, chastising scientists for being "perennial prophets of doom" who should, instead put their faith in technology to solve the big problems.

> The broad consensus among climate scientists is that humans have poured out so many pollutants into the atmosphere that we are now on the verge of altering the planet's climate irreversibly. While the current bushfires may be unprecedented, no one should be claiming they were unexpected. Climate and fire scientists have been warning for years that the catastrophes we are enduring would become more frequent due to climate change. To reject the warnings of scientists about the dangers of inaction while at the same time admonishing us to put our faith into technological fixes (developed by other scientists) is irresponsible.[275]

I think that it is high time for Christians to seriously get "religious" about climate change by revisiting and actually understanding what the Bible would say to us about it. In his *Systematic Theology (Vol. II)*, Robert Jensen says that Genesis' creation story makes it clear that human beings are *gardeners* of someone else's garden. "We are to *tend* our area of creation on behalf of the Creator to whom it continues to belong, taking our own subsistence from his generosity."[276] Contrary to what many Christians seem to believe, this earth and material creation is not some temporary detour from our heavenly home. This earth is the *very good* abode created by God. Creation is not "some icky, regrettable mistake on God's part. It is the product of his *love*."[277]

Earlier this year, I attended a campus lecture by Ellen Davis, Professor of Bible and Practical Theology at Duke Divinity School. Her lecture was entitled "The Bible, Earth & Our Imagination." She called our attention to the fact that Genesis 2:7 tells us that the Lord God formed Adam (Hebrew for humankind) from the fertile soil (Hebrew: Adamah) of the ground and breathed into his nostrils the breath of life. This is how man became a living being. Dr. Davis stressed that the Bible is telling us that we are attached to the land. We are from "fertile soil," literally from the earth. Humans come from humus. "Remember that you are dust, and to dust you shall return" (Genesis 3:19). She went on to show how the land is included in the covenant that God makes with humankind. In Leviticus 26:42 God promises, "I will remember my covenant with Jacob and my covenant with Isaac and my covenant with Abraham, and I will remember the land." The order here goes backwards in time. The land comes first. The land gave us life and thus deserves our respect. She encouraged us to read the Bible "through agrarian eyes." The soil of Israel has crucial significance here, since the topsoil (the fertile soil) there is very thin. Jesus himself invoked this image in his teachings in Mark 4 and elsewhere. At minimum, our callous disregard for the earth works against our best interests as a species, and at worst, it is an egregious sort of sin against the Creator.

It seems to me that we have arrived at a point of no return on this issue. If what the climate scientists are telling us is true, we have little or no margin for error. We are on the cusp of a Faustian bargain that makes short-term economic gain our primary goal and kicks the ecological can down the road, leaving it to our children and grandchildren to reckon with. We are rolling the dice between now and the future. Charles Eisenstein graphically illustrates our dilemma:

> Imagine you are President of the World and receive the following offer from the aliens Supreme Leader: "A sustainable gross world product (GWP) is $10 trillion a year. We would like to make you an offer: $600 trillion for the entire earth. True, we plan to extract all of its resources, destroy the topsoil, poison the oceans, turn the forest into deserts, and use it as a radioactive dump. But think of it—$600 trillion! You'll all be rich!" Of course you would say no, but collectively today we are essentially saying yes to this offer. We are carrying out the alien's plan to a tee, making over the next ten years perhaps $600 trillion (current GWP is $60 trillion a year). Through a million little choices every day, we are cashing in the earth.[278]

Is this kind of bargain at all viable to us as Christians? Why have we been so silent in the face of a continual assault upon our waterways, air and topsoil by monied interests whose primary concern is short-term profit? We rise up indignantly over anything that we think threatens our freedom of religion, yet we sit silently by as the freedom to live in a healthy world is virtually stolen away from us by people who worship money. Are we this unconcerned about the future lives of our children and grandchildren? Is it possible, that the American church has become so acclimatized to the "American dream" that we are blind to what a nightmare it could easily become, if it hasn't already?

Some years ago a faculty colleague told me that no student was truly educated if she did not grasp "the tragedy of the commons." This phrase applies to the well-known sociological phenomenon wherein individual users of a shared-resource system, acting independently according to their own self-interests, behave contrary to the common good of all users by depleting or spoiling the shared resources. So, when certain industries pollute Flint, Michigan's water systems—shared resources that provide drinking water to the people—we see the tragedy of the commons. Charles Eisenstein is correct when he says that it may well be that *the* essential purpose of government is to serve as the trustee of the commons. And he adds that "the commons includes the surface of the earth, the minerals under the earth, the water on and under the ground, the richness of the soil, the electromagnetic spectrum, the planetary genome, the biota of local and global ecosystems, the atmosphere, the centuries-long accumulation of human knowledge and technology, and the artistic, musical, and literary treasures of our ancestors."[279] How could it possibly be all right for corporations, or even governments, to make decisions that adversely affect the lives of people in the way that the handling of water supply issues in Flint has? Why is it permissible to violate treaties and run oil pipelines through the sacred lands of our indigenous peoples? Why is it considered business as usual for energy companies to be heavily subsidized by the government even while they turn huge annual profits and are among the worst polluters of our air? Is this the bargain we are prepared to make? We must listen carefully and soberly to Eisenstein's prophetic words: "When every forest has been converted into board feet, when every ecosystem has been paved over, when every human relationship has been replaced by a service, the very processes of planetary and social life will cease. All that will be left is cold, dead money, as forewarned by the myth of King Midas so many centuries ago. We will be dead—but very, very rich."[280] Rather than sitting out the environmental crisis, awaiting the rapture, the church must embrace its stewardship of creation in a way that both honors its biblical vocation and takes the findings of science seriously. The church must insist that stewardship is about much more than money, it is about our relationship to the earth. The church can adopt practices that model creation care by the way it uses resources and serves the eco-concerns of its local communities. And the church must recover its prophetic voice to speak out against the idols of rampant consumerism, and all modern gods that devour and poison God's good earth.[281]

The thing that the church must not do is to fall into some false hope that science will stumble onto some grand ecological solution that will save the day. I have endeavored to show my deep appreciation for science and the people who dedicate their lives to it; however, I always want to remember that while scientific technology gave us penicillin, computers, and microwave popcorn, it also gave us Hiroshima, acid rain, and Texas-sized islands of plastic in the ocean. Science alone is not the answer. We must not forget this. In his book, *Why Liberalism Failed*, Patrick Deneen writes,

> As the farmer and author Wendell Berry has written, if modern science and technology were conceived as a "war against nature," then, "it is a war in every sense—nature is fighting us as much as we are fighting it. And . . . it appears that we are losing." Many elements of what we today call our environmental crisis—climate change, resource depletion, ground water contamination and

scarcity, species extinction—are signs of battles won but a war being lost. Today we are accustomed to arguing that we should follow science in an issue such as climate change, ignoring that our crisis is the result of long-standing triumphs of science and technology in which "following science" was tantamount to civilizational progress. Our carbon-saturated world is the hangover of a 150 year old party in which until the very end, we believed we achieved the dream of liberation from nature's constraints. We still hold the incoherent view that science can liberate us from limits while solving the attendant consequences of that project.[282]

I've been wondering if we could put creation stewardship into a Pascal's-wager form. If we were to adopt sound ecological practices and discover years from now that the predicted planetary disaster would never have happened anyway, what would be lost? Some forms of work and industry, I suppose, although the adoption of clean energy, for example, seems not to cost jobs but to hold the promise of replacing old ones with new ones. At worst we might have adopted, unnecessarily, some lifestyle changes that we found inconvenient. On the other hand, if we ignore climate science and do nothing, and the dire predictions for our world begin to come true, I shudder to imagine the pain and suffering, especially for those who can least afford to bear it. And, in truth, there is some question about whether it actually *can* be endured.

I don't know what it will require to get American Christians to take their vocational stewardship seriously. But I hope and pray that the church will find its voice and call its people to honor our Creator by loving God's good world. In Romans 8, Paul considers that our present sufferings are not worth comparing with the glory that will be revealed in us (vs. 18). I suppose that most people read those words and immediately think of the glories of heavenly life. But Paul is very "earthbound" in this text. He reminds us of the stake that the entire creation has in the revealing of God's children (vs. 19). And then he tells us that the creation, subjected to frustration by choices not its own, awaits its liberation from bondage and decay so that it, too, can experience the freedom and glory of God's thoroughly redeemed world. Paul presents the image of a pregnant woman who eagerly anticipates welcoming her child to help us grasp how ardently God's world longs to be liberated. Liberators! That's what we are called to be. And that liberation is not some far-off future assignment. It is part and parcel of our purpose on earth from this moment on.

Chapter 9

Too Wounded to Heal[283]

> GOD BLESS THE WHOLE WORLD: NO EXCEPTIONS. Nothing sucks more than to realize that for many people, church is the place where they've learned who they should reject, and feel righteous doing so. As Anne Lamott has said, "you can safely assume you've created God in your own image when it turns out that God hates all the same people you do." . . . . The church's first calling is to announce the good news—that news that you are loved in spite of everything, in spite of the crap you and everyone else have done or left undone. The church fails to deliver this good news every day, and it rips my heart into jigsaw pieces. But frustration is no excuse for allowing such absurd failure to continue.
>
> —Jacqueline Bussie[284]

Author Henri Nouwen popularized the phrase "wounded healer"[285] as descriptive of the type of Christian most enabled for a ministry of empathy and true compassion. And he's right: all of us are "wounded" in some sense or another, and embracing our brokenness allows us to be authentic in our service to God and others. So it follows that the church is a collection of wounded healers. What else could it be? As Eugene Peterson used to say, "The church is a community of sinners, and one of those sinners is called pastor." We do, in fact, have this treasure in earthen vessels (2 Cor. 4:7). The church is a community of redeemed sinners at various points on a journey towards wholeness. And, in the sufficiencies of God's grace, this gathering of wounded, broken people—earthen vessels—can become a community of healing and hope.

The image of "wounded healer" is not only truthful, it is reassuring. Portraying the church as some idyllic family where everyone has their act together isn't likely to be taken at all seriously by our reality-TV culture. But the wounded healer metaphor also comes with a possible downside. We are reassured when our health-care providers are empathetic to various frailties and maladies, but we don't want to entrust ourselves to someone whose health is in worse shape than ours! No one willingly goes to a doctor they believe to be sicker than they are!

Given the image of the church as "wounded healer," we might then ask, "could the church be perceived as being too wounded to heal?" Could there be those who view the church as so impaired that the idea of it being it a healthy, whole community is beyond credulity? This appears to be the case if we listen to the words of some of the church's critics. And while it may be that such critiques originate from experiences or prejudices that lurk in the complicated recesses of modern culture, we can't simply dismiss such ideas as invalid perceptions. Remember, "That which is perceived *as* real, *is* real in its consequences." So even though a church filled with broken people can be a positive influence on society, growing numbers of people, particularly millennials and younger, look at the church these days and respond with the proverbial challenge, "Physician, heal yourself!" Such skepticism is rife among the "nones," the growing numbers of Americans who claim no religious affiliations, and I think that skepticism can be traced at least in part to the church's perceived attention, or inattention, to specific issues. None of these issues are new, but they keep popping up and reminding us that they are unresolved.

In her book *The Mystic Way of Evangelism*,[286] Elaine Heath describes the contemporary church using the phrase "the church in the night." By this, she refers to the church being thrust onto the margins of the culture with the disappearance of the "home field advantage" that "Christendom" often provided. Foremost among the daunting challenges faced by today's "post-Christendom" church as it pursues its mission in the world are what Heath describes as "the three great wounds of the church," racism, sexism, and classism. I believe that these three "wounds" present virtually insurmountable barriers to large numbers of people who can't find their way into the church. Heath contends that the American church has lost much of its credibility because women and people of diverse ethnicity are senators, physicians, lawyers, and professors in the wider culture, but they remain segregated, silenced, excluded, and invisible in the church. The consequence of this reality is a widespread and growing skepticism towards the church. For all the talk these days about the evangelical church being "missional," its inability to actually embody anything like its "healing community" ideal creates the sort of fundamental contradiction that becomes too much for the culture to accept. In Heath's words, "There is no greater challenge to the church in the night than to relinquish its idolatrous and syncretistic attachment to sexism, racism, and classism, for this trio of evil ideologies has been embedded in the American church from the time Christianity made its way across the Atlantic with the first explorers."[287] This is a provocative, yet fundamentally true claim. The essential truth is that racism, sexism, and classism can be found lurking in the evangelical churches of our day and time, and if we desire to be taken seriously by an ever more skeptical culture, the church must find some way to address these three visibly persistent contradictions, whatever gaps there might be between "real" and "perceived." The alternative is a church too wounded to heal.

THE MATTER OF BLACK LIVES

The virus of racism has always been there in the church, long before and long after Martin Luter King Jr's observation about Sunday morning eleven o'clock being the most segregated hour in American life. At times it has lurked below the surface, sporadically revealed by events in the culture or in the church itself. In recent times Ferguson, Charleston, Charlottesville, and now, "I can't breathe" have blown America's race problem into the open. It can't be ignored. Anyone who claims that the American church is free of this festering wound has never tried to have a conversation about white privilege in a predominantly white congregation. Barack Obama's election made it far too easy and convenient for some in the white church to assume that race was no longer a big deal. As one black author put it, "Barack Obama governs a nation enlightened enough to send an African-American to the White House, but not enlightened enough to accept a black man as its president."[288] Charlottesville and its aftermath demonstrated that the country had a long way yet to go in its response to racism. White supremacy is real, and it serves as a powerful and painful reminder of the white church's capacity to be in denial or to cluelessly insist that racism doesn't affect them personally.

As an editor at *The Christian Century* observed recently, "Never have I ever looked myself in the mirror and said, 'I'm white.'" To which he concluded, "we don't consider 'white' a race. We consider 'white' normal." I remember the first time I saw an African-American person wearing a shirt that said, "It's a Black thing, you wouldn't understand." To be honest, it annoyed me until I began to grasp what David Gushee calls the "epistemological privilege of the oppressed." Gushee says that this means that people of color understand the realities of racial bias and injustice a whole lot better than white people do. "They see it more clearly because their sense of moral well-being and self-worth does not require them to lie to themselves about what is really going on."[289] This is what the white Christians who counter "Black Lives Matter" with signs reading "All Lives Matter" can't quite comprehend. When has there *ever* been a time when white lives didn't matter? In America, white lives have *always* mattered. With regard to "All Lives Matter," John Seed wrote, "Black people perceive such statements as a form of aggression. They see it this way because such words completely discount Black history and the existential day-to-day reality of Black communities."[290]

Without a doubt, the best student I ever had in twenty years of teaching preaching was a young African-American man from Chicago. He was amazingly gifted for Christian ministry and even had a singing voice of professional quality. A few weeks following his graduation, he was driving through western New York on his way to graduate school in Boston, so we met one July morning at an area restaurant for breakfast. I could barely disguise my unease in the wake of the "innocent" verdict handed down the day before in the shooting death of Trayvon Martin. The white man who shot him claimed self-defense, which I found ludicrous given the details of the shooting. I looked across the table at my gifted friend and tried to express my sorrow and anguish at such a travesty. He looked at me and said that he wasn't at all surprised by the verdict; it was what the African-American community had come to expect in America.

He then told me about his mother giving him "the talk" as he prepared to drive from Chicago to New York and then on to Massachusetts. I was both outraged and ashamed as I listened to him tell me the strict instructions his mother gave him about how to conduct himself should he be stopped by a police officer. Saying such things to my son never ever occurred to me for the simple reason that we were white! As I watch, horrified, at the ongoing murders of young black men in this country under questionable circumstances, I am unwilling to bear the tired litany of excuses offered by a privileged white community, particularly when that community claims to be "Christian." Even this very day as I write these words, I am confronted with the latest public murder of a black man in Minnesota, who died with a policeman's knee on his neck. Lord have mercy! Gary Dorrien was absolutely right when he said that "White racism has been the rocket fuel . . . of every form of authoritarian nationalism to gain power in the past century, and it still is."[291] Let evangelicalism's "81 percent" take careful note of that!

If the Charlottesville debacle revealed anything, it revealed the breadth and depth to which racist attitudes persist, yes, even in the church. The majority of those men who marched at Charlottesville were likely "Christian" in one sense or another. In the aftermath of that sad moment in our history, many of the participants were identified due to the proliferation of cell-phone cameras and social media. They cried "Foul!" and tried to claim "this is not who we are!" The painful truth is that, yes it is! It's exactly who we are! Those men who marched are the sort of people who have been produced by our nation, our culture, and sadly, in many cases, by our churches. In his article, "White Supremacy Versus the Gospel in Charlottesville," David Potter noted that, "Many surprised observations have been made that the demonstrators were students and professionals, largely undifferentiated from the hypothetical young white man living next door, or sitting in a pew on Sunday morning. The desire to project the problem of white supremacy onto the recesses of society is simply too convenient. The same air these angry extremists are breathing also exists in my lungs."[292] Potter goes on to pose this question: "How long could a polo-shirt wearing, tiki torch bearing, white nationalist attend your evangelical church before hearing something from the pulpit that would contradict his worldview?"[293] How long, indeed?

The typical white evangelical Christian seems woefully uninformed as to the patent inequality that continues to shadow the lives of our minority populations. According to Harvard sociologist Devah Pager, "Between 1983 and 1997, the number of African-Americans admitted to prison for drug offenses increased more than twenty-six fold, relative to a sevenfold increase for whites . . . By 2001, there were more than twice as many African-Americans as whites in state prison for drug offenses."[294] "African-Americans typically raise their children to protect themselves against a presumed hostility from white teachers, white police officers, white supervisors, and white co-workers."[295]

For a while I had the opportunity to teach seminary classes in which the majority of my students were African-American pastors. Man, did I get an education! Like most white people, I didn't know what I didn't know. As I read their papers chronicling the daily struggles of the African-American community, I almost despaired of any remediating steps that might bring about real change. Listening to their words in class, how weighted they were with frustration and sadness, evoked in me a profound sense of embarrassment and horror on behalf of my race's complicity in their circumstances. But hope was renewed as I observed the incredible fortitude, faithfulness, and amazing graciousness of these men and women. America's black churches epitomize the "city set on a hill."

Unfortunately, racism appears to be more overt in the recent days since the election of Donald Trump. In his study of the 2016 election, political scientist Philip Klinker found that "the most predictive question for understanding whether a voter favored Hilary Clinton or Donald Trump was, 'Is Barack Obama a Muslim?'"[296] Honestly, I do not want to believe that, and yet I can't legitimately question Klinker's findings. *Mother Jones* magazine found, based on pre-election polling data, that "if you only tallied the popular vote of 'white America' to derive the 2016 electoral votes, Trump would defeat Clinton 389 to 81, with the remaining 68 votes either a 'toss-up' or unknown."[297] Trump promised to "Make America Great Again," sounding the call to white Americans to return to simpler, better days. But, as Michael Eric Dyson reminds us, "the golden age of the past is a fiction, a projection of nostalgia that selects what is most comforting to remember. It summons a past that was not great for all; in fact, it is a past that was not great at all, not with racism and sexism clouding the culture. Going back to a time that was great depends on deliberate disremembering. One of the great perks of being white in America is to forget at will."[298] Forgetting the past is not a luxury afforded to people of color in America. The late African-American theologian James Cone grew up in rural Arkansas in those days that so many white people remember as days of America's "greatness." Cone tells a different story.

> As a child, I remember worrying about my father when he did not come home from work at the usual time in the evening. My brothers and I would watch anxiously out the window, hoping that the lights from every vehicle would be the lights from his pick-up truck. My mother worried too, but she tried to assure us that "God would protect Daddy from any harm that whites could do to him," and that he would arrive home soon. I wanted to believe that, but I had heard too much about white people killing black people to believe what she said without deep questioning. When my father would finally make it home safely, I would run and jump into his arms, happy as I could be. For that moment, at least, my faith was renewed.[299]

Those words break my heart every time I read them. Moreover, the fact that so many white evangelical Christians seem unconcerned about the racial hate that has been accelerated by the most recent presidential election causes me to wonder whether Donald Trump's presidency was largely the result of white supremacy. That statement is sure to evoke a quick and passionate rebuttal by some, but the fact remains that, right now, there's not a great deal for people of color to celebrate, and the uneasy silence of so many white churches and white pastors creates a huge stone in the shoe of a growing number of American Christians. In his excellent book, *Johnny Cash and the Great American Contradiction*, Rodney Clapp says that, "The United States is without doubt a great actor in and on world history, but nothing holds it back from becoming a democracy for grownups so much as the myth of innocence . . . American innocence with its plenitude of dangerous and infantilizing effects, can be maintained only by forgetting American history from its very inception. There was no golden age of absolute innocence; slavery and racism cannot be recognized as minor (and so now negligible) subplots in the American story. African Americans, slaves in the land of the free, incarnated America's deepest contradiction."[300] Forgoing America's "myth of innocence" requires much more than simply accepting a slightly altered understanding of our history. It means fully coming to grips with the truth, as Jim Wallis put it, that, "The United States of America was established as a white society, founded upon the genocide of another race and then the enslavement of yet another."[301] If the evangelical church in America has any designs on being the kind of healing community God intends it to be, it must speak out and act out against America's original sin and its deepest contradiction.

SUPPORTING THE SISTERS

I learned about gender equality by virtue of my environment. I had six older sisters and one younger one who is the toughest of them all! My sisters taught me they were not to be trifled with, that any of my juvenile chauvinisms were out of bounds, and I'm all the better for it. Beyond that, I grew up in a small holiness church in the Midwest where women pastors were fairly commonplace. In fact, one of my earliest ministerial models was an ordained woman. So I freely admit that I come to this particular wound with nowhere near the anecdotal "skin in the game" that others might bring. The idea of gender equality and women in ministry has never seemed that big of a reach for me. But because I have spent much of my life as a ministerial educator, I have often witnessed firsthand the pain of young women, clearly dealing with calls to ministry, who sit in my office wondering if they can endure the kind of gender bias that seems to come with the territory. They have been blocked and discouraged, often foremost and ironically, by the very churches that have nurtured and discipled them. I heard many stories that were distressingly similar in how these women were gently patronized and steered towards non-ordained forms of ministry. In some cases, colleagues and I were able to convince these young women to persevere and see the process through, waiting to see what doors God might open for them. In other cases, I watched gifted women walk away sorrowfully from their vocational callings. I can say without hesitation, that by and large, the best ministerial students my department produced on an annual basis were women. The fact that so many of them faced a lifetime of barriers and resistance was and is a source of great sadness for me.

Of course, the problem of sexism goes far beyond issues surrounding the ordination of women. Many very real glass ceilings impede and prevent the advancement of women—disparities in income and in access to adequate health care are but two of the ways this particular "wound" continues to hamper women in the modern world. That such biases also flourish in the church makes this issue doubly problematic. Elaine Heath suggests that "patriarchy is the first systemic evil found in the Bible, emerging from original wounds."[302] That statement might be incendiary to some, but if you want to understand why growing numbers of young people do not see the church as a credible witness to human wholeness, I suggest that you need look no further than the patriarchalism that hovers over so much of the church, like L.A. smog on a hot day. Perhaps it doesn't register with everyone in the church, but today's younger generation is increasingly egalitarian in the way that it views gender roles and relations. Moreover, this wound of sexism has profound implications, not only for the way the church is perceived, but for the actual well-being of women in our world.

I once listened to a TED Talk by former President Jimmy Carter entitled, "Why I believe the mistreatment of women is the number one human rights issue." He claimed that the abuse of women and girls is the most neglected human rights issue on earth and suggested three reasons for the neglect. After citing the misinterpretation of religious writings like the Bible, and then discussing increased injustice towards women embodied in domestic violence, human trafficking, etc., he gave his third reason.

"In general," he said, "men don't give a damn!"

My fear is that he's spot on, and to the extent that this kind of indifference to sexism exists in the church today, well, "Houston, we have a problem."

The defense of sexism inside the church has historically been marked by the all-too-familiar tactic of gathering the texts which seem to support this position and firing away. While taking Scripture seriously clearly matters, yet one more review of biblical texts on this subject is beyond the scope of this book, and frankly, beyond my capacity to endure. Flinging Bible verses at this issue doesn't seem to resolve much, if anything. There are, however, some broad biblical themes that require our attention if the church is to embrace, as I would hope, an egalitarian view towards gender.

First, we must weigh what the creation texts are and are not saying with regards to women and their place in the human hierarchy. While the argument is made that woman's subservience to men is some kind of 'creation mandate," Genesis 3:16 actually views any sort of patriarchy as grounded in the fall and the conflicted relationship it fostered between men and women. Patriarchy is not grounded in creation itself.[303] Further, the account of the creation of woman in Genesis 2 emphasizes the *similarity* of men and women, contrasted against the rest of the animals. "The creation of the woman is not narrated, first of all, as a means for humankind's achieving 'fruitfulness,' but rather as an antidote to the problem of aloneness."[304] Eve is called Adam's "helper," which is a word used to describe God in other Old Testament texts (C.F., Ex. 18:4; Deut. 33:29; Psalm, 10:14, 27:9, 118:7). John Walton concludes that, "through the account in Genesis 2, it is shown that woman is not just another creature but was like the man, in fact, his other half sharing his nature and was therefore suitable as his ally."[305] Yes, the cultures in which the Bible was written were clearly ordered along the lines of patriarchy, but that must not be viewed as normative in terms of God's intentions for humankind. Richard Middleton argues that,

> The Genesis creation account provides a normative basis to critique inter-human injustice or the misuse of power over others, whether in individual cases or in systemic social formations. Specifically, since both male and female are made in God's image with a joint mandate to rule (Gen. 1:27–28), this calls into question the inequities of power between men and women that have arisen in patriarchal social systems and various forms of sexism throughout history. And since the imago Dei is prior to any ethnic, racial, or national divisions (see Gen. 10), this provides an alternative to ethnocentrism, racism, or any form of national superiority; beneath the legitimate diversity of cultures that have developed in the world, people constitute one human family.[306]

Although the kind of "alternative" approach to individual and social formations that Middleton speaks about here is rarely seen in the heavily patriarchal texts of the Old Testament, in the New Testament the narrative clearly shifts. Nowhere is this more evident than in the gospels where Jesus' relationship with women is breathtakingly revolutionary. It is unfortunate that so many Christians fail to grasp just how revolutionary Jesus' interactions with women truly were, given the social norms and practices of that day and time. N.T. Wright says that the fact that women are the first to see the risen Jesus, the first to be entrusted with the news that he has been raised from the dead, is of "incalculable significance. Mary Magdalene and the others are apostles to the apostles."[307] Wright also cites as particularly important, the episode of Jesus' visit to the house of Mary and Martha as completely overturning the social conventions of that day.

> Far more obvious to any first-century reader, and to many readers in Turkey, the Middle East, and many other parts of the world to this day, would be the fact that Mary was sitting at Jesus's feet in the male part of the house rather than being kept in the back rooms with the other women. This, I am pretty sure, is what really bothered Martha; no doubt she was cross at being left to do all the work, but the real problem behind that was that Mary had cut clean across one of the most basic social conventions.... We have our own clear but unstated rules about whose space is which. So did they, and Mary has just flouted them. And Jesus declares that she is right to do so. She "sat at the master's feet," a phrase that doesn't mean what it would mean today—the adoring student gazing up in admiration and love at the wonderful teacher. As is clear from the use of the phrase elsewhere in the New Testament (for instance, Paul with Gamaliel), to sit at the teacher's feet is a way of saying you are being a student and picking up the teacher's wisdom and learning; in that very practical world, you wouldn't do this just for the sake of informing your own mind and heart, but in order to become yourself a teacher, a rabbi.[308]

It appears to be the case that Jesus' teachings, along with his personal modeling of a radical new way of relating to women, had a huge impact upon and within the early church. In fact, some of the so-called "problem texts" that seem to prohibit the participation of women in the church are much better understood as the church trying to find its balance in the "new creation" of God's kingdom, which has arrived, yet is still to come in its fullness. The Apostle Paul seems very keen to try to help the church walk a fine line between the revolutionary freedom that the gospel has proclaimed (especially for women) versus the risk of scandalizing the witness of the church in the eyes of its surrounding culture. James Brownson contends that the "New Testament's seemingly patriarchal injunctions can be understood as various attempts to rein in imbalances in the 'already/not yet' tension of New Testament eschatology."[309] He writes, "the church must not assume that it has passed completely from this world into the age to come. It must not . . . assume that the structures of this world are completely done away with. Yet, at the same time, where the life of the age to come can be experienced with peaceableness and harmony, it is to be embraced: women lead, teach, pray, prophesy, host churches, and model a new form of equality that stood markedly apart from the prevailing Greco-Roman culture."[310]

Though the early church had to experience the necessary "growing pains" of finding its way in the regnant culture (and, to be sure, this presented some huge hurdles), it nevertheless, forged a new path in terms of male/female relationships. If the contemporary evangelical church wants to be viewed as a healing community, it must discover the freedom of living eschatologically, or modeling what life in the kingdom of God is fully intended to be. That means it must find its way beyond sexism. Is it too much to hope that the American evangelical church can actually incarnate Paul's vision? "There is neither Jew nor Gentile, neither slave nor free, nor is there male and female, for you are all one in Christ Jesus" (Gal. 3:28). Brother and sister evangelicals, it's time to give a damn.

CLASS DISMISSED

In the second chapter of the Epistle of James, the issue of classism, or as James puts it, "favoritism," is addressed. To James, the humiliation of the poor is evidence of how the church has been polluted by the world. It betrays the misguided idea that the church has the ability, or even the right, to judge the value of others (something James insists is the province of God alone). But beyond all else, James says that this kind of behavior cannot be in any way compatible with faith in "our glorious Lord Jesus Christ." Jesus' complete refusal to adhere to the class distinctions of his day is all we need to know about the unacceptability of class distinctions in the church. But the pressures of a materialistic culture weigh heavily, and they easily subvert the church's message when class becomes an issue in the faith community. Socio-economic factors are the primary determinants of class structure, even more so than race, except in extreme cases. Many white people wouldn't mind if Michael Jordan, Oprah Winfrey, or some other wealthy African-American were their neighbor, but if "lower-class" neighbors were to materialize, there would be difficulties.

Class, by and large, is a matter of wealth or the lack thereof. In America, the richest country in the history of the world, classism is primarily about poverty, and there is an unmistakable link between poverty and justice. The wounds of injustice in America are predominantly the stories of "haves and have-nots." The United States now stands among the worst countries in its "Gini" index, a measure of inequality in the distribution of family income.[311] Gar Alperovitz says that "virtually all the gains of the entire economic system have gone to a tiny, tiny group at the top for at least three decades."[312] He says that "almost fifty million Americans live in officially defined poverty, and the rate is higher now than it was in the 1960's."[313] And, despite the American propensity to wave our finger at the world, claiming our status as number one, Alperovitz details that, "The United States now ranks lowest or close to lowest among advanced "affluent" nations in connection with inequality (21st out of 21), poverty (21st out of 21), life expectancy (21st out of 21), infant mortality (21st out of 21), mental health (18th out of 20), obesity (18th out of 18), public spending on social programs as a percentage of GDP (19th out of 21), maternity leave (21st out of 21), paid annual leave (20th out of 20), the "material well-being of children" (19th out of 21), and overall environmental performance (21st out of 21)."[314] This data is all the more alarming given that a mere four hundred Americans now own more wealth than the entire bottom one hundred and eighty million Americans put together, a degree of wealth concentration that Alperovitz calls "medieval."[315] Something in the system is clearly wrong. Awakening to such inequities should convince the church that the call to social justice is not some liberal scheme to distract the church from the gospel. On the contrary, social justice is at the heart of the gospel. The late missiologist David Bosch said: "Once we recognize the identification of Jesus with the poor, we cannot any longer consider our own relation to the poor as a social ethics question; it is a gospel question. Or, to put it in the words of Nicholas Berdyaev: While the problem of my own bread is a material issue, the problem of my neighbor's bread is a spiritual issue."[316]

As is the case with racism and sexism, grasping the complexities of classism requires some understanding of systemic evil and how easily, even if unwittingly, we become participants in such destructive realities. Like the people in James' illustration, we can easily show favor to the rich, knowingly or unwittingly guided by assumptions that their class has earned them special treatment. We can also point fingers of shame at the poor all around us, finding ways in which they are to blame them for their own circumstances. We may have never considered how stacked the deck is against them, in significant ways. Poverty is not simply the result of making poor choices. It's much more complicated than that. Generally speaking, I have found that American Christians find it far too easy to hurl blanket condemnations at the liberation theologies of Central and South America without ever having taken seriously the kind of class injustice that gave rise to such theologies in the first place. It's far too simplistic to brand the poor as "lazy" or preferring to live off the government, but this kind of outlook allows us to escape more complicated and painful explanations.

I find that many Christians seldom, if ever, think about the class implications of things like the location of new church plants, accessibility of ministerial and theological training in our cities, or the affordable-housing crises spawned by the gentrification of urban areas. It can be easy to ignore issues of class because the people in the lower strata are used to being invisible. But a close look at Scripture reveals that such matters were considered extremely significant to God's people as they lived in covenant with Him. In the *Sojourners* call-to-renewal document "From Poverty to Opportunity: A Covenant for a New America," these words warrant careful consideration:

> The Hebrew prophets consistently say that the measure of a nation's righteousness and integrity is how it treats its most vulnerable. And Jesus says the nations will be judged by how they treat "the least of these" (Matthew 25). As our religious forebears declared that slavery was morally intolerable, we now insist that widespread poverty in the midst of plenty is a moral wrong we refuse to accept any longer. Poverty is the new slavery. It is time to lift up practical policies and practices that help people escape poverty and clearly challenge the increasing wealth gap between rich and poor. The Bible condemns extremes of wealth and poverty. Across the globe, inequality is on the rise. The disproportionate impact of poverty on woman and people of color is a further indictment of our society.[317]

As this document implies, wealth inequality and the problems associated with poverty are not the inescapable consequences of economic development. Instead, they are largely the product of laws related to property rights, tax structures, and the way our government spends its money. For example, if minimum wages kept pace with the increase in CEO pay scales over the last twenty years, it would be $23 per hour.[318] But minimum wage rates fall far short of that. How can the church view that as acceptable? The church must use its voice to move government and business into practices that help to reduce the unbearable burdens of poverty in our land of abundance. As Jim Wallis says, "Christians must learn to judge our social and economic choices by whether they empower the powerless, protect the earth, and foster true democracy."[319] The American evangelical church faces a clear "put up or shut up" moment with regards to using its voice to call for economic justice and an end to an aggressive and destructive form of classism.

HEALING THE WOUNDS

The current presence of these wounds does not mean to imply that nothing has changed in the church in recent times. Progress has been made, but for the most part, the evangelical church in America continues to struggle with patriarchy, racism, and class inequities. Even if we agree that these "wounds" are huge barriers in contemporary America, actually doing something about them is another thing entirely. "Diagnosis is cheap—remedy is expensive," as the saying goes. Much of the "expense" lies in making the church acknowledge the deeper reality of such wounds. As Richard Middleton observed, "In the realm of the 'sacred,' we are quite willing to declare the equality of all people and to share the gospel (understood in a minimalist sense, as the way to 'heaven'); but in the 'secular' realm of realpolitik on earth, we horde our wealth and cling to our (national, class, economic) privilege. Granted, perhaps we might give away some of our wealth as charitable giving or tithing, but this requires no substantial change in our way of life, in our this-worldly (well-nigh idolatrous) commitments to success, material progress, and national identity.[320] I'm fairly confident that there's not a pastor among us who relishes the thought of taking on these wounds in his or her congregation, but we do well to recall the prophet's warning to those who "dress the wound of my people as though it were not serious. Peace, peace, they say where there is no peace." (Jeremiah 8:11).

One of the major challenges for evangelical churches in this regard is to resist the temptation to take refuge in our "orthodoxy" in certain front-page issues while looking the other way when it comes to the church's three great wounds. Considering ourselves "right" on theological issues, or even on cultural controversies like abortion, are ultimately undermined by the contradictory presence of these all-too-visible wounds. The late Rabbi Abraham Joshua Heschel, who became friends with Martin Luther King Jr., warned frequently of the dangers of theological and religious shallowness, of our tendency to "worry more about the purity of dogma than about the integrity of love."[321] No amount of "orthodoxy" on select issues exempts the evangelical church from dealing with its wounds. The immediate need is for the church's shepherds to reckon with the grievous contradiction of a wounded church trying to do its mission in the world as if nothing is out of order. Again, the prophet's words are telling: "Since my people are crushed, I am crushed; I mourn, and horror grips me. Is there no balm in Gilead? Is there no physician there? Why then is there no healing for the wound of my people?" (Jeremiah 8:21–22). Until the leaders of the church can recognize the unseemliness of a "too wounded" church, the healing balm that is available will go wanting. But this is our task. Elaine Heath writes, "The church . .

. is being called to own and renounce its threefold syncretistic attachment to sexism, racism, and classism. These attachments have wounded the church and have caused the church to wound the world for too long. Painful self-reflection, repentance, and much theological work are needed to retrieve the egalitarian ethos of the gospel."[322] Let me suggest four theological pathways that might be pursued as part of that "theological work" in finding the balm that can heal a wounded church.

First, we begin by affirming and embodying the implications of the *imago dei*. One of the first Christian writers to influence me was a Quaker philosopher by the name of David Elton Trueblood. He wrote a book in 1967 entitled *The Incendiary Fellowship*. In it, Trueblood argues that "the strongest reason for racial justice is a doctrine, and that doctrine is concerned with creation."[323] It's more than ironic, given the evangelical church's interest in creation, that we too often fail to take full measure of what it means to claim that *all* human persons are made in the image of the Creator. If the church cannot agree on its fundamental anthropological claim, and then embrace the implications and consequences of that claim, there is no way out of the contradictions of the three great wounds.

Second, we must insist on the "catholicity" (or universality) of the church, and this can only be accomplished by recovering our theology of baptism. Rodney Clapp reminds us that "in terms of identity and destiny, biblically speaking, there was no more fundamental divide than that between Jew and Gentile. This division broke humanity into two fundamental parts. Citizenship in the commonwealth of Israel is that basic, that determinative."[324] This is what made Peter's baptism of the household of Cornelius so revolutionary. Baptism effectively drew in and adopted Gentiles into the commonwealth of Israel. And, as Paul put it, this created "one new humanity in place of the two" (Eph. 2:15). "You are children of God through faith in Christ Jesus, for all of you who were baptized in Christ have clothed yourselves with Christ. There is no longer Jew or Greek, there is no longer slave or free, there is no longer male and female; for all of you are one in Jesus Christ (Gal. 3:26–27). As Clapp puts it, "Baptism 'naturalizes' the Gentile, incorporates him or her into the body of the Jew Jesus Christ, and grants him or her citizenship in the commonwealth of Israel . . . Nothing can more basically or comprehensively define the Christian than baptism."[325] Here again, we see how the church has tended to sell short, or better, live short of its theology. The church is "catholic," it is universal, and the boundary to the church has nothing to do with race, gender, or class, but everything to do with baptism. As Barbara Brown-Taylor reminds us, "At least one of the purposes of church is to remind us that God has other children, easily as precious as we are. Baptism and narcissism cancel each other out."[326]

Third, the great wounds of the church remain potent and hurtful as long as the church fails to embody its role as an eschatological community. The church is to be a "sacrament," a sign of God's presence in the world, and of God's intentions for the world. But to incarnate the kingdom in that matter involves taking Jesus much more seriously than often seems to be the case. American churches are very good at "believing *in* Jesus" as the Savior and as the offering for our sins. Many of those same churches seem much less committed to actually believing Jesus—believing that what He taught and embodied Himself is actually what He expects of His church, namely, the continuation of His earthly mission. I can conceive of no scenario under which the Kingdom of God, fully come to this earth, excludes persons on the basis of race, gender, or socioeconomic class. The church of the future, in a world where Jesus is Lord, can no longer evidence the hurtful and denigrating actions and attitudes that too often are laid at its door by today's ecclesial critics. As Paul essentially said over and again to the church, "become what you are!" The church needs to begin living out its destiny, here and now.

Finally—and this is without a doubt the most painful and daunting part of the challenge to wholeness—the church must repent. Writing this chapter has brought to my mind Jesus' teachings about the so-called "unpardonable sin." The sin that is unpardonable is the sin that is unacknowledged, unconfessed. What greater irony can there be than for a body which owes its very existence to confession and repentance, to become so resistant to it in terms of these specific issues? We stubbornly cling to our insistence that racism, sexism, and classism cannot be found among us. And as long as the church clings to its insistence of innocence, wholeness will continue to evade it. Stanley Hauerwas, speaking to the problem of racism, reminds us that,

> "Standing up to evil" or "Resisting hate" or "Equality not hate" are laudable sentiments but, from a Christian perspective, they're just that, sentiments. They are so because they are insufficiently Christian. The word justice is unintelligible for Christians apart from the content named by Jesus Christ. Appeals to equality are likewise spurious for Christians, for Christians can rightly remember our nation's history and we know the white men who wrote about equality at our founding were all slaveholders. And hate and evil aren't specific enough words for Christians to describe racism. Sin is the word Christians must use first. Our sin of racism is how the Power of Sin, and our

bondage to it, manifests itself in the world. If there's a contribution Christians can make to the public square when it comes to race, it's speaking Christian. Christians must resist racism as Christians not as Americans. . . For Christians, particularly white progressive Christians, the first step in combating racism and privilege is acknowledging one's own culpability and blindness; that is, confession."[327]

There it is. Can we reframe all of the church's wounded-ness into the theological language of sin? We must do nothing less. The church must confess its sins that it might be healed.

In dealing with John 8:31–36, the infamous "the truth will set you free" passage, F.D. Brunner ponders the crowd's response to Jesus, insisting that they have no need of such "liberation," and then writes, "It is apparently very difficult for some persons to think that they need much of anything. It is very difficult for such persons . . . to become 'real' disciples. Indeed it is precisely self-satisfied persons who will prove in the long run to be Jesus' main enemies."[328] God forbid that the church squander its opportunity for mission in this needy culture due to its failure to acknowledge its own wounds.

In the dark days that saw the German church accommodate itself to Hitler and the nightmare of National Socialism, Dietrich Bonhoeffer said to that church, "only he who cries out for the Jews dares to sing Gregorian chants."[329] It was his way of telling a compromised church that they can't go on with business as usual. The worship of God is expressly tied to matters of justice and embodied love. The church does not exist in a vacuum; it exists in the world and for the world. To paraphrase Bonhoeffer, only those who long for the day of true justice to dawn upon all citizens regardless of one's race dare sing, "In Christ there is no East or West, In Him no South or North; but one great fellowship of love throughout the whole wide earth." Only those who anguish over the way women have so often been marginalized both inside and outside the church dare sing, "May the mind of Christ my Savior, live in me from day to day, By His love and power controlling all I do and say." Only those who weep for the homeless, the hungry, the refugees, the migrants and the prisoners, dare sing, "Children of the heavenly Father, safely in His bosom gather." It is now time for Christians to understand that for those on the outside, the authenticity of the church is more likely measured by the sincerity of its tears than by the volume of its worship.

Elaine Heath envisions that day when the church can walk with authority and integrity into an unbelieving world. She writes, "As the church is healed from the damaging threefold wound, it will regain the moral authority it needs to speak to a world hurtling toward chaos. Delivered of its demonic attachment to oppressive power, the church will find its God-given conscience towards all living things that have suffered under the centripetal force of domination. The earth and all its creatures will once again become the primary foci of the good news, that God is redeeming not just fallen humans but the whole of creation"[330] God is redeeming not just fallen humans but the whole of creation. How can the church not be the centerpiece of that hope? I listened, some time ago, to a guest preacher in my home church. This eloquent African-American man took as his text, Romans 8:18–21, where Paul speaks of the hope that creation has in God completing His great redemptive work. The preacher particularly noted verse 19, which says, "the creation waits in eager expectation for the children of God to be revealed." He urged us to not simply view that verse through the lens of a long-range future, but to see it as part of our calling and mission as the church here and now. And then, he said this: If the church can't get it right, how will the world ever know it can be better?"

Epilogue
What Now?

> Our only recourse is to hang on by our teeth, that is, to have faith and hope, and to love this possibility of an impossible and unmasterable future which is not in our hands. Love and hope and faith are the virtues of the impossible, taking the measure of the immeasurable future. The borders of the possible are safe but flat, sure but narrow, well defined but confining, and they may stake out the lines of a salted and mediocre life, without a passionate hope, where nothing *really* happens and all present systems will do just fine. If at the end of our lives we find that all our hopes have been sensible and moderate and measured by the horizon of our future present, if we have never been astir with the impossible, then we shall also find that on the whole life has passed us by. If safe is what you want, forget religion and find yourself a conservative investment counselor.
>
> —John Caputo[331]

In their book, *Romans Disarmed*, Sylvia Keesmaat and Brian Walsh contend that a lot of people are suffering from what they term "Post-Evangelical Traumatic Stress Disorder," (PETSD).[332] They are talking about people who have been spiritually and emotionally traumatized by a kind of evangelicalism that has pushed many of them to the brink of abandoning Christian faith. I sometimes think that I am one of those people, although I have never seriously considered giving up my faith, just the church. But, here I am, still hanging in, after many years of frustration and disappointment at the direction and pace of change in American evangelicalism. Writing this book has been something of a catharsis for me, in that I have at least expressed myself in ways that I never have previously. Even during the writing, I have found myself wondering "What will so and so think of that statement?" Or, "How will this affect my standing with that group?" Writing these words has brought me face to face with my own cowardice, my incessant need for the approval of others, and my almost pathological efforts to avoid controversy at any cost. But as John Caputo reminds us, playing it safe all the time is the quickest route to having life pass us by. So, I have taken on this project with an attitude of grim uncertainty over what it will augur in my life going forward and whether it will prove helpful to my fellow PETSD companions. Having emptied the stones out of my shoes, I would bring my "confessions of an evangelical outlier" to a close by reaffirming a few salient points about what I have written and its meaning and significance for the evangelical church.

First, I hope that these pages have revealed my utter fascination with and admiration of Jesus Christ. If these pages have been nothing more than one properly contextualized and extended "come to Jesus" moment, my efforts have been rightly directed. Colin Morris, whose book has been in the back of my mind throughout this writing, said that, "If it is possible to make sense of a world that brutalizes millions then Jesus is the sense of it. And Jesus is all the church has got left."[333] But, there is nothing to fear in Morris' stark assessment of the church's resources, because Jesus has always been enough. Morris goes on to remind us that "Stripping down Christianity to what is sneeringly called a Jesus-cult need not be the first step to the nearest Unitarian church . . . A combination of Christ-devotion and Christ action . . . leads to a majestic conception of God . . . Relentlessly [Jesus] drives me on, eluding all my efforts to pin down His essence, smashing His way out of every structure I build around Him."[334] Through all my frustrations and irritations with the church that bears his name, I have found Christ to be an unending source of inspiration and motivation. The evangelical church must do everything in its power to keep the person and work of Jesus Christ at the absolute center of its mission and being in the world. This means allowing Jesus to speak into *this present world*, in *this present moment*.

> Our greatest resource in post-Christendom is Jesus. In a society that is heartily and understandably sick of institutional Christianity, Jesus still commands interest and respect. However garbled his teachings have become, and however little his story is known, many people suspect Jesus is good news, despite the shortcomings they see in our churches and the distaste with which they regard our evangelistic activities. We may agree that "to become an admirer of Jesus" (Kierkegaard's term) is much

easier than to become a follower, but admiration—or even curiosity... offers us a starting point.

Our priority must be to rediscover how to tell the story of Jesus and present his life, teaching, death and resurrection—recognizing past attempts have seriously missed the mark. We cannot continue to present Jesus only as the savior from a guilt few feel in post-Christendom. Nor can we invite people to follow a Jesus who merely guarantees life after death to those who are otherwise comfortable or a Jesus whose lordship affects only a limited range of personal moral decisions. We can no longer present a safe establishment Jesus who represents order and stability rather than justice, who appeals to the powerful and privileged for all the wrong reasons. Nor can we reduce Jesus to dogmatic statements in simplistic evangelistic courses or perpetuate the overemphasis on his divinity at the expense of his humanity that Christendom required.

Instead we must present Jesus as (among much else) friend of sinners, good news to the poor, defender of the powerless, reconciler of communities, pioneer of a new age, freedom fighter, breaker of chains, liberator and peacemaker, the one who unmasks systems of oppression, identifies with the vulnerable and brings hope.[335]

If the church has any hope, it is because of Jesus. As Brian McLaren aptly said, "We are stuck with Jesus and he won't go away."[336] Thank God for that! Because of Jesus' unending love for the church, we dare believe that the church can, in fact, rise to the momentousness of the present time and truly represent itself as the bride of Christ.

To do so, the church needs to get crystal-clear about its mission. Apart from such clarity, the church becomes just one more organization trying to "do some good" in the world. Can the church actually offer something to a world staggering with injustice? Can the church appeal to that world in a way that doesn't immediately condemn, judge, or alienate? Can the church effectively engage the poor without patronizing them or offering them "stones for bread"? That requires a church committed to being different. Being different, by definition, puts the church at risk. But when has it ever been safe to be the church in a world that has collectively turned its back on God?

To be that kind of church will require a radical commitment to the translatability of the gospel. The evangelical church must be willing to forgo the old wineskins of "Christian America" and instead discover new wineskins into which to pour the vintage of its renewed witness to this culture, because we are embracing how things really are instead of how we wish they were. As Will Willimon put it, "Christians are every bit as 'realistic' as anyone else. We simply have a fundamental quarrel with the world's conventional definitions of what is real."[337] And our take on reality is shaped first and foremost by the story of Jesus Christ, his life, teachings, crucifixion, and resurrection.

The church's witness must be characterized by humility and a willingness to listen. In *Jim and Casper Go to Church*, Jim Henderson asks his atheist friend, Matt Casper, what he would like Christians to hear from people like him. Casper replies,

> I guess I'd just like Christians and church leaders to be more honest. Not just with me, but with everyone in their churches. Stop treating faith as a fact. Call it hope. Call it confidence, not certainty. I guess I'd like some straight shooting. 'Hi. Life is challenging. But we've found that being followers of Jesus has helped us. Maybe it could help you, too.' That'd be *refreshing*. And I'd be interested in hearing more and asking questions. In short, I'd be interested in having a conversation.[338]

The evangelical church must enable its members to be confident enough in the gospel to truly listen to what other have to say, to invite the questions that people have about matters of the spirit and how God actually relates to real human beings. As Darrel Guder reminds us, "As an alternative social reality, the church is called to teach people how to talk, how to act, how to fight, how to love, how to see the world in a peculiar way—a Christ-like way."[339] The ability to see the world through God's eyes is the promise of the Holy Spirit in the believer's life. There has never been a time when such vision is more necessary in the church. The challenges of these days are overwhelming. The temptation is to withdraw and content ourselves with the ecclesial status quo. But that is to move counter to the Spirit, who sends the church into the world as Christ's witnesses. Again, Guder: "The church's proclamation of the gospel has validity and relevance only when it confronts head-on the often terrifying circumstances of human life, when it expresses hope in the face of despair, when it honestly and realistically accepts its vocation to convert hostility into hospitality."[340] At this moment in history, confronted with a worldwide pandemic, economic uncertainty, and political polarization the likes of which we've never seen before, Guder's words take on special poignancy. The conversion of hostility into hospitality can seem like a dream to observers of the church, including outliers like myself, but I've seen it happen, and I want to believe with all my heart that I'll see it again, that it's not an impossible dream.

I'd be lying if I didn't admit to hoping that outliers like me experience that hospitable welcome, even if others view some of the positions I've taken in this book as coloring outside the lines. My ardent hope is that even if I should be wrong about some things, which is entirely possible, I can still be part of the family. As one of my colleagues put it, "I suspect that Jesus is going to ask me more questions about my commitment to follow him and love the people around me than he is my determination to defend a doctrinal statement."[341] As it happens, "orthodoxy" literally means "straight praise," which reminds us that being orthodox isn't about having all your beliefs perfectly in line with some particular expression of dogma, but it's about uttering authentic words of praise to God. Sometimes saying "I don't know" is the best evidence of our orthodoxy.

So here I am, trying to figure out where I stand in the midst of a church which I have known all my life, but which feels increasingly strange to me. I don't know what the future holds for people like me. I confess that I do not care for that kind of uncertainty, but before God, I have honestly tried to engage the church of my birth and lifetime in a conversation aimed at trying to find enough common ground to continue walking together. I don't know if what I have written will be sufficient to bring that to pass. All I can do is bear witness to the conviction that Jesus Christ has completely ruined my life in the best possible way. In his book, *The Responsible Self: An Essay in Christian Moral Philosophy*, H. Richard Niebuhr wrote these words which I have read and re-read across the years because they describe so well my own heart, and my own experience as an outlier:

> I call myself a Christian, though there are those who challenge my right to that name, either because they require a Christian to maintain some one of various sets of beliefs that I do not hold, or because they require a Christian to live up to various sets of moral standards, including those of my own conscience, to which I do not conform. I call myself a Christian simply because I also am a follower of Jesus Christ, though I travel at a great distance from him, not only in time, but in the spirit of my traveling; because I believe that my way of thinking about life, myself, my human companions and our destiny has been so modified by his presence in our history, that I cannot get away from his influence; and also because I do not want to get away from it; above all I call myself a Christian because my relationship to God has been, so far as I can see, deeply conditioned by the presence of Jesus Christ in my history and in our history.[342]

EPILOGUE

My own claim to the label "Christian" resides not in what I've written in these pages, but what is written deeply on my heart and in my feeble attempts to love as God loves.

Many years ago, when I was eighteen, I was caught smoking marijuana in the desert foothills of Tucson, along with six of my friends. At that time, such an offense was a felony, but the narcotics officer in charge was after "bigger fish" than us, so instead of being carted off to jail, we were all accompanied home by an officer to apprise our parents of what we had been doing. Honestly, I would rather have gone to jail than awaken my parents at 5:00 on a Saturday morning with the admission that a narcotics officer needed to talk with them. It remains one of the worst moments of my life. My parents were devastated, of course, but they didn't say all that much to me. Home was not all that comfortable a place for me in the following days. Eight days after this, a Sunday, I walked a block or so from my house to our local convenience store to buy a Sunday paper. As I approached the store, I saw a familiar vehicle and was immediately accosted by Bob, one of my friends who had been involved in the drug bust eight days earlier. He was a mess. His father had thrown him out of the house, and it was obvious that he had been living in his car. He clearly hadn't bathed in a few days. He asked me to help him get something to eat. I didn't have any money to give him. I hoped that would lead to him getting into his car and leaving, but he was not to be denied, begging me to get him some food. Finally, I told him to come with me, and we began to walk back to my house. The last thing I wanted was for my neighbors to see me walking down the street with this disheveled creature, so I took him down the alley that ran behind our house. I told him to wait outside the fence in the alley while I went in to try to get him some food.

Sunday dinner at our house was a big deal. With both of my parents working full-time, it was the one occasion during the week where the entire family ate together. The idea of interrupting Sunday dinner, of now adding to the guilt I was already carrying, was not an appealing prospect at all. I hoped to be able to grab some food, take it out to Bob, and see him off. When I explained to my mother why I needed the food, suddenly the situation was taken completely out of my hands. The next thing I knew, I was sitting at Sunday dinner in the Walters' house, and my druggie friend Bob was sitting next to my father being treated like the long-lost prodigal son. I can't adequately explain how surreal this was to me. Bob, sitting there, eating Sunday dinner, conversing with my father like a member of the family. Afterwards, Bob left, through the front door, with an invitation to come back. To this day, so many years later, that remains the single most powerful image I have of what authentic Christian faith is all about.

Having flipped over a few tables in the church, I know that there is one table that is, thankfully, "unflippable." It is our Lord's table. It is the table of gracious, welcoming, and hospitable love. And it is the church's most effective witness to a world filled with prodigals.

So now, duly noting the irony of it all, I find myself, an outlier, a bit of a prodigal, I suppose, standing in the alley outside the house, wondering if I'll be invited in. I hope so. But I don't know.

Endnotes

CHAPTER 1

1. Bebbington, https://www.nae.net/what-is-an-evangelical/
2. Oden, *Classic Christianity*.
3. www.dictionary.com
4. Bussie, *Outlaw Christian*, 17.
5. Morris, *Include Me Out!*, 45.
6. Bonhoeffer, *Life Together*, 1954), 110.
7. Butler-Bass, *Christianity for the Rest of Us*, 198.
8. Berger and Zijdeveldm, *In Praise of Doubt*, 32.
9. Murphy, *Beyond Liberalism and Fundamentalism*, 1.
10. Bonhoeffer, *Life Together*, 25–26.
11. Pavlovitz, *A Bigger Table*, 80.
12. Butler-Bass, *Christianity for the Rest of Us*, 189.
13. 10Worthen, *Apostles of Reason*, Introduction, Kindle.
14. Ibid., Chapter 11, Kindle.
15. Tomlinson, *The Post-Evangelical*, 64.
16. Knoll, *The Scandal of the Evangelical Mind*, 239.
17. Bosch, *Transforming Mission*, 373.
18. Morris, *Include Me Out*, 31.
19. Cited in Tomlinson, *The Post-Evangelical*, 13.

CHAPTER 2

20. Guiness, *Prophetic Untimeliness*, 77.
21. Duin, *Quitting Church*, 13.
22. Hammet, *Reaching People Under 40*, Chapter 1, Kindle.
23. Morey and Gibbs, *Embodying Our Faith*, Introduction, Kindle.
24. McNeal, *The Present Future*.174, Kindle.
25. Ibid., 1.
26. Kinnaman and Lyons, *UnChristian*, 26.
27. Ibid., 11.
28. McNeal, *Present Future*, 4.
29. Duin, *Quitting Church*, 21.

30. McNeal, *Present Future*, 4.
31. Duin, *Quitting Church*, 109.
32. Nancarrow, "Rethink Church," (blog) http://www.maggienancarrow.com, 11/3/2015.
33. Morey and Gibbs, *Embodying Our Faith*, Introduction, Kindle.
34. Guder, *The Continuing Conversion of the Church*, 196–197.
35. McNeal, *Present Future*, Kindle, 167.
36. Held Evans, "Want millennials back in the pews? Stop trying to make church 'cool,'" *The Washington Post*, April 30, 2015.
37. McLaren, *Everything Must Change*, 299.
38. Keesmaat and Walsh, *Romans Disarmed*, 8.
39. Guder, *The Continuing Conversion of the Church*, 146.
40. Guder, *Missional Church*, 2–3.
41. 22. Cited in, Morey and Gibbs, *Embodying Our Faith*, Introduction, Kindle.
42. Hunter, *To Change the World*, 158.
43. Held-Evans, "Want millennials back in the pews?"
44. Guder, *Missional Church*, 98.
45. . Grenz, *Revisioning Evangelical Theology*, 181.
46. Frost, *Seeing God in the Ordinary*, 6–7.
47. Ibid., 52
48. McLaren, *The Church on the Other Side*, 37.
49. Frost and Hirsch, *Re-Jesus*, 122.
50. Guder, *Missional Church*, 84.
51. Held-Evans, "Want millennials back in the pews?"
52. Lyons, *The Next Christians*, 170.
53. Guiness, *Prophetic Untimeliness*, 12, 15.
54. Wax, *Holy Subversions*, 13.
55. Grentz, *Revisioning Evangelical Theology*, 16.
56. Hauerwas and Willimon, *Resident Aliens*, 94.

CHAPTER 3

57. Lyons, *The Next Christians*, 52.
58. Smith, *The Bible Made Impossible*, 7. Rethinking Human Knowledge, Authority and Understanding, Kindle.
59. Brown-Taylor, *Leaving Church*, 106.
60. Blevins, *How to Read the Bible Without Losing Your Mind*, Chapter 2, Kindle.
61. Enns, *The Bible Tells Me So*, 163.
62. Grentz, *Revisioning Evangelical Theology*, 113.
63. Knoll, *The Scandal of the Evangelical Mind*, 52.
64. Lyons, *The Next Christians*, 55–56.
65. Dobson, *Bitten by a Camel*, 81.
66. Smith, *The Bible Made Impossible*, Subsidiary Problems with Biblicism, Kindle.
67. Gorman, *Reading Revelation Responsibly*, Chapter Four, Kindle.
68. Ibid. Chapter Four, Kindle.
69. Smith, *The Bible Made Impossible*, The Christocentric Hermeneutical Key, Kindle.

ENDNOTES

70. Wall and Castello, "Rethinking the Bible," *Wesleyan Theological Journal*, Fall 2018.
71. Ibid.
72. Barth, *Church Dogmatics*, 1/2:720.
73. Boyd, *Cross Vision*, 21.
74. Cited in, Murray. *Post-Christendom*, 312.
75. Wright, *Surprised by Scripture*, 28.
76. Smith, *The Bible Made Impossible*, The Christocentric Hermeneutical Key, Kindle.
77. Ibid. The Christocentric Hermeneutical Key, Kindle.

CHAPTER 4

78. Pavlovitz, *A Bigger Table*, 100.
79. Zahnd, *A Farewell to Mars*, Chapter 2: Repairing the World, Kindle.
80. Bosch, *Transforming Mission*, 409.
81. Ibid., 409–410.
82. Wicker, *The Fall of the Evangelical Nation*, 135.
83. McNeal, *The Present Future*, 36.
84. Hirsch and Ford, *Right Here Right Now*, Debriefing Right Now, Kindle.
85. Pavlovitz, *A Bigger Table*, 166.
86. Dobson, *Bitten by a Camel*, 42.
87. Fitch and Holsclaw, *Prodigal Christianity*, Signpost Two: Missio Dei, Kindle.
88. Wright, *Surprised by Scripture*, 84.
89. . Zahnd, *A Farewell to Mars*, Chapter 2: Repairing the World, Kindle.
90. Middleton, *A New Heaven and a New Earth*, 240.
91. Ibid. 71.
92. Hirsch and Ford, *Right Here Right Now*, Section One: Putting Our Hearts Into It, Kindle.
93. McLaren, *Everything Must Change*, 81.
94. Ibid.
95. Heath, *The Mystic Way of Evangelism*, 13.
96. Middleton, *A New Heaven and a New Earth*, 79.
97. McLaren, *Everything Must Change*, 96.
98. Willimon, *Pastor*, 231.
99. Dobson, *Bitten by a Camel*, 111.
100. Butler-Bass, *Christianity for the Rest of Us*, 76.
101. Heath, *The Mystic Way of Evangelism*, 13.
102. Donovan, *Christianity Rediscovered*, 79.
103. Guder, *The Continuing Conversion of the Church*, 131.
104. Kinlaw, *Let's Start with Jesus*, Chapter Two: The Level of Intimacy God Desires, Kindle.
105. Henderson, *Evangelism Without the Additives*, 138.
106. McLaren, *More Ready Than You Realize*, 141..
107. Howard-Merritt, *ReFraming Hope*, Chapter Four, Kindle.
108. Bosch, *Transforming Mission*, 411.
109. Willimon, *Pastor*, 205.

110. Morey and Gibbs, *Embodying Our Faith*, Chapter Two: Same Wine, Different Skin, Kindle.
111. Ibid. Chapter Two: Same Wine, Different Skin, Kindle.
112. McLaren, *Everything Must Change*, 244.
113. Willard, *Renovation of the Heart*, 244.
114. Ibid. 238–239.
115. Kinnaman, *You Lost Me*, Part 2. Disconnections: Shallow, Kindle,
116. Guder, *The Continuing Conversion of the Church*, 26.
117. Henderson, *Evangelism Without the Additives*, 28–29.
118. Morey and Gibbs, *Embodying the Faith*, Chapter 6: Communal Faith, Kindle.

CHAPTER 5

119. Smedes, *Sex for Christians*, 95.
120. Regnerus, *Forbidden Fruit*, 83.
121. Hauerwas, *A Community of Character*, 75.
122. Regnerus, *Forbidden Fruit*, 127.
123. Ibid. 3.
124. Ibid. 22.
125. Smedes, *Sex for Christians*, 9.
126. Cited in, Winner, *Real Sex*, 152.
127. Simon, *Bringing Sex Intro Focus*, Conclusion: Toward Sexual Integrity, Kindle.
128. Fitch and Holsclaw, *Prodigal Christianity*, Signpost Eight: Prodigal Relationships, Kindle.
129. Regnerus, *Forbidden Fruit*, 59.
130. Ibid.
131. Brownson, *Bible, Gender, Sexuality*, 165.
132. Ibid. 110.
133. Ibid. 103.
134. Smedes, *Sex for Christians*, 366.
135. Ibid.
136. Bell, *Sex God*, 40.
137. Smedes, *Sex for Christians*, 194.
138. Gushee,, *A Letter to My Anxious Christian Friends*, 68,
139. Regnerus, *Forbidden Fruit*, 115.
140. Floyd-Thomas, Floyd-Thomas, and Toulouse, *The Altars Where We Worship*, Chapter 1, Kindle.
141. Gardner, *Making Chastity Sexy*, 4.
142. Ibid. Kindle, 5.
143. Wicker, *The Fall of the Evangelical Nation*, 81.
144. Bolz-Webber, *Shameless*, 122–123..
145. Gardner, *Making Chastity Sexy*, 12.
146. Kinnaman, *You Lost Me*, Part 2. Disconnections, Kindle.
147. Gardner, *Making Chastity Sexy*, 187.
148. Winner, *Real Sex*, 17.
149. Ibid. 15.
150. Smedes, *Sex for Christians*, 72.

151. Struthers, *Wired for Intimacy*, Chapter 7, Kindle.
152. Simon, *Bringing Sex into Focus*, The Dominant Covenantal Lens in Christian Society, Kindle.
153. Smedes, *Sex for Christians*, 111.
154. Bell, *Sex God*, 157, Kindle.
155. Smedes, *Sex for Christians*, 20.
156. Struthers, *Wired for Intimacy*, Chapter 4, Kindle.
157. Hauerwas, *A Community of Character*, 177.
158. Winner, *Real Sex*, 50.
159. Kinnaman, *You Lost Me*, Part 2. Disconnections: Repressive, Kindle.
160. Hauerwas, *A Community of Character*, 180.
161. Hauerwas and Willimon, *Resident Aliens*, 63–64.
162. Kinnaman, *You Lost Me*, Part 2. Disconnections: Repressive, Kindle.
163. Hauerwas, *A Community of Character*, 182.

CHAPTER 6

164. Cone, *God of the Oppressed*, 41.
165. Pavlovitz,. *A Bigger Table*, Introduction, Kindle.
166. Hauerwas and Willimon, *Resident Aliens*, 30.
167. Gushee, *A Letter to My Anxious Christian Friends*, 21.
168. Fitch, and Holsclaw, *Prodigal Christianity*, Signpost Ten: Prodigal Openness, Kindle.
169. McLaren, *Everything Must Change*, 285.
170. Hunter, *To Change the World*, 171.
171. Gushee, *A Letter to My Anxious Christian Friends*, 43.
172. Hunter, *To Change the World*, 12.
173. Ibid. 95.
174. Ibid. 08.
175. Ibid. 175.
176. Bell and Golden: *Jesus Wants to Save Christians*, 161.
177. Gushee, *A Letter to My Anxious Christian Friends.*, 60.
178. Keesmaat and Walsh, *Romans Disarmed*, 279–280.
179. Ibid, 133.
180. Ibid. 290–291.
181. Alperovitz, *What Then Must We Do*, Part V. 22, Kindle.
182. Deneen, *Why Liberalism Failed*, Introduction, Kindle.
183. Hauerwas and Willimon *Resident Aliens*, 32.
184. Deneen *Why Liberalism Failed*, 178.
185. Ibid. Preface, Kindle.
186. Morris, *Include Me Out*, 97.
187. Meyers, *Binding the Strong Man*, 417.
188. Keesmaat and Walsh, *Romans Disarmed*, 21.
189. Vanhoozer, Anderson, and Sleasman. *Everyday Theology*, 58.
190. Hauerwas and Willimon, *Resident Aliens*, 83.
191. Smith, *Awaiting the King*, 53.
192. Leithart, *Against Christianity*, 136.

193. Hunter, *To Change the World*, 95.
194. Butler-Bass, *Christianity for the Rest of Us*, 263.

CHAPTER 7

195. Floyd-Thomas, Floyd-Thomas, and Toulouse, *The Altars Where We Worship*, Introduction, Kindle..
196. Lenker, *Luther's Large Catechism*,44.
197. Gorman, *Reading Revelation Responsibly*, Chapter Three, Kindle.
198. Ibid. Chapter Three, Kindle.
199. Butler-Bass, *Christianity for the Rest of Us*, 30.
200. Gorman, *Reading Revelation Responsibly*, Chapter Two, Kindle.
201. Fea, *Was America Founded as a Christian Nation?*, Preface, Kindle.
202. Ibid. Introduction, Kindle 470. Fea cites the example of David Barton, well-known founder of WallBuilders, a ministry devoted to "presenting America's forgotten history and heroes with an emphasis on our moral, religious, and constitutional heritage." He writes, "It is hard to separate Barton's historical work from his political passions. He served eight years as the vice chair of the Texas Republic Party, the same political organization whose 2004 platform included the line: "the United States of America is a Christian nation." Barton's books and videos about America's Christian heritage have sold thousands of copies, and he speaks widely on the subject to large evangelical audiences, both in person and through his radio and television ministry. In 2005 Time named Barton one of the twenty-five most influential evangelicals in America." Chapter Four, Kindle.
203. Ibid. Chapter Four, Kindle. Barton, for example, has listed several "unconfirmed quotations" on his Web site that critics have discovered were fabricated or drawn from secondary sources that inaccurately attributed them to founders.
204. https://twitter.com/rainnwilson/status/1157736650274828288?lang=en
205. Bell and Golden, *Jesus Wants to Save Christians*, 18, Kindle.
206. Zahnd, *A Farewell to Mars*, Chapter 1: "That Preacher of Peace," Kindle.
207. Ibid. Chapter 1, Kindle.
208. Hirsch and Ford, *Right Here Right Now,* Section Two: Wrapping Our Heads Around It, Kindle.
209. Keesmaat and Walsh, *Romans Disarmed*, 252.
210. Smith, *You Are What You Love*, 52.
211. Foster, *A Celebration of Discipline,* 80.
212. Bessenecker, *The New Friars*, 158.
213. Keesmaat and Walsh, *Romans Disarmed*, 227,
214. Ibid. 115.
215. Ibid. 97.
216. *The Christian Century*, February 12, 2020.
217. Keesmaat and Walsh, *Romans Disarmed*, 259.
218. Bacevich, *Washington Rules*
219. Ibid. 29,
220. Ibid. 225.
221. Ibid. 182.
222. Ibid. 189.

223. Ibid. 223.
224. Middleton, *A New Heaven and a New Earth*, 56.
225. Ryan, "The Rejection of Military Service by the Early Christians." http://cdn.theologicalstudies.net/13/13.1/13.1.1.pdf
226. Gushee, *A Letter to My Anxious Christian Friends*, 82.
227. Ibid.
228. Hauerwas and Willimon, *Resident Aliens*, 131.
229. . Atwood, *America and Its Guns*, 22.
230. Ibid. 3.
231. Ibid. 5.
232. Ibid. 24.
233. Ibid. 52.
234. Ibid. 160.
235. Ibid. 204.
236. Cited in, Atwood, *American and Its Guns*, 52.
237. Hunter, *To Change the World*, 157.
238. McLaren, *Everything Must Change*, 159.
239. Boyd, *The Myth of a Christian Nation*, 90.
240. Zahnd, *Sinners in the Hands of a Loving God*, 169.

CHAPTER 8

241. Gibberson and Collins. *The Language of Science and Faith*, 17.
242. Collins, *The Language of God*, 172.
243. Gibberson and Collins, *The Language of Faith and Scripture*, 131.
244. Collins, *The Language of God*, 176.
245. Gibberson and Collins, *The Language of Faith and Scripture*, 73.
246. Ibid. 74.
247. Ibid. 75.
248. Ibid.
249. Ibid. 158.
250. Collins, *The Language of God*, 206.
251. Giberson and Collins, *The Language of Faith and Scripture*, 51.
252. Walton, *The Lost World of Adam and Eve*, 21.
253. Ibid. 77.
254. Ibid. 136.
255. Enns, *The Evolution of Adam*, Part 1.1, Kindle.
256. Collins, *The Language of God*, 58.
257. Polkinghorne and Beale. *Questions of Truth*, 7.
258. Collins, *The Language of God*, 6.
259. Cited in Wright, *Surprised by Scripture*, 142.
260. Collins, *The Language of God*, 6.
261. Knoll, *The Scandal of the Evangelical Mind*, 198–199.
262. Polkinghorne and Beale, *Questions of Truth*, 13.
263. Ibid. 44.
264. cited in, Keller, *The Reason for God*, 130.
265. Giberson and Collins, *The Language of Faith and Scripture*, 189.

266. Ibid. 182.
267. Ibid. 183.
268. Ibid., 176.
269. https://www.nationalgeographic.com/news/2013/1/
270. https://courses.lumenlearning.com/atd-fscj-introastronomy/chapter/the-circumstellar-habitable-zone/
271. Bosch, *Transforming Mission*, 343.
272. Wright, *Surprised by Scripture*, 84.
273. Ibid. 95.
274. Eisenstein, *Sacred Economics*, 173.
275. Michael Clarke, "Pardon me for getting 'religious' about climate change," https://www.abc.net.au/religion/
276. Jensen, *Systematic Theology: Volume II*, 115.
277. Smith, *You Are What You Love*, 171.
278. Eisenstein, *Sacred Economics*, 233.
279. Ibid. 187.
280. Ibid. 79,
281. Heath, *The Mystic Way of Evangelism*, 171.
282. Deneen, *Why Liberalism Failed*, 14.

CHAPTER 9

283. Portions of this chapter are taken from J. Michael Walters, *Too Wounded to Heal: The Church's Uncomfortable Challenge to Wholeness*, presented at "Evangelical Theology: New Challenges New Opportunities," Rochester, NY, October 2017.
284. Bussie, *Outlaw Christian*, (Nashville: Thomas Nelson, 2016), 142–143.
285. Nouwen, *The Wounded Healer* 1990.
286. Heath, *The Mystic Way of Evangelism*,
287. Ibid. 99.
288. Coates, *We Were Eight Years in Power*, 124.
289. Gushee, *A Letter to My Anxious Christian Friends*, 55.
290. Seed, "Do Black Lives Matter? What's Your Frame?," *Evangelicals for Social Action*, July 28, 2016
291. Dorrien, "Saving Democracy," *The Christian Century*, June 21, 2017.
292. Potter, "White Supremacy Versus the Gospel in Charlottesville," *Sojourners*, August 2017.
293. Ibid.
294. Coates, *We Were Eight Years in Power*, 256.
295. Ibid. 312.
296. Ibid. 325.
297. Ibid. 346.
298. Dyson, *Tears We Cannot Stop*,78.
299. Cone, *The Cross and the Lynching Tree*, 153.
300. Clapp, *Johnny Cash and the Great American Contradiction*, 84.
301. Wallis, "America's Original Sin: The Legacy of White Racism."
302. Heath, *The Mystic Way of Evangelism*, 55.
303. Brownson, *Bible, Gender, Sexuality*, 58..

304. Ibid. 89.
305. Walton, *The Lost World of Adam and Eve*, 80.
306. Middleton, *A New Heaven and a New Earth*, 52.
307. Wright, *Surprised by Scripture*, 69.
308. Ibid. 70.
309. Brownson, *Bible, Gender, Sexuality*, 71.
310. Ibid. 77.
311. Blevins, *How to Read the Bible Without Losing Your Mind*, Chapter 6, Kindle.
312. Alperovitz, *What Then Must We Do?*, Introduction, Kindle.
313. Ibid. Introduction, Kindle.
314. Ibid. Part I.1, Kindle.
315. Ibid. Part II.5, Kindle.
316. Bosch, *Transforming Mission*, 429.
317. Cited in Hunter, *To Change the World*, 138.
318. Hirsch and Ford, *Right Here Right Now*, Section Two: Wrapping Our Heads Around It, Kindle.
319. Hunter, *To Change the World*, 139.
320. Middleton, *A New Heaven and a New Earth*, 274.
321. George Yancy, "Is Your God Dead?,"
322. Heath, *The Mystic Way of Evangelism*, 100.
323. Trueblood, *The Incendiary Fellowship*, 62.
324. Clapp, *Johnny Cash and the Great American Contradiction*, 122.
325. Ibid., 122-123.
326. Brown-Taylor, *Leaving Church*, 95.
327. Micheli, "Stanley Hauerwas: Racism, Reconciliation, and White Guilt."
328. Brunner, *The Gospel of John*, 533.
329. Bonhoeffer, *Meditating on the Word*.
330. Heath, *The Mystic Way of Evangelism*, 100.

EPILOGUE

331. Caputo, *On Religion*, 14.
332. Keesmaat and Walsh, *Romans Disarmed*, 367.
333. Morris, *Include Me Out*, 96.
334. Ibid. 96-97.
335. Murray, *Post-Christendom*, 316-317.
336. McLaren, *A New Kind of Christian*, 240.
337. Willimon, *Pastor*, 2002), 264.
338. Henderson and Casper, *Jim and Casper Go To Church*, 144-145.
339. Guder, *Missional Church*, 152.
340. Ibid. 176.
341. Case, *Around the Table*, Chapter 1, Kindle.
342. Niebuhr, *The Responsible Self*, 43-44.

Bibliography

Adeney, Frances S. *Graceful Evangelism*. Grand Rapids: Baker Academic. Kindle.
Alperovitz, Gar. *What Then Must We Do?: Straight Talk about the Next American Revolution*. White River Junction, VT: Chelsea Green, 2013. Kindle.
Atwood, James E. *America and Its Guns*. Eugene, OR: Cascade 2013. Kindle.
Bacevich, Andrew. *Washington Rules: America's Path to Permanent War*. New York: Metropolitan, 2010.
Baker, Sharon. *Razing Hell*. Louisville: Westminster John Knox, 2010. Kindle.
Barth, Karl. *Church Dogmatics*. T.F. Torrance and Geoffrey Bromiley, eds. Peabody, MA, Hedrickson, 2010
Bell, Rob & Don Golden: *Jesus Wants to Save Christians: A Manifesto for the Church in Exile*. San Francisco: HarperOne, 2008. Kindle.
Bell, Rob. *Love Wins: A Book About Heaven, Hell, and Every Person Who Ever Lives*. San Francisco: HarperCollins. Kindle.
———. *Sex God: Exploring the Endless Connection Between Sexuality and Spirituality*. Grand Rapids: Zondervan, 2007
———. *What is the Bible?: How an Ancient Library of Poems, Letters, and Stories Can Transform the Way You Think and Feel About Everything*. San Francisco: HarperOne, 2016.
Berger, Peter L., and Anton C. Zijdeveld. *In Praise of Doubt: How to Have Convictions Without Becoming a Fanatic*. San Francisco: Harper Collins, 2010. Kindle.
Bessenecker, Scott A. *The New Friars: The Emerging Movement Serving the World's Poor.*. Downers Grove, IL: InterVarsity, 2006
Blevins, Kent. *How to Read the Bible Without Losing Your Mind*. Eugene, OR: Wipf and Stock. 2014, Kindle.
Bolz-Webber, Nadia. *Pastrix: The Cranky Beautiful Faith of a Sinner & Saint*. New York: Jericho, 2014.
———. *Shameless: A Sexual Reformation*. New York: Convergen, 2019. Kindle.
Bonhoeffer, Dietrich, *Life Together: A Discussion of Christian Fellowship*. San Francisco: HarperCollins, 1954.
———. *Meditating on the Word*. New York: Rowman & Littlefield, 1986.
Bosch, David Jacobus. *Transforming Mission: Paradigm Shifts in Theology of Mission*. Maryknoll, NY: Orbis, 1991.
Boyd, Gregory, *Cross Vision: How the Crucifixion of Jesus Makes Sense of Old Testament Violence*. Minneapolis: Fortress, 2017. Kindle.
———. *The Myth of a Christian Nation*. Grand Rapids: Zondervan, 2005.

Bracevich, Andrew *Washington Rules: America's Path to Permanent War* .New York: Metropolitan, 2010.
Brown-Taylor, Barbara. *Leaving Church: A Memoir of Faith*. San Francisco: Harper, 2007.
Brownson, James V. *Bible, Gender, Sexuality: Reframing the Church's Debate on Same-Sex Relationships,* Grand Rapids: Wm. B. Eerdmans Co., 2013.
Bruner, Frederick Dale. *The Gospel of John: A Commentary*. Grand Rapids: Wm. B. Eerdmans, 2012.
Bussie, Jacqueline. *Love Without Limits*. Minneapolis: Fortress, 2018. Kindle.
———. *Outlaw Christian*. Nashville: Thomas Nelson, 2016. Kindle.
Butler-Bass, Diana. *Christianity for the Rest of Us*. San Francisco: Harper Collins, 2007. Kindle.
Caputo, John. *On Religion*. New York: Routledge, 2019. Kindle.
Carlson, Kent, and Mike Lucken. *Renovation of the Chuurch: What Happens When a Seeker Church Discovers Spiritual Formation*. Downers Grove, IL: IVP, 2011. Kindle.
Case, Jonathan P. *Around the Table: Talking Graciously About God*. Eugene, OR: Cascade, 2019.
Clapp, Rodney. *Johnny Cash and the Great American Contradiction*. Louisville: Westminster John Knox, 2008.
Coates, Ta-Nehisi. *We Were Eight Years in Power: An American Tragedy*. New York: One World, 2017. Kindle.
Collins, Francis. *The Language of God: A Scientist Presents Evidence for Belief*. New York: Free Press, 2006.
Cone, James. *God of the Oppressed*. Maryknoll, NY: Orbis, 2012.
———. *The Cross and the Lynching Tree*. Maryknoll: Orbis, 2011.
Deneen, Patrick J. *Why Liberalism Failed*. New Haven: Yale University Press, 2018.
Dobson, Kent. *Bitten by a Camel: Leaving Church Finding God*. Minneapolis: Fortress, 2017. Kindle.
Donovan, Vincent J. *Christianity Rediscovered*. Maryknoll, NY: Orbis, 2003.
Duffy, Michael F. *Making Sense of Sex: Responsible Decision Making for Young Singles*. Louisville: Westminster John Knox, 2011. Kindle.
Duin, Julia. *Quitting Church: Why the Faithful are Fleeing*. Grand Rapids: Baker, 2008.
Dyson, Michael Eric. *Tears We Cannot Stop: A Sermon to White America..* New York: St. Martin's, 2017. Kindle.
Eisenstein, Charles. *Sacred Economics*. Berkeley CA: Evolver Editions, 2011.
Enns, Peter. *The Bible Tells Me So: Why Defending Scripture has Made Us Unable to Read It*. San Francisco: Harper One, Kindle.
———. *The Evolution of Adam: What the Bible Does and Doesn't Say About Human Origins*. Grand Rapids: Brazos, 2001. Kindle.
Fea, John. *Was America Founded as a Christian Nation?.* Louisville: Westminster John Knox, 2011. Kindle.
Fitch, David. *Faithful Presence: Seven Disciplines that Shape the Church for Mission*. Downers Grove IL: IVP, 2016. Kindle.
Fitch, David E., and Geoffrey Holsclaw. *Prodigal Christianity: 10 Signposts into the Missional Frontier*. San Francisco: Josey-Bass, 2013. Kindle.

Floyd-Thomas, Juan, Stacey M. Floyd-Thomas, and Mark G. Toulouse. *The Altars Where We Worship: The Religious Significance of Popular Culture*. Louisville: Westminster John Knox, 2016.
Frost, Michael. *Seeing God in the Ordinary: A Theology of the Everyday*. Peabody, MA: Hendrickson, 2005.
Frost, Michael, and Alan Hirsch. *The Shaping of Things to Come*. Peabody, MA: Hendrickson, 2003.
———. *Re-Jesus: A Wild Messiah for a Missional Church*. Peabody, MA: Hendrickson, 2009.
Gardner, Christine J. *Making Chastity Sexy: The Rhetoric of Evangelical Abstinence Campaigns*. Berkeley, CA: University of California Press, 2011. Kindle.
Gibberson, Karl W. and Francis S. Collins, *The Language of Faith and Scripture: Straight Answers to Genuine Questions*. Downers Grove, IL: IVP, 2011. Kindle.
Gibbs, Eddie, and Ryan K. Bolger. *Emerging Churches: Creating Christian Community in Postmodern Culture*. Grand Rapids: Baker Academic, 2005.
Gorman, Michael. *Reading Revelation Responsibly*. Eugene, OR: Cascade, 2011. Kindle.
Grenz, Stanley J. *Revisioning Evangelical Theology*. Downers Grove: InterVarsity, 1993
Guder, Darrell L. *Missional Church: A Vision for the Sending of the Church in North America: The People of God Sent on a Mission*. Grand Rapids: Wm. B. Eerdmans, 1998.
———. *The Continuing Conversion of the Church*. Grand Rapids: Wm. B. Eerdmans, 2000.
Guiness, Os. *Prophetic Untimeliness: A Challenge to the Idol of Relevance* Grand Rapids: Baker, 2003.
Gushee, David P. *A Letter to My Anxious Christian Friends: From Fear to Faith in Troubled Times*. Louisville: Westminster John Knox, 2016. Kindle.
Hammet, Edward H. *Reaching People Under 40 While Keeping People Over 60*. St. Louis: Chalice, 2007. Kindle.
Hart, David Bentley. *That All Shall Be Saved: Heaven, Hell, and Universal Salvation*. New Haven, CT: Yale University Press, 2019. Kindle.
Hauerwas, Stanley. *A Community of Character: Toward a Constructive Christian Social Ethic*. Notre Dame: University of Notre Dame Press, 1981.
Hauerwas, Stanley, and William Willimon. *Resident Aliens: Life in the Christian Colony*. Nashville: Abingdon, 1989.
Heath, Elaine A. *The Mystic Way of Evangelism: A Contemplative Vision for Outreach*. Grand Rapids: Baker Academic, 2008.
Held-Evans, Rachel. "Want Millennials back in the pews? Stop trying to make church 'cool.'" *The Washington Post*, April 30, 2015.
Henderson, Jim. *Evangelism Without the Additives: What if Sharing Your Faith Meant Being Yourself?*. Colorado Springs: Waterbrook, 2007.
Henderson, Jim, and Matt Casper. *Jim and Casper Go To Church*. Ventura, CA: Barna, 2007.
Hiestand, Gerald, and Todd A. Wilson. *The Pastor Theologian: Resurrecting an Ancient Vision*. Grand Rapids: Zondervan, 2015.
Hirsch, Alan, and Lance Ford. *Right Here Right Now: Everyday Mission for Everyday People*. Grand Rapids: Baker, 2011. Kindle.
Hirsch, Alan. *The Forgotten Ways*. Grand Rapids: Brazos, 2006.

Hunter, James Davison. *To Change the World: The Irony, Tragedy, and Possibility of Christianity in the Late Modern World.* New York: Oxford University Press, 2010. Kindle.

Jensen, Robert. *Systematic Theology: Vol. II The Works of God.* Oxford: Oxford University Press, 1999. Kindle.

Keesmaat, Sylvia C., and Brian J. Walsh. *Romans Disarmed: Resisting Empire, Demanding Justice.* Grand Rapids: Brazos, 2019.

Keller, Tim. *The Reason for God: Belief in an Age of Skepticism.* New York: Penguin, 2008.

Kinnaman, David and Gabe Lyons. *Unchristian: What a New Generation Thinks about Christianity . . .And Why it Matters.* Grand Rapids: Baker, 2012.

Kinnaman, David. *You Lost Me: Why Young Christians are Leaving Church . . .And Rethinking Faith.* Grand Rapids: Baker, 2016. Kindle.

Kinlaw, Dennis F. *Let's Start With Jesus: A New Way of Doing Theology.* Grand Rapids: Zondervan Academic, 2005. Kindle.

Knoll, Mark A. *The Scandal of the Evangelical Mind.* Grand Rapids: Wm. B. Erdmans, 1995.

Leithart, Peter. *Against Christianity.* Moscow, ID: Canon, 2002.

Lenker, John Nicholas. *Luther's Larger Catechism.* Minneapolis: Luther, 1908.

Lyons, Gabe. *The Next Christians: The Good News About the End of Christian America.* New York: Doubleday, 2010.

MacDonald, Gregory. *The Evangelical Universalist.* Eugene, OR: Cascade, 2006.

McLaren, Brian D. *A New Kind of Christian: A Tale of Two Friends on a Spiritual Journey.* San Francisco: Josey-Bass, 2001.

———. *A New Kind of Christianity.* New York: HarperOne, 2010.

———. *Everything Must Change: When the World's Greatest Problems and Jesus' Good News Collide.* Nashville: Thomas Nelson, 2007.

———. *More Ready Than You Realize. The Power of Everyday Conversations* Grand Rapids: Zondervan, 2002.

———. *The Church on the Other Side.* Grand Rapids: Zondervan, 1998.

———. *The Last Word: And the Word After That.* San Francisco: Josey-Bass, 2005.

McNeal, Reggie. *The Present Future: Six Tough Questions for the Church.* San Francisco: Josey-Bass, 2003.

Merrit-Howard, Carol. *ReFraming Hope: Vital Ministry in a New Generation,* Herndon, VA: The Alban Institute, 2010.

———. *Tribal Church: Ministering to the Missing Generation.* Herndon, VA: The Alban Institute, 2007.

Micheli, Jason. "Stanley Hauerwas: Racism, Reconciliation, and White Guilt." http://Facebook, August 11, 2017.

Middleton, Richard J. *A New Heaven and a New Earth: Reclaiming Biblical Eschatology.* Grand Rapids: Baker Academic, 2014.

Morey, Tim, and Eddie Gibbs. *Embodying Our Faith: Becoming a Living, Sharing, Practicing Church.* Downers Grove, IL: IVP, 2009. Kindle.

Morris, Colin. *Include Me Out: The Confessions of an Ecclesiastical Coward.* London: Epworth, 1968.

Murphy, Nancey. *Beyond Liberalism and Fundamentalism.* Harrisburg: Trinity, 1996.

Murray, Stuart. *Post-Christendom: Church and Mission in a Strange World.* Bletchley, U.K.: Paternoster, 2005.

BIBLIOGRAPHY

Meyers, Ched. *Binding the Strong Man: A Political Reading of Mark's Story of Jesus.* Maryknoll, NY: Orbis, 2015.

Nancarrow, Maggie. "Rethinking Church." (Blog) http://www.maggienancarrow.com.

Niebuhr, H. Richard. *The Responsible Self: An Essay in Christian Moral Philosophy.* New York: Harper & Row, 1969.

Oden, Thomas C. *Classic Christianity: A Systematic Theology.* San Francisco: Harper One, 2009.

Parry, Robin A. and Christopher H. Partridge, EDS. *Universal Salvation: The Current Debate.* Grand Rapids: Wm. B. Eerdmans Publishing Co., 2003. Kindle.

Pavlovitz, John. *A Bigger Table: Building Messy, Authentic, and Hopeful Spiritual Community.* Louisville: Westminster John Knox, 2017. Kindle.

Peterson, Eugene H. *Working the Angles: The Shape of Pastoral Integrity.* Grand Rapids: Eerdmans, 1987.

Peterson, Jim, and Mike Shamy. *The Insider: Bringing the Kingdom of God into Your Everyday World.* NavPress, 2003. Kindle.

Polkinghorne, John, and Nicolas Beale. *Questions of Truth: Fifty-One Responses to Questions about God, Science, and Belief.* Louisville: Westminster John Knox, 2009.

Ranier, Thom S., and Eric Geiger. *Simple Church.* Nashville: B&H, 2006.

Regnerus, Mark D. *Forbidden Fruit: Sex & Religion in the Lives of American Teenagers.* New York: Oxford University Press, 2007.

Robinson, Anthony B. and Robert W. Wall. *Called to Lead.* Grand Rapids: Wm. B. Eerdmans., 2012 Kindle.

Rohr, Richard. *Falling Upward: A Spirituality for the Two-Halves of Life.* San Francisco: Josey-Bass, 2011. Kindle.

Ryan, Edward J. SJ. „The Rejection of Military Service by the Early Christians." http://cdn.theologicalstudies.net.

Simon, Caroline J. *Bringing Sex Intro Focus: The Quest for Sexual Integrity.* Downers Grove, IL: IVP, 2011. Kindle.

Smedes, Lewis. *Sex for Christians.* Grand Rapids: Wm. B. Eerdmans, 1976

Smith, Christian. *The Bible Made Impossible: Why Biblicism is Not a Truly Evangelical Reading of Scripture.* Grand Rapids: Brazos, 2011. Kindle.

———. *Soul Searching: The Religious and Spiritual Lives of American Teenagers.* New York: Oxford University Press, 2005.

Smith, James K. A. *Awaiting the King: Reforming Public Theology.* Grand Rapids: Baker Academic, 2017. Kindle.

———. *Desiring the Kingdom: Worship, Worldview, and Cultural Formation.* Grand Rapids: Baker Academic, 2009.

———. *You Are What You Love: The Spiritual Power of Habit.* Grand Rapids: Brazos, 2016. Kindle.

Stassen, Harold Glen. *A Thicker Jesus.* Louisville: Westminster John Knox, 2012. Kindle.

Struthers, William M. *Wired for Intimacy: How Pornography Hijacks the Male Mind.* Downers Grove: IVP, 2009. Kindle

Talbot, Thomas. *The Inescapable Love of God.* Eugene OR: Cascade, 2014.

Tomlinson, Dave. *The Post-Evangelical.* Grand Rapids: Zondervan, 2003.

Trueblood, David Elton. *The Incendiary Fellowship.* New York: Harper and Row, 1967.

Vanhoozer, Kevin, Charles A. Anderson, and Michael J. Sleasman. *Everyday Theology: How To Read Cultural Texts and Interpret Trends.* Grand Rapids: Baker Academic, 2007.

Vanhoozer, Kevin. *The Pastor as Public Theologian: Reclaiming a Lost Vision.* Grand Rapids: Baker Academic, 2015.

Wall, Rob and Daniel Castello. "Rethinking the Bible." *Wesleyan Theological Journal,* Fall, 2018.

Wallis, Jim. "America's Original Sin: The Legacy of White Racism." www.jstor.ohttpsrg/stable1244661363?seq=1.

Walters, J. Michael. "Too Wounded to Heal: The Church's Challenge to Wholeness." Presented at "Evangelical Theology: New Challenges, New Opportunities," Rochester, NY, October 2017.

Walton, John H. *The Lost World of Adam and Eve: Genesis 2–3 and the Human Origins Debate..* Downers Grove, IL: InterVarsity, 2015. Kindle.

Ward, Pete. *Liquid Church.* Peabody, MA: Hendrickson, 2002.

Wax, Trevor. *Holy Subversions: Allegiance to Christ in an Age of Rivals.* Wheaton, IL: Crossway, 2010.

Wicker, Christine. *The Fall of the Evangelical Nation: The Surprising Crisis Within the Church.* New York: HarperOne, 2008.

Willard, Dallas. *Renovation of the Heart: Putting on the Character of Christ.* Colorado Springs: NavPress, 2002.

Willimon, William H. *Pastor: The Theology and Practice of Ordained Ministry.* Nashville: Abingdon, 2002.

Winner, Lauren. *Real Sex: The Naked Truth about Chastity.* Grand Rapids: Brazos, 2005.

Worthen, Molly. *Apostles of Reason: The Crisis of Authority in American Evangelicalism..* New York: Oxford University Press, 2014. Kindle.

Wright, N.T. *Surprised by Scripture: Engaging Contemporary Issues.* San Francisco: Harper Collins, 2014. Kindle.

Yancy, George. "Is Your God Dead?" http://Facebook, July 2017.

Zahnd, Brian. *A Farewell to Mars: An Evangelical Pastor's Journey Toward the Gospel of Peace.* Elgin, IL: David C. Cook, 2014.

———. *Sinners in the Hands of a Loving God.* Colorado Springs: Waterproof, 2017. Kindle.

www.ingramcontent.com/pod-product-compliance
Lightning Source LLC
Chambersburg PA
CBHW071419160426
43195CB00013B/1743